Women of Devotion
HISTORY OF AN ANGLICAN
RELIGIOUS COMMUNITY

Women of Devotion
HISTORY OF AN ANGLICAN RELIGIOUS COMMUNITY
Begun in 1898

SISTER MONICA MARY HEYES, CT

ORANGE *frazer* PRESS
Wilmington, Ohio

ISBN 978-1939710-048
Copyright©2014 Society of the Transfiguration

No part of this publication may be reproduced in any material form (including photo-copying or storing in any medium by electronic means and whether or not transiently or incidentally to some other use of this publication) without the written permission of the copyright holder except in accordance with the provisions of the Copyright, Designs and Patents Act 1988.

Published for Society of the Transfiguration by:
Orange Frazer Press
P.O. Box 214
Wilmington, OH 45177
Telephone: 800.852.9332 for price and shipping information.
Website: *www.orangefrazer.com*
www.orangefrazercustombooks.com

Book and cover design: Brittany Lament and Orange Frazer Press
Cover Original Painting by Sister Julia Margaret Hayes, CT (1899-1975)

Library of Congress Control Number 2014930233

I dedicate this book to all of my Sisters of the Transfiguration, past, present, and future. To all of my family and friends who have supported me in this endeavor, and to all whose lives have been touched by the Sisters.

TABLE OF CONTENTS

PREFACE *By Bishop Epting* ... ix
FOREWORD ... xi
INTRODUCTION *Mother Eva's Version* ... xv

PART ONE *Time of Beginnings (1896-1928)*
CHAPTER 1 *Foundation of the Community (August 6, 1898)* ... 3
CHAPTER 2 *A Time of Decision* ... 14
CHAPTER 3 *Bethany Mission House* ... 18
CHAPTER 4 *Bethany Home for Children* ... 30
CHAPTER 5 *Trip to England* ... 35
CHAPTER 6 *Bethany Home Grows* ... 46
CHAPTER 7 *The Community and the Diocese of Southern Ohio* ... 52
CHAPTER 8 *The Community Grows* ... 60
CHAPTER 9 *The Rule in the Development of Community Life* ... 66
CHAPTER 10 *The Novitiate* ... 78
CHAPTER 11 *The Associates and Oblates* ... 86
CHAPTER 12 *Outreach for Ministry* ... 89
CHAPTER 13 *Mother Eva's Last Years* ... 101
CHAPTER 14 *The Story of the Chapel* ... 105
CHAPTER 15 *Liturgy and Music* ... 121

PART TWO *The Community Continues*
CHAPTER 16 *Depression and World War II* ... 131
CHAPTER 17 *End of War and Transition* ... 142
CHAPTER 18 *Reviewing the Past, Preparing for the Future* ... 158

EPILOGUE *Sister Teresa Marie* ... 169

APPENDIX I

CHRONOLOGY OF COMMUNITY HISTORY	181
LIST OF LIFE PROFESSED SISTERS BETWEEN 1911 AND 2008	185
DECLARATION OF NOVICES REGARDING COMMUNITY PRACTICES	199
BISHOP VINCENT'S SERMON	201

APPENDIX II

BAT CAVE, NORTH CAROLINA, MINISTRY	215
NORTHERN OHIO 1909–1979	219
CHINA	221
ST. ANDREW'S PRIORY SCHOOL FOR GIRLS HONOLULU, HAWAII	243
THE SISTERS OF THE TRANSFIGURATION IN CALIFORNIA	251
ST. SIMON OF CYRENE AND ST. MONICA'S CENTER LINCOLN HEIGHTS, OHIO	259
PUERTO RICO	281
JAPAN 1955–1979	285
MCKINNEY AND DALLAS, TEXAS	289
ST. LUKE'S HOUSE 1979–1988 LINCOLNTON, N.C.	291
THE DOMINICAN REPUBLIC 1980–PRESENT	297

INDEX 305

PREFACE
BY BISHOP EPTING

When I was privileged to lead a long retreat for the Community of the Transfiguration in the early 1990s, little did I know that it would lead to more than two decades serving as the Sisters' "Bishop Visitor," companion and friend. Each year has been a blessing to me and that is why I am so pleased that this "History of An American Religious Community" has been completed.

Each word in that subtitle is important. This is a "history" captured for us from prior material—articles and documents—and from the priceless recollections of aging Sisters who are still with us and whose oral remembrances fill in important blanks never before recorded by the Community.

This is a quintessentially "American" religious community. Their democratic form of government and commitment to and involvement with The Episcopal Church was always part of Mother Eva's dream—not to import English or European monasticism, but to develop a distinctively American form of it.

It is, however, clearly an "Anglican" community, committed to the Anglican Communion around the world and appreciative of the heritage they have received from the Church of England. It is certainly a "Religious" community, rooted and grounded in the Divine Office, Daily Eucharist, prayer, study, and silence. The Sisters have always sought to maintain the difficult balance of a contemplative life yielding forth its fruit in active ministry and tireless mission.

Finally, of course, this is a "Community." These women share their lives and resources, their joys and sorrows, and attempt to do so, guided by their motto, "Benignitas, Simplicitas, Hilaritas" (Kindness, Simplicity, and Joy). It has been an enormous privilege for me to walk with these amazing women over the years, to experience their kindness, to marvel at their simplicity, and sometimes to laugh so hard with them that I have shared their tears of joy.

May God continue richly to bless this "American...Religious...Community."

—C. Christopher Epting, VIII Bishop of Iowa Bishop Visitor, CT, Friday, May 04, 2012

FOREWORD

Eva Lee Matthews in 1898 founded the Community of the Transfiguration, an Anglican Religious Community for Women in Cincinnati, Ohio. Mother Eva chose the name Community because she wanted her Sisters to be like a family. So in one sense this is a history of a family of Sisters rather than of an organization or institution.

Sister Beatrice Martha, CT, co-foundress of the Community wrote a history of the first 33 years of the Community of the Transfiguration, after the completion of her second term as Superior of the Community, in 1940. Her book, *A Follower's Story* exists only in manuscript. Lengthy excerpts from *A Follower's Story* are included in this history. There have been two biographies of Mother Eva, one by her sister, Grace Cleveland, *Mother Eva, C.T., and The Story of a Foundation*, written soon after her death in 1928. Another later biography was written, *Windfall of Light* (1968) by Sybil Harton, a visitor from England and an admirer, but one who did not know Mother Eva personally.

I have been in this Community for over fifty years and have served in many of its branch ministries. Thanks to the long lives of many Sisters, I have known personally some of the earliest ones, albeit in their old age, including Sister Beatrice. We come from many different parts of the country, different backgrounds of education, family and church affiliations. We learn to live together and to respect each other's ideas. My own experience of living in the community has been fulfillment of my life vocation in serving God and my Sisters.

This book includes much of *A Follower's Story*, and information from the two biographies. It also makes use of the *Bethany Home Chronicle*, from 1911 to 1945, which was produced by the students at Bethany Home School on the convent grounds at Glendale, Ohio. *The Transfiguration Quarterly*, begun in 1945, has information regarding the period since Mother Eva's death and contains a great deal of other valuable, historical information. Oral traditions in the Community, which have been passed down among the Sisters, and my own memories, as well as records of meetings of the Community, provide rich substance as well. Accounts of some ministries have come from Sisters who have been personally involved in them.

This history is an effort to weave together all of this information into a comprehensive story of the growth and development of the Community over many years, and an effort to see how the various changes have fit into Mother Eva's vision.

I chose to arrange the history chronologically according to the terms of each Superior. Mother Eva Mary was the Superior of the Community until her death in 1928. She was succeeded by Sister Beatrice Martha, fifteen years younger, who had followed Mother Eva from the beginning and carried on in her footsteps. The Superior is elected for a five-year term and may not serve more than two consecutive terms. Each succeeding Superior has made her own contribution and so has every Sister, but all have endeavored to carry on in the spirit of Mother Eva. This history shows how there have been changes in the Community in keeping with the needs of the changes in the Episcopal Church and in society in general.

There have been high points and low points in the course of 110 years. There was a low point in the late 1960s, after the death of eighteen Life Professed Sisters and fewer newcomers. In 1970–71, we had a time of "renewal." At the times of our Visitations from our Episcopal Visitor, 2001 and in 2006–2007, as required by the House of Bishops, the Community was urged to look back to our roots and to the vision of our Mother Foundress to help us as we look forward to the future.

This history is written to show the life of the Community during its first century and for the benefit of present and future Sisters and as a tribute to our Mother Foundress Eva Mary, her first companion and co-foundress, Sister Beatrice Martha, and to all other Sisters. We appreciate the support of our Associates and Oblates and the many friends who have served God with them.

I wish to thank the Rt. Rev. C. Christopher Epting for his prayerful support, and his contributions to the book; Sister Teresa Marie, C.T. (our present Superior) for her encouragement, Sister Ann Margaret and the Sisters and friends of the Transfiguration who have helped me in the writing of this book. Especially I thank Sister Eleanor Grace, CT, Sister Jacqueline Marie, CT, Sister Carina Elsa, N/CT, her brother, Eric Spendel, Zenwizard Studios, who provided important technical assistance at the end, and Dr. Mattie Decker, Oblate CT, whose enthusiasm and energy encouraged me to continue and whose understanding of computer skills and interest made it possible. I also thank Sister Hilary Mary, CT, and Eve Morrow, Oblate, for their painstaking help in finding information in the Community Archives, especially photographs, and the many Sisters who have contributed from their experience in the Community, particularly in the Branch Houses.

I am grateful to the Rev. Deacon Ellen Deuell, and the Rev. Lisa Tolliver who helped me get started and to the many other Associates and friends who have contributed in various ways.

—*Sister Monica Mary, CT*

INTRODUCTION
MOTHER EVA'S VISION

Mother Eva's vision for the Community is stated in the Prologue to our Rule: Her choice of the mystery of the Transfiguration as the dedication of the Community is symbolic of the purpose to which she believed the Community was called—a

Mother Eva Mary.

life of prayer, of service, and of showing forth the Good News of Jesus Christ to others. Her original thought was to name it the "Community of St. Mary and St. Martha of Bethany." Traditionally, Mary who sat at Jesus' feet and listened has represented the life of prayer, and Martha who served the life of action. But at that time there was another Community, which had taken that name.

In her interview with the bishop of Southern Ohio, Bishop Vincent, he asked her if she had a favorite Collect. She replied, "the Collect for the Transfiguration." This was new in the American Prayer book of 1892. The Bishop replied, "The very thing! An American Collect for an American community." And so the name was chosen. The account of the Transfiguration, described in the Gospels, Matthew 1-8.14-21, Mark 9:2-8, `4-29, 37-43 and Luke 9:28-36, tells that Jesus went up to a high mountain, taking with him the disciples, Peter, James, and John. As they watched, Jesus was transfigured before them; his body was transformed and seen in a vision of light. Moses and Elijah, prophets of old, were seen in the glory with him. As they came down the mountain a man begged Jesus to heal his son possessed by a demon. Jesus did so.

As related above, Mother Eva chose to name her Community for the mystery of the Transfiguration. The event of the Transfiguration of Our Lord, followed so closely by the healing of the epileptic boy, seemed appropriate for a life given to prayer and active works of mercy, which was the thought behind Mother Eva's original choice of Mary and Martha of Bethany. As she said, "As his disciples, we see in the Transfiguration the union of the heavenly and the earthly, the sacramental presence of God. The vision of the King in his beauty is given that the light may shine through us and guide others to know, love and glorify him."

Mother Eva knew that there would be disparate views of the religious life among the people in the Episcopal Church. At that time the friction between the Roman Catholic and non-Roman churches was intense. For some in the Episcopal Church, the emphasis on the sacramental and liturgical life was too similar to Roman practices. Mother Eva was able to persuade her Bishop of her loyalty to the Episcopal Church. His sermon, given at the inauguration of the Community on August 6, 1898, which follows, shows his support and understanding of her vision.

She saw a need in the Church for an Order that would be distinctly American, one, that while based on the best traditions of the Religious Life, should yet be free, with the true democratic American spirit, to develop along these lines: "personal freedom with Community unity in the love of Christ. Personality should be developed without being molded into a set form or suppressed into the Superior's idea of a medieval Religious" (from the Prologue to the Rule).

Collect of the Transfiguration (BCP 1892)
O God, who on the holy mount didst reveal to chosen

witnesses thine only-begotten Son, wonderfully transfigured, in raiment white and glistering: Mercifully grant that we, being delivered from the disquietude of this world, may be permitted to behold the King in His beauty; who with thee, O Father, and thee, O Holy Ghost, liveth and reigneth, one God, world without end. Amen.

Women of Devotion
HISTORY OF AN ANGLICAN
RELIGIOUS COMMUNITY

PART ONE
Time of Beginnings (1896-1928)

1 FOUNDATION OF THE COMMUNITY

On the Feast of the Transfiguration, August 6, 1898, a very unusual event took place in the Episcopal Diocese of Southern Ohio. Two young women, Miss Eva Lee Matthews, 36, and Miss Beatrice Henderson, 21, made Religious vows of Poverty, Chastity, and Obedience. The service was presided over by the Rt. Rev. Boyd Vincent, Bishop of Southern Ohio, who received their vows and preached the sermon. This service marks the formal establishment of the Community of the Transfiguration. Miss Matthews and Miss Henderson, better known by their Religious names, Mother Eva Mary and Sister Beatrice Martha, had been living a Community life under a Religious Rule for about a year prior to their formal taking of vows. Although made with the expectation of a life commitment, these first vows were temporary. Mother Eva wisely refrained from permanent vows until after a further time of testing. She made her life vows on the Feast of the Transfiguration, 1903, Sister Beatrice on March 8, 1905.

On August 10, 1898, the Community was incorporated under the laws of the State of Ohio as the Society of the Transfigura-

Mother Eva Mary and Sr. Beatrice Martha.

tion, a non-profit corporation organized for the worship of God and for work religious, charitable, and educational in the Diocese of Southern Ohio and elsewhere. Those elected to the first Board of Trustees were the Rt. Rev. Boyd Vincent, Bishop of Southern Ohio, Eva's brother, the Rev. Paul Matthews, her elder brother, Mr. Mortimer Matthews, Mr. Harlan Cleveland (husband of her sister Grace Matthews Cleveland), Mother Eva Mary and Sister Beatrice Martha. The first meeting of the Board of Trustees of the Society was held on September 26. The Trustees were responsible for the financial and legal affairs of the Society. At first they met annually. In recent years the full board has met three times a year. The Sister Trustees meet almost weekly. Canon Law of the Episcopal Church requires every Religious Community to have a Bishop Visitor. He is responsible for the temporal affairs of the community. He is often the Diocesan Bishop but this is not required. At the beginning Bishop Vincent, our Diocesan, was our Visitor.

This was a courageous venture on the part of Eva Lee Matthews and also of Bishop Vincent. It was then only fifty years since the revival of the Religious Life in the Anglican Communion, one of the fruits of the Catholic Movement in the Church. Both in England and the United States, Sisters had won grudging acceptance because of their work as nurses in the Crimea and in cholera epidemics in cities of England. In the United States there was the mar-

Bishop Vincent.

tyrdom of Sister Constance and Companions of the Community of St. Mary in the Yellow Fever epidemic in Memphis in 1878, now commemorated in *Lesser Feasts and Fasts*. Still, many fellow churchmen looked upon Sisters as "Romanizers," disloyal to the Anglican Church. The Diocese of Southern Ohio, a stronghold of Evangelical Churchmanship, could not be expected to provide a sympathetic atmosphere for a Religious Community. It took real courage to even try. At the end of the nineteenth century there was little understanding of the purpose of the monastic life in the Anglican Communion in general. However, Eva Matthews was able to persuade Bishop Vincent of her loyalty to the Church, the reasonableness of life vows, and the need for an established community, and obtained his consent. The sermon he preached on the occasion of receiving their vows showed that he had learned to appreciate the value of the Religious Life, and he required all of his clergy to attend.

The sermon is long but is important to include in part, here with the conclusion, because it provides an understanding of the context in which the Sisters would be ministering. It is both an apologia to the congregation and a Charge to the two new Sisters. The complete Sermon is included in Appendix I.

> "The Rule of these Sisters is entirely simple and reasonable, and its service practical and blessed beyond all question. May God bless and enlarge it more and more.
>
> "And now as for you, my daughters in the Lord: in the Name of Christ and his Church I bid each of you a personal God-speed in what you are doing. You know how carefully and prayerfully I have watched you and have advised with you, and finally how warmly I have approved your purpose and work. You have been perfectly loyal

to your Bishop and your Church, and I feel sure that my confidence in you in this respect will never be disturbed. Let me now congratulate you especially on the name you have at last chosen for your Order, and on the day you have chosen for this service. No name could more fitly embody the essential idea of the Sisterhood Life than that of "the Transfiguration," and no words more beautifully set forth its motive than the Collect for this Feast.

"As those chosen disciples of old, then, being delivered from the disquietude of this world, were (for a moment) permitted to see the King in His Beauty—so day by day may it be with you. As that marvelous manifestation was his reassurance and theirs of the indwelling of the divine in the human and of the glory to come after the humiliation here—such may it be to you. As they really, even with the bodily eye, looked upon him who is 'God of God and Light of Light' so may you be able to see with the inner eye of faith. As they with the natural ear really heard that voice from heaven, 'This is my beloved Son: hear Him'—so indeed may you hear with the inner ear of faith and be always ready to obey. As He, 'even while he prayed, was transfigured before them' so may it be with you inwardly in your own life of devotion. As He, descending from the Mount, straightway delivered one possessed of the devil—such may your work be of overcoming evil as you come forth from that life of devotion.

"In short, to all of us who are Christians, our Lord's Transfiguration is the incentive and promise of our own, and that in two ways: in body, at the last, when he will 'fashion anew the body of our humiliation that it may be conformed to the body of his glory;' in spirit, even now since 'we all, with unveiled face reflecting as a mirror the glory of the Lord, are (ourselves) transformed into the same image from glory to glory, even as from the Lord to the Spirit.' This, as I understand you, my daughters, is the special desire of your hearts. May God in his goodness grant it to you in full measure!"

(Sermon delivered by the Rt. Rev. Boyd Vincent, Bishop of Southern Ohio, on Transfiguration Day, August 6, 1898, at St. Luke's Church, Cincinnati, OH.)

Not all of the Church people of the Diocese shared their Bishop's understanding, but the Community was spared the persecutions that were the lot of many Anglican Religious Orders in the early days, suspected of being disloyal to the Anglican Church. It was also helpful that Mother Eva had the strong support of her family, both the Matthews family and the Proctor family, with whom she was closely related. Her two brothers, Mortimer and Paul had each married a daughter of William A. Proctor, a prominent citizen of Glendale and one of the founders of the Proctor and Gamble Company. The people of Glendale quickly came to appreciate the work the Sisters were doing for children, but the rest of the diocese was not convinced. Sister Beatrice reported her memory of the first diocesan convention which Mother Eva attended as a delegate:

> "It was held in an up-state city not long after we had taken our first vows and were wearing the Religious habit. She was the delegate from the Mothers' Meeting branch of the Women's Auxiliary. We were so completely shunned that no one would speak to us or make us welcome. After spending the night at a hotel and having to entertain our-

selves, we went home. Southern Ohio has long since made up for this uncomfortable and unfriendly meeting."

Mother Eva wrote to her sister at this time, "Prejudice is so strong that it amounts to social ostracism. I am unclassed by my own class—not that I care very much. It is a small matter to me to be judged of man's judgement. And, He himself had little honor from the rich and worldly." Mother Eva's is a story of vocation that is born in this world yet reaches beyond the social boundaries of the wealthy, to serve His children. Here is her story.

Life of Eva Lee Matthews (Mother Eva Mary)

Eva Lee Matthews was the daughter of Stanley and Mary Ann Matthews. Stanley was a prominent lawyer of Cincinnati, later a United States Senator from Ohio and, from 1881 to 1889, a Justice of the United States Supreme Court. Eva, born on February 9, 1862, was the eighth child of her parents, the first four having died in an epidemic of scarlet fever several years before Eva was born. Eva, a very frail baby, was baptized in infancy at home by the Presbyterian minister. The close-knit family included her brother, Mortimer, who had survived the epidemic, her older sister, Jane, her younger sister Grace, and younger brother Paul. They grew up in the Presbyterian Church and were active in its affairs. In 1877 the family moved to Washington, DC. Eva was a quiet, thoughtful child, not interested in the social life of Glendale or of Washington. She was a voluminous reader in both English and French. She attended Wellesley College for two years, where she was very happy with the availability of books in the college library, but her health made it necessary for her to withdraw. After her mother died in 1885 Eva was without a real home. Her sisters had both married.

Paul was studying for the Presbyterian ministry at Princeton Theological Seminary, but his studies in Church history convinced him that the Episcopal Church was closer to the church of the apostles, and he transferred to the General Theological Seminary of the Episcopal Church in the United States, in New York City. Eva did not follow him into the Episcopal Church then, but stayed with him at the seminary. She then accompanied Paul to the University of Oxford, England, where he spent another year in his studies. He took lodging in the town and Eva kept house for him.

Experience at Oxford

The Oxford Movement was a response to the preceding movement toward Protestant Evangelicalism. This movement focused on personal prayer and spirituality, keeping Sunday as a day of rest, and centering the family around Christian morality and prayer. The Oxford Movement sought to restore the Catholic Sacraments and rituals observed in the seventeenth century. This included weekly celebration of the Eucharist, candles on the altars, choirs dressed in surplices, Religious Orders and parish missions. Many who opposed the Movement were afraid that it would lead back to Roman Catholicism. Discussions between scholars and theologians on both sides could be dynamic. The result was a revival of high-church practices while maintaining their identity as the Church of England. This gave birth to the Anglo-Catholic movement.

Eva had the opportunity to meet and hear preaching by some of its most notable members, including Charles Gore, who became the founder of the Community of the Resurrection, and later Bishop of Oxford. He was then Librarian of Pusey House. It was at Oxford that she learned to appreciate the sacramental life of the Episcopal Church and decided to enter it. However, she was not confirmed until their return to the United States where she was confirmed by Bishop Vincent at Christ Church, Glendale.

It was in England that Eva also became more aware of the restoration of the Religious Life in the Anglican Church. Eva had of course read in history of the Roman Catholic Religious, and knew that there were now Anglican communities, but in Oxford she had the opportunity of seeing members of these communities. Anglican Sisterhoods usually had a ministry of education and help to the sick and poor. In Oxford she might have seen Sisters of the Holy and Undivided Trinity, the All Saints Sisters of the Poor, and the Community of St. John the Baptist. There was also the Society of St. John the Evangelist, the first men's Community to become permanently established. It had a foundation in the United States in Cambridge, Massachusetts. Three English Communities of women already had foundations in the U.S.: the All Saints Sisters of the Poor in Baltimore, Maryland, the Sisters of St. John the Baptist in Mendham, New Jersey, and the Society of St. Margaret in Boston, Massachusetts. No doubt the seed of Religious vocation was planted here.

After their return from England, Eva accompanied Paul to Omaha, Nebraska, to assist him in his ministry at the mission there. Her experience in Omaha was a determining factor in Eva's future course of life, leading to the founding of the Community of the Transfiguration. Her life story is woven with the story of the Community from its foundation until her death on July 6, 1928.

Life of Beatrice Henderson (Mother Beatrice Martha)

Beatrice McCobb Henderson, who is remembered as Sister Beatrice Martha, made her vows with Eva Matthews on August 6, 1898 and is considered the co-foundress of the Community of the Transfiguration. Beatrice was born April 12, 1877 in Lake Forest, Illinois. Her family moved to Colorado because of her father's tuberculosis, and later to Omaha. Beatrice was only 15 years old when she first met Eva Lee Matthews who was teaching in the parochial school of the Associate Mission in Omaha. Eva taught French, but Beatrice wrote that she learned much more from her than French. Beatrice was not then a member of the Episcopal Church. At the age of six she had been baptized at home by a Congregational minister at the same time as a younger sister who later died. But she was rather turned off from religion by a revival preacher who could not answer her question as to why God made the devil, and she considered herself a free-thinker. Irving Johnson's religion class at the school caused her to change her attitude, although she would not admit it at first. On the Eve of St. John Baptist Day, 1894, she was confirmed by Bishop Worthington of the Diocese of Nebraska at a private service at St. Augustine's Chapel, which she had been attending because her mother played the organ there. Mrs. Henderson required Beatrice to attend church at least once on Sunday, and she found St. Augustine's the least objectionable. Mrs. Henderson attended the Congregational Church Sunday mornings and was not happy at first that Beatrice had elected to become an Episcopalian.

Eva took an interest in Beatrice and asked her to help her in some secretarial work, and when the House of Women was started, Beatrice was thrilled to be invited to be one of the members. There were four young girls who continued to be pupils in the school plus three adults, Miss Matthews and Sister Ellis Victoria, then a member of the Community of St. Monica (a Community of widows which was failing). Later Beatrice became a pupil-teacher in the school. As Beatrice describes it in A Follower's Story:

"Miss Matthews was like a stranger to the rest of the household, so much that they often sat through meals in silence, tongue-tied in her presence—so much so that Eva was disturbed and asked Pauline Welles, a teacher in the school and sister of Samuel Welles, who became a member of the Associate Mission, to do something about it. Pauline and I undertook to remedy the situation by recounting amusing situations from the school," (*A Follower's Story*, p. 7).

Beatrice was dismayed when she heard that Miss Matthews was "going to be a Sister." But she was cheered when, before she left for the Holy Land, Eva explained to her that she was not quite sure of her plans for the future, but she asked Beatrice not to engage herself to any other work until she heard from her. Beatrice resolutely trusted her future to Eva Matthews. She had been praying for months that if she could be of any help to the Church of God through Eva, that God would let her serve Him with her through life. The House of Women continued for another year, now with only five members. Pauline Welles was in charge of the charitable and social work, and Beatrice was responsible for the spiritual life of the family, the keeping of rules and the happiness of the household.

From this beginning Beatrice Henderson continued to follow Eva Matthews, eventually joining her in the foundation of the Community of the Transfiguration. As Eva had chosen *Mary* as her name in Religion, Beatrice took the name of *Martha*. "In both the prayer of Mary and the work of Martha shall the Sisters of the Transfiguration find their strength." Beatrice took her first vows at the same time as Eva on August 6, 1898, but when Eva made her life vows on August 6, 1903, Beatrice did not join her on that day. Her delay in taking her life vows demonstrates Beatrice's ability to decide for herself and not blindly follow Eva. At the same time she regretted her delay for the anxiety it would have caused Eva. When she did make her decision, in Lent, 1905, she asked to have the service on Ash Wednesday, February 16, when they would not be able to celebrate. After Mother Eva's death in 1928, Sister Beatrice succeeded her as Superior.

A TIME OF DECISION   2

After his ordination to the diaconate, Paul Matthews, along with his friend, the Rev. Irving Johnson, and some others, had volunteered for the mission field and were accepted by Bishop George Worthington of Nebraska to form an Associate Mission in Omaha, Nebraska. They had first offered themselves to two other bishops in missionary districts but were turned down because they were too "Catholic." Nebraska was already a diocese but aided by the national church and was really a missionary field. Of the original group of volunteers only Paul and Irving actually went. They were ordained to the priesthood along with John Albert Williams, "a Colored (sic) Deacon of the Diocese of Nebraska, on St. Luke's Day, October 18, 1891, at St. Matthias Church, Omaha," (*A Follower's Story*, p. 15). They pledged themselves to serve for three years and to remain unmarried for that time. They worked

Paul Matthews.

together from a common center, serving four missions in Omaha and assisting in St. Barnabas parish. Paul's sister Eva Matthews accompanied the two men to do the housekeeping and to assist in the mission work.

Omaha was a frontier city. It had not yet recovered from the panic of 1893 which was caused by a period of depression. For the first time Eva found herself living among people in poverty. Among the men's other projects, they started a parochial school, and Eva was one of the teachers. It was through this school that Eva became acquainted with Beatrice Henderson who later joined her in the foundation of the Community. Eva took an interest in Beatrice and asked for her help in some secretarial work.

After a few months more clergy came, requiring more space, so Paul and Eva moved into their own house. The three year pledge was extended to four. A new, larger clergy house was built. Paul moved into it.

✠

House of Women, 1894–96

It was then that Eva conceived the idea of a "House of Women." Paul Matthews dates the beginnings of the Community of the Transfiguration to the organization of the House of Women in Omaha (Quarterly 1:2). When the House of Women was started, Beatrice was thrilled to be invited to be one of the members. The group also included Irving Johnson's fiancée Grace Keese, Pauline Welles, and Sister Ellis Victoria. Each member was assigned to a particular church. In describing the work of the House of Women in Omaha, Eva wrote to her sister in March, 1894:

> "There are several objects in view. One is the doing of Church work that cannot be done in the ordinary way of

guilds or that requires some special fitness; another is the training of women in Church work, so that wherever they may be, they can always take an active and perhaps a leading part in the work that is always there to be done. Then, there are women who could always spare a few months every year away from home who cannot, either from circumstances or from disinclination, make up their minds to give it up entirely. They would be greatly benefited in their spiritual life if, instead of spending their three months at the seaside or in the mountains, they would sometimes spend it in a religious house where the rule of life would not be so strict as to exclude them," (Cleveland, p. 8).

Eva Decides

In 1896, as Eva already knew, there were several Anglican Religious Orders of women in the United States which were extensions of English Communities. There was also the Community of St. Mary at Peekskill, New York, the first American foundation to become permanently established (1865). Eva became an Associate of the Community of St. Mary and her original intent was to join it. Her family was unenthusiastic about this desire, fearing that it would separate her from them. She had then no intention of founding a community herself. On November 5, 1893, she wrote to her sister Jane, that Paul had consented to her entering the Sisterhood of St. Mary next summer and that her heart was set on it. In a letter to the same sister, March 28, 1894 she tells of her intention to form a house of women with a life formed on a religious rule and that all would take part in the work of the parish—either in Omaha or in Cincinnati. In the intervening time she had been persuaded by her brother, the Rev. Paul Matthews, later Bishop of New Jersey, and his good friend, the Rev. Irving Peake Johnson, later Bishop of Colorado, to found a new Community in Southern Ohio. Eva made her decision. Her plans developed gradually.

Paul and Eva's Pilgrimage to the Holy Land

First, when his period of service in Omaha ended, Paul and Eva made a pilgrimage to the Holy Land. From abroad she writes on December 11, 1895, to her ever-sympathetic sister Grace, living in Glendale, Ohio:

> "I am growing daily more satisfied in my vocation, and while I can hardly expect to feel the joy of it until I take some active step towards fulfilling it, I see it there waiting for me when the time shall come. What you tell me about the Bishop [Vincent] openly declaring his intention of starting a Sisterhood in Cincinnati, has been a wonderful relief to me. I feel now that he means to include me in Paul's work."

While in the Holy Land, Eva furthered her call. It was there that she chose the Jerusalem cross, the Crusaders' cross, as insignia for the Community. She liked its connection with Jerusalem, and to her the four crosslets around the central cross, symbolized the spread of the gospel to the four corners of the earth.

Sister Beatrice reported that it was while in Palestine that Eva visualized her future Sisters dressed as the women of Bethlehem, in blue with white veils. "Those are some of the fruits of her meditations. She was a pioneer by nature and far from being a coward in any way. If this were God's will for her, she would not refuse Him" (*A Follower's Story,* p. 25).

BETHANY MISSION HOUSE 3

Upon their return from the Holy Land, Paul Matthews was appointed by Bishop Vincent to be in charge of St. Luke's Church in Cincinnati. Eva and Beatrice followed him. The first home of the little Community was at 1711 Freeman Street, across the street from Paul's house, and not far from St. Luke's Church, of which Paul was in charge.

It was a typical West End building. The ground floor contained the drawing room with double doors separating it from the back room. There was a large dining room and ample kitchen. The Sisters used the back room as their workroom. It was here that people came for counsel and relief. On the second floor was an alcove with a connecting door which made a suitable chancel and the connecting front room was large enough to serve as the Chapel. It held a little pipe organ from the Matthews residence in Glendale, and six small pews. (These were later moved to the Oratory of the Convent in Glendale, and were burned in the fire in 1957. There was a small Altar which was later taken to the house at Bat Cave, N.C.) There were three bedrooms on the second floor; one being used for Eva's private office. We have been told that Mother Eva's desk is now in the library workroom in the Convent. The third floor was only over the front half of the building. Beatrice and the other helpers lived here.

Parish and Social Service Work

Mother Eva and Sister Beatrice, with a few helpers, visited the families in the section where they lived, visited sick people, and helped in whatever way they could. For instance, by an arrangement with a coal firm, they bought the coal for the people at a wholesale price and had it delivered to them. They also visited the hospital and formed a Hospital guild. In particular, they worked with mothers and children, and it was from this that Bethany Home was conceived. The helpers pledged themselves for one year, and wore a uniform dress, which for Eva and Beatrice was their postulants' dress. Beatrice's mother and her sisters Marion and Julia were among the helpers. Marion had to return to the West and join her brother because of the Cincinnati climate. Julia was there for four months but died of typhoid fever. Beatrice stayed in the house and supervised the work of the women who cleaned and washed walls and woodwork, windows and floors, and received furniture. They went into official residence on July 17, 1896, and on November 10 Bishop Vincent blessed the house. The work at the Mission House was in connection with Paul's church, St. Luke's, and was under his direction.

They tried everything in the way of church organizations: Sunday School, Sewing School, and Mother's Meetings which grew quickly. Most of the time was spent in sewing clothes and household goods for themselves and their families, and some church linens.

The work at the Bethany Mission House passed through several stages. Many things were tried and methods changed but good was always done. In *A Follower's Story*, Beatrice wrote:

"Mothers' Meetings were filled to capacity. It started with three women meeting in the Mission House. There were soon one-hundred or more on the roll. They were able to select and take the most needy. It became a sort of social club for West End mothers, and some of them frankly said they came as much for pleasure as for the garments they made. Tea and cakes were served at three-thirty, just in time for the children to share it with mothers and grandmothers. The meeting closed with a service held upstairs in the Church where hymns were sung lustily. "I Need Thee Every Hour," "Stand Up, Stand Up for Jesus," and "He Leadeth Me" were some of the favorites. A short address was given to them by the priest, containing much good doctrine and spiritual advice. There was usually a congregation of about one hundred and fifty, including howling babies, tired out by this time. Later, they learned to leave the babies downstairs with a mother or two to take care of them. No one was excused to go home before this service. From this group a special branch of the Women's Auxiliary was formed and functioned for years, sending in its contributions and electing Sister Eva Mary as one of its delegates to the Diocesan Convention," (*A Follower's Story* p. 35-36).

Beatrice described the work:

"Mother Eva Mary shopped in the early summer for the Mothers' Meeting, putting in several hundred dollars worth of material—unbleached muslin for sheets, pillow-cases, nightgowns, and underwear—pretty outing flannel for children's dresses, women's skirts, and boy's shirts; white outing for infants' wear, cotton plaids for children's Sunday dresses and bright, pretty gingham for children's school dresses and women's aprons. These good, solid, portly women of German stock—quite content to be comfortable rather than stylish—were all warmly and completely clad. One garment in four had to be a child's garment. They were allowed two large sheets a year, four pillowcases, two each of wearing apparel and once in two years they could tuft a warm comforter. They paid no dues but all of their work was sewn by hand and had to pass an inspector before they were allowed to order a new piece, or take the finished garment home. The inspector gave them a card which entitled them to order the next garment. Sheets usually took two weeks in making; they did not want to run the risk of having that center overcast seam ripped open. I remember when a newcomer named Mrs. Sheets brought her work to the inspector for the first time. The inspector asked the usual questions: "Garment finished?" Answer—"Sheet." "Garment wanted for next week?" "Sheet." "Name, please?" "Sheets." The bewildered Sister did some more questioning. This was the mother who said of her cute, five months-old baby, the youngest of several children, 'He is new seven times a day.' Mother Eva cut the ordered garments for Mothers' Meetings for several years and then she gave me that fun," (*A Follower's Story* p. 35-36).

After they moved to Glendale, the work at the Mission House continued, involving Sister Beatrice and Mother Eva with a fifteen mile train trip and a street car to the Church every day. From *A Follower's Story:*

"When Father Paul Matthews became Dean of St. Paul's Cathedral in Cincinnati, he asked the Sisters to direct a Mothers' Meeting down there. This we did and carried it on with the help of some of the parishioners for several years. The mothers came largely from the slum district abutting the Cathedral on Plum Street. Here also the meetings soon grew to capacity. We also tried to work for a short time at St. Andrew's Colored (sic) Church, but for some reason this was not successful. I think there was some lack of co-operation or a feeling that white leadership was not necessary—maybe it was not. These were the only works we undertook in the city not connected with St. Luke's Church," (*A Follower's Story* p. 38).

There was much calling done on members of the Mother's Meeting and Sewing School. Sunday school was recruited from these. This school grew so large that for some time there was a second session held on Sunday afternoon. The classes in the morning session were all very large and taxed the ability of the teachers. Miss Nellie Bechtel had a class of thirty-eight and Sister Beatrice's numbered nearly thirty. The Sewing School was organized before there were any classes in Domestic Science in the public schools. They had 235 children on the roll and the large Sunday school room was crowded, so some classes had to be held in other smaller rooms. The meeting opened with prayer. It was divided into two sessions. In the first session they worked on their practice clothes. During the second session they worked on their clothes which they could take home with them when finished. Some of the graduates were able to obtain good positions on their merits and record of satisfactory accomplishment in the Sewing School. The Sewing School was discontinued when the public schools began offering Domestic Science.

At Thanksgiving and Christmas the members of both Mothers' Meeting and Sewing School were given small gifts of fruit and candy. In the early days they gave Thanksgiving Day dinner to a hundred or more children who were admitted by invitation card.

There were many brought for baptism and confirmation as the result of this visiting and the contacts made through the Mothers' Meetings and the Sewing School and Sunday school. Of all the works tried, not counting the regular parish organizations, only the Mothers' Meetings and the Sewing School lasted through several rectorates of St. Luke's. The others were gradually dropped as circumstances changed and the Mission House closed.

The Church League was started soon after Father Matthews began work at St. Luke's. Members of this League were the Catholic minded Church men and women in and about Cincinnati—a sort of oasis in a very dry land. It was a small but vitally interested group who met once a month to read and discuss some Church paper written for the occasion. Mother Eva contributed several very good papers which were printed in the "Church Evangelist," a paper printed by this group. She also contributed some poems and other writings to the "Evangelist." Mother Eva was active in all general Church work in the city. She attended the Flower Guild, the Maternity Society, and the meetings of the Children's Hospital Cooperative Society and took part in all activities connected especially with St. Luke's.

"Fresh Air Camp"

In the summer of 1897 Mother Eva told Sister Beatrice that although she had been helping all types of people, she had been doing very little for very young children and for those not able to come out for school or meetings. So she had rented the old Allen homestead on Congress and Fountain Avenue in Glendale to be used as a kind of "fresh air camp" for families to give them relief from the hot city. Beatrice was placed in charge, with two friends to help her, as well as the mothers who came. Beatrice was then 20 years old. Nearly 200 people benefited that summer from a "whiff of fresh air".

At the end of the summer there were several children, mostly babies, who they realized could not be taken back to the impossible conditions in the city. Mother Eva rented a house next door to provide a home for these children. Sister Beatrice, whose father had been a physician, was very good at taking care of sick babies. They learned many things in that first short year and one was that the city was not the ideal place for a children's home. The dirt of the city and the lack of clean fresh air were not good for the children.

So, early in the spring of 1898, Mother Eva, with her brother Mortimer's help, purchased the old "Huston Hall," also known as the Crafts Wright Place, in Glendale. She paid $4,125.00 for it. She had expected to use it simply as a summer home for a year or two and as a vacation house for city workers, but instead it became the site of the present Convent. After they moved to Glendale, Mother Eva kept up her work in the city. She spent more time in Glendale, but her principal work was still in Cincinnati. It was later in that year that the Sisters made their first vows.

Life is Working His Purpose Out

Sister Beatrice remembered 1899 as serious testing time for the new little Community. She says, "God is working His purpose out." A Religious Community could not be established with the first two members of it living fifteen miles apart. Mother Eva was still keeping up her work in the city and Sister Beatrice was in Glendale. There was a good deal of sickness among the children and Sister Beatrice herself developed symptoms of consumption which alarmed the doctors. She had nursed her father with tuberculosis in Omaha, and her sister who had come with her to Glendale, was dying of it. Sister Beatrice refused to believe there was anything wrong with her, but the doctor gave her six weeks to live unless she went away and devoted herself completely to getting well. Father Matthews suggested Oakland, Maryland, which was within easy reach of Glendale and had a good mountainous climate and good physicians. Mother Eva asked Sister Beatrice hesitatingly if she would go, and Sister Beatrice reluctantly did so. It meant leaving her sister Marion who was slowly dying and her mother to bear this heavy burden without her and Mother Eva to carry the responsibility of it all alone. It was a hard decision to make, however she went. Sister Beatrice carried out all the advice she had ever heard about treatments. Many were praying for her. After two months the doctor said that her recovery was remarkable. She was not allowed to return in August for her sister's funeral lest it undo all that had been done, but she returned to Glendale in the fall. Beatrice believed that her life had been given back to her by God to be used for his work. She learned later that Mother Eva feared that she could not continue without her. This long strain of anxiety and sickness began to show its effects on Mother Eva, who wrote to her sister in October, 1899:

> "I have been in Retreat all this week and it has been most helpful and refreshing. I went into it tired out and discouraged with a sense of being overburdened in the long and apparently unceasing trial of sickness that has borne so

heavily on me this last year, and I came out of it fresh and strong once more, feeling ready and able both to bear and to do God's Will. It is impossible to measure the value of spiritual retreats, to both soul and body. The subject was the Holy Angels and the meditations and instructions were full of beautiful suggestions and helpful teaching, and I feel in much closer touch than ever before with these bright and blessed spirits, our champions in the conflict with the devil and his angels, our elder brethren in the Church of God. We had a beautiful service in the Chapel on St. Michael and All Angels' Day, the twenty-ninth of September. Grace was received as an Associate, and Sister Ethel renewed her postulate. She is not old enough yet to take the novitiate. Some came from the village and a good many came from town. Most of our Associates were there, and after the service we had luncheon and a very enjoyable social hour before they scattered."

Sister Eva Mary was living most faithfully her spiritual life and Rule and working just as hard as she ever had but it required greater physical effort. Her brother, Father Matthews, said truly of her, "She has too much steam for her boilers." Her slight, delicate body was not strong enough to bear all she wanted to put upon it; she suffered from almost constant pain and fatigue. She called it rheumatism and she felt it mostly in her eyes. Frequently she had to stay in a dark room, the slightest ray of light causing acute pain. Sister Beatrice and the others were all very anxious.

Mother Eva still kept up her work in the city. The workrooms, the Mothers' Meetings; the Sewing and Sunday Schools, were all under her care, and she also kept up her general interest in the diocese. She began to come out every night to Glendale, hoping to get more rest, and also because she wanted to watch some volunteer workers who had come to help us there. In April she wrote to her sister,

> "I have been feeling so badly that it has been a great effort for me to do anything. I still have the rheumatic pain that seems to come on every night, though I am comparatively free from it during the day, but feel weak and languid and rather stiff-jointed. I did go in town to close the Mothers' Meeting for the year and we had a very interesting afternoon. There was a little program of music with the usual annual report and then a very bright little talk from Paul closing, to my astonishment, with a presentation of a very pretty china clock, the gift of the mothers to me. I was very much touched by it. There was ice cream and cake—the ice cream being given by Grace, and then Sister Beatrice hurried me off, as she was afraid I would overdo myself. And indeed, I was very tired and have hardly recovered from it yet. Tomorrow I go in to close the Sewing School."

Health and Start at Bat Cave

That fall seems to have been an unhealthy one for the House. Beatrice remembered they had fifteen severe cases of tonsillitis at one time. Eventually almost everyone in the Home, adults and children alike, suffered from it, including Mother Eva herself.

This prostration, weakness and insomnia, with the rheumatic pain, caused such extreme suffering that it alarmed the doctors and they ordered absolute rest for her away from any responsibilities. She had tried resting in Glendale but that was too near her work so plans were made to spend the summer in Hickory Nut Gap, North Carolina. She wrote Colonel Turner of Esmeralda

Inn to inquire if they could rent a cabin somewhere near his place where they could keep house. Sister Eva was always restive and felt out of place in a hotel. The Colonel wrote back to come to the Inn and he would quickly finish a small building he was planning to build on his property. This plan pleased Mother Eva, and she brought her little summer family to the mountains with her. This family consisted besides herself, of Sister Ethel, Rosemary, a two year-old, and Sister Beatrice. They left Mrs. Henderson in charge of Bethany Home. Another helper was in charge of the city work. It was during this summer that they decided that they should have a real vacation house of their very own in these mountains. They first planned to lease the place from the man who furnished their milk, butter, and eggs, on a long-term lease. On one of the visits of Mother Eva's brother Father Paul Matthews and her brother-in-law, Harlan Cleveland, visited this property and accepted the proposition. John Dotson agreed to remodel the small house on the place and this ideal spot became a delightful vacation house. It was a little cottage of three rooms, quite high and commanding a beautiful view, about a mile from the village. Eva wrote of it to her older sister:

> "We leased it for twenty-five dollars a year, and Paul drew plans for improvements that will cost about one hundred and fifty dollars, ($150.00) enlarging one of the present rooms and adding another, with a long, wide verandah in front and a grape arbor at the back and the house to be ceiled throughout with seasoned pine. It is on a natural terrace that can be made very pretty with flowers, and there is a beautiful knoll crowned with chestnuts where we can have a summer house, and there is room at the back of the house for a garden. It will not take much to fur-

nish it as she would make the same sort of rustic furnishings that I have here, shelves draped with chintz, and the chairs I already have, and beds that Paul is going to send me from Cincinnati. Paul said they must have a horse of their own, and a very good opportunity presenting itself, I bought one yesterday. It is a pretty bay, young—only seven years old, and strong and perfectly gentle, well used to the mountains having been reared five miles from here, quite fast, and with a good single foot gait for riding and all for sixty dollars. (His name was Thomas.) The man who owned it had to sell to pay off a mortgage on his land or I think I could not have gotten such a good bargain."

Thomas the horse.

This was the beginning of our time at Bat Cave, North Carolina, first as a place for rest and recuperation, and later a place with opportunities for ministry. Sister Beatrice felt that this was God's way of preparing Mother Eva for the work she was intended to do.

BETHANY HOME FOR CHILDREN 4

The Original House, Glendale, Ohio

The property they had purchased in Glendale, the old Huston Hall, also known as the Crafts Wright place, was an old farmhouse in Glendale. It became Bethany Home (which eventually became Bethany School) and the Convent of the Transfiguration. Mother Eva and Sister Beatrice moved to the new place on July 3, 1898. It was in deplorable condition, and they had to camp out that summer while the house, a fine old farmhouse, was made ready for its new occupants. The people of Glendale were very generous, providing milk, provisions, ice, hammocks and furnishings. By September the house was ready and was blessed by the Rt. Rev. Boyd Vincent, Bishop of Southern Ohio, on September 29, 1902, the Feast of St. Michael and All Angels. That was always observed as Bethany Home's birthday, and the tradition has continued in Bethany School.

The home had opened with five babies. The annual reports for the first few years give the number of children received, the number of deaths and the number returned to their parents. At that time they received children from many places, including several from Alaska. Later, when Bethany Home became a Community Chest recipient, they had to restrict admissions to local children. In September, 1900, there were twenty-four children in the Home.

Life at the Home

At the beginning Sisters and children lived together. A Sister often shared her room with an infant. A woman was employed to help with the babies. After she left our employment, we decided not to take any children under two years old because of the difficulty caring for young babies. This gave more space for the older children. There were gardens and pets and domestic animals to care for. Children and Sisters did housework together.

Bethany Home.

The Home received much help, in money and in contributions of clothing, from individual donors and from church groups. The women of the Presbyterian and Episcopal Churches, including a group called the Bethany Home Aid Society, did a great deal of sewing for the children.

Old Oratory.

One of the first priorities when preparing the original building for occupancy was the provision of a Chapel. The former ball room of the old farmhouse was used for this. This room was enlarged in 1905, but it was still very crowded, for there were now 62 children in the Home. The stairway leading to Mother Eva's apartment was just outside the chapel and older

Sisters reminiscing about that period said that many of the children sat outside on the stairway. A fund for a new Chapel was started in 1906 with the gift of one dollar from a child, followed by a $25 gift from a friend. The fund grew slowly. The Sisters say that the fund grew by many small gifts. In 1925 the Sisters decided that there was enough money to start building a new Chapel. After the new Chapel was built the original one was called the Oratory.

The home in Bethany "where Jesus was wont to visit as a Friend and where Mary and Martha typified the life of prayer and service in their consecrated lives," was always a favorite subject of meditation for Mother Eva. She wanted her home to be a Bethany home. She wanted it to be a real home, a happy home, with happy memories of their childhood. The children wore uniforms, but were allowed to wear their own clothes when visiting their families. The children and the adult helpers did most of the house work and the Bethany Home girls were well trained.

Schooling

Because of the loss of school days during epidemics, and to provide greater time for the children's religious education, it was decided that Bethany Home should have its own school rather than the children attending the Public Schools. Two school rooms were built. For many years Bethany Home had its own high school. By that time the Community had several Sisters who were qualified to be high school teachers. And they were able after several years to receive the standard of Grade A from the State Board of Education.

Confirmation class 1936.

Mother Eva wanted to give the children of the poor the same opportunities as other children had. They were encouraged to develop any special talents. Scholarships in music were donated by Professor W. S. Sterling of the Metropolitan College of Music in Cincinnati. A Scholarship in Art was given by Miss Devou, principal of the Glendale College, and to the Cathedral Schools for one in Ecclesiastical embroidery. Professor Sterling and Mrs. Sterling retired to a cottage on the Bethany Home grounds and there he also taught some of the Sisters.

The Sisters wanted to train the girls to be good citizens and, if possible, leaders in their parishes wherever they might live. At the beginning, children were accepted from anywhere and there were children from twenty-seven states, Alaska, Canada, China, and the Philippines. When they came under the Community Chest, in 1919, they were not allowed to take any from outside of Hamilton County unless their parents paid board.

✠

Bethany Home for Boys

In 1907 the Community undertook the management of an already established work, a Boys' Home, which was operated in conjunction with Bethany Home for Girls. The Home had been founded in the city of Cincinnati by the Rev. Samuel S.G. Welles, assistant to the Rev. Paul Matthews at St. Luke's Church. It was originally a house of detention for boys on parole. They were trained in manual arts. There were difficulties in finding suitable places for them to work. And after Father Welles left, difficulties in finding adequate administrators. It was called the Church Home for Boys. Father Paul Matthews called this to the attention of William Cooper Proctor, and the Sisters of the Transfiguration were invited to take charge. It became Bethany Home for Boys. (It is of interest that Miss Caroline Cochran and Miss Deborah Powell who helped with the Boys' Home before it came to the Community became our Sisters Caroline Mary and Deborah Ruth.)

For a few years Bethany Home for Boys was operated in conjunction with Bethany Home for Girls. The boys were moved from the Home in the city. From the spring of 1909 until July, 1918, the boys were housed in a building on the convent grounds and shared in the care and the privileges of the Bethany Home for Girls. In 1918 a house of their own was built for them on property purchased nearby. There was room for about 20 boys, aged six to fifteen.

Sister Clara Elizabeth was put in charge of the boys in 1911 and was responsible for their teaching and care. She mothered and fathered the boys for several years. The boys flourished in the new atmosphere away from the city. Their health improved from the more nourishing food, and so did their behavior. The property was a little farm. Under Sister Clara's leadership the boys built a barn for their cows and the Swiss Chapel through which she taught them the art of woodcarving. The boys attended Public School and some of them joined the Boy Scouts. For a time the boys were taught at home because of the distance. Sister Clara's health broke down and she and Mother Eva felt that the boys would do better under the supervision of a man. Father Boggess took charge of the work but gave it up after a few years. In 1922 the Community relinquished administration of the Boys' Home, and sold the property to the Diocese, and it was reorganized as St. Edmund's Home, later known as St. Edmund's Camp. In 1995 the property was sold to private developers. The Chapel which had been built by Sr. Clara and the boys was purchased by a group in Glendale and moved to a new site near the village square.

5 TRIP TO ENGLAND

Mother Eva was aware of her lack of training in the Religious Life. During these formative years especially, Mother Eva Mary had the wisdom to follow the guidance of the Holy Spirit and the initiative to seek guidance when contrary advice was given or pressure was brought upon her by outsiders, sometimes even by most interested friends. She frequently said she did not want to be under the special training of any one of our Religious Orders for men. She wanted to be free to use any of them for Retreats and as specialists in spiritual matters, but she did not want to be under them officially. She thought it better that the regular house Chaplain of our Community should be a married priest.

Travel Arrangements

Father F. C. Powell, a member of the Society of St. John the Evangelist (SSJE), who later founded the Order of St. Anne, took a great interest in us and frequently visited Bethany Home. Already a member of an established Community, he had knowledge of the Religious Life which Mother Eva valued. Fr. Powell had a great influence on Mother Eva. It was he who suggested our motto, Benignitas, Simplicitas, Hilaritas. Mother Eva had originally favored St. Paul's "In whatever state I am, therewith to be content." Sister Beatrice says she voted in favor of Fr. Powell's suggestion.

It was Father Powell who suggested and made possible the trip to England to visit Communities there. After the death of Sister Beatrice's mother in 1907, Mother Eva thought it expedient to make the trip. Fr. Powell obtained invitations to visit St. Margaret's in East Grinsted and the St. John Baptist Community in Clewer. He gave them letters of introduction which procured for Mother Eva and Sister Beatrice several weeks of valuable experiences.

The works at home were well organized and could safely be left for several months. Mother Eva learned from her cousin, Sister Lydia Margaret, Society of St. Margaret's, about the New England Teachers' Travel Bureau, and for a small fee she joined it.

This very practical travelers' bureau gave lists and addresses of respectable, moderate pensions in the British Isles, names of good doctors and dentists, and other practical hints. They determined to travel third class in England which they learned later was really the best and most interesting way.

Mother Eva knew herself to be a very poor ocean traveler. Sister Beatrice was an unknown quantity. So they took passage on the S.A. Minnehaha of the Atlantic Transport. Because these ships transported cows, who suffer from seasickness, these boats are built broad, sacrificing speed for steadiness. It made a ten days' passage to England. Sister Beatrice was young and enthusiastic. Let her start the story:

> "England looked like a tidy flower garden. I blushed to remember the railroad entrances into our cities, the big or

small towns alike: dumps, tumble down back yards full of trash, garbage cans and gray wash out on lines. Here window boxes, neat hedgerows, flower beds, quaint houses quite like our 'Spotless Town' pictures at home. Even the railroads seemed like toys with the cute 'goods trains' and gaily painted but powerful engines to the passenger trains. And those shrill, high pitched whistles quite in keeping with the gay engines. I was thrilled!"

Pilgrimage to Holy Places

Their plan was to make a pilgrimage to England's holy places before visiting the Convents. Sister Beatrice's first view of St. Paul's great Cathedral was at an early service in one of St. Paul's side chapels, the morning after they arrived in London. They did little sight-seeing in London at this time, for after a few days spent in arranging the trip they started on their tour. They went up the east side of England to Cambridge, which became Sister Beatrice's first love for college towns, on to Bury St. Edmund and saw the Inn with its room and big bed where Queen Elizabeth I had spent a night. Then they went to Ely Cathedral rising a glorious pile out of flat fen country, pilgrims here spending but a night, then in rapid succession Peterborough, Ripon, Lincoln. They went on to York and Whitby and then went on to Durham. The verger there gave Sister Beatrice some fragments of St. Cuthbert's original coffin. These tiny bits of wood are in a handsome silver reliquary placed in and behind the reredos on the Gospel side of our High Altar in Glendale.

The trip continued to Lindisfarne, the Holy Isle, to Edinburgh, through the Trossachs and Rob Roy country to Fort Williams and down the Caledonian Canal to Obad. Sister Beatrice loved Obad. From Obad they sailed around the Island of Mull to Fingal's Cave but even more thrilling, on to Iona, the isle of the Saints. They went down the west coast through the Grinning canal stopping in Glasgow, then to Carlisle where the old unfinished Cathedral interested Sister Beatrice, showing much of the transition state or development of architecture through the centuries. They went on to Chester where they had rooms in a quaint, damp house on the wall and looked down on the river Dee. Chester was most interesting in every way with its quaint unspoiled buildings. They visited the "Lake Country" seeing the Falls of Lahore, rowed over the beautiful Derwentwater, then on to Tintern Abbey ruins.

"Tourists"

After seeing St. Alban's they passed from the pilgrimage atmosphere into the tourist, seeing Stratford-on-Avon, Warwick with its commercialized castle, Kennilworth and Oxford. Geography, history, both Church and secular, past and present, literature, art, in fact education in innumerable ways both ancient and modern, each with its proper emotional appeal. To this should be added Canterbury Cathedral and St. Martin's in the Fields where it is said that King Ethelbert was baptized.

Back in London they missed nothing Sister Beatrice had ever heard about: the Tower of London, British art galleries and museums. They "did" them all. They made several visits to Westminster Abbey, though they wasted little time in looking at the tombs which Sister Beatrice considered atrocities, but which clutter up the nave of that dignified Minster. All this was the preparation for their visits to the Religious Houses.

Perhaps the verger at Durham gave Sister Beatrice the idea, for she acquired the habit of picking up a stone at each of the holy places they visited, later to be made into a pavement in front

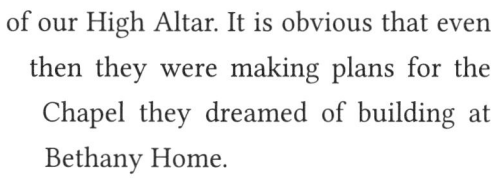

St. Paul's Cathedral, London, England.

of our High Altar. It is obvious that even then they were making plans for the Chapel they dreamed of building at Bethany Home.

In St. Paul's Cathedral work was going on in the dome where glorious mosaics glitter down on the worshipers. Here Sister Beatrice picked up some discarded bits of mosaic for her collection of holy stones. The verger scorned her pickings and got her some fresh, new bits. These now outline the pavement of English stones before the Altar, the idea here being the continuity of the Church. One of these stones is from an ancient Chapel deep down under Chester Cathedral dating from the days of King Harold. She felt very Saxon about that. The verger at Westminster Abbey gave her a piece of Purbec marble. He said it was a bit of a pillar which fell one night in St Faith's Chapel, one of the oldest parts of the Abbey. Beatrice's holy stones are now, as she planned, imbedded in the stone in front of the Altar in the beautiful chapel in Glendale, symbolic that the priests serving at our Altar are standing on an Anglican foundation. The stones which she brought later from the Holy Land are in the Altar Stone. There are diagrams of these hanging in the narthex of the Chapel.

Visits to Convents

After a few days of London they set out on the second part of their journey, the visits to Convents. Sister Beatrice was very nervous about these having heard about English reserve and airs of superiority. She was happily surprised.

"The excitement of sightseeing, along with the accompanying physical weariness was over and we were about to enter a cloister where we had neither duties nor responsibilities and she wondered if the weary days would drag themselves into weeks. They had heard how austere the Community of St. Margaret's was, and how spacious and beautiful the Convent buildings, how well trained and numerous the Sisters were."

Sister Beatrice felt herself to be very small and presumptuous and insignificant.

All her fears proved to be groundless, except that the buildings were cold, so damp and cold that she learned the meaning of marrow, chilled marrow at that. Extra wool clothing made little difference. Furnaces were not started until November first regardless of the weather and the weather was cold rain.

After the first few days when they were left very much to themselves with no one except the Guest Mistress apparently knowing they were there, they were quite suddenly adopted into the warm heart of the Community. Evidently they had been weighed in invisible balances and not found wanting. They had passed whatever test it was for they now found the Community as warm in its heart as the Community room was with its wide fireplace glowing and bright and dear old Sisters who sat chatting around it. Sisters found time to take the visiting Sisters for walks in beautiful woods clothed in autumn colors. The Chapels and Sacristies held much of interest and the Sacristans were most kind in their teaching. Sister Beatrice found the services were beautiful although she never quite got used to the English Mass. She enjoyed Vespers especially because there were rows of sweet-faced little girls so like the dear ones at home.

Mother Eva spent hours with the Reverend Mother or the Chaplain or the Mistress of novices, as she did in each Convent they visited, while Beatrice spent profitable hours with the lesser dignitaries or younger Professed. After two weeks in East Grinsted they regretted that they could stay no longer but must hurry on to Clewer to visit the Sisters of St. John the Baptist. Sister Beatrice remembered "Our first love will always be St. Margaret's in East Grinsted where pleasant memories warm the chill of remembered physical discomfort."

To Sister Beatrice's relief they found the Mother House of the Sisters of St. John the Baptist in Clewer in England warm and cordial and full of darling Sisters who made them most welcome. They did not go through any initial chilling stage of inspection; maybe coming from East Grinsted assured them of their integrity. Here again Mother Eva consulted those in authority and learned much.

Sister Beatrice wrote that she learned much about taking care of children from the Sister in charge of their Children's Home.

> "We had just arrived in the development of our own Home where our first little girls were going through their adolescence and they had found it hard to understand the rather sudden change from little care-free girls to girls rebellious and giving all kinds of trouble. We had tried putting some of them out to service with no good results—others we returned to parents which was not really kind, or as a last resort we sent them to a Good Shepherd Convent for reformation. We felt we were shirking our own responsibility in each case, but we knew the girls were a bad influence on the younger children" (*A Follower's Story*).

This competent Sister (also named Sister Beatrice) gave them words of real wisdom which long proved true. She said, "Girls reaching adolescent age could not understand themselves any more than we could understand them. They should be loved through this difficult age and that almost as suddenly as they had changed at twelve or thereabouts they would change again into fine young women a few years later. Love was the solution to all of their problems, love, patience, and understanding. She also told them that it was important to have an older group—those who had gone through it—in the family for they would be a steadying influence and the younger children could look up to them as their examples rather than to those going through their difficult years." Sister Beatrice added that they had acted on her advice ever since and sent no more children away except those who were deficient or incorrigible. She believed that it was worth a trip to England to learn this valuable advice from one so experienced: "Love, patience and quiet good sense and sympathetic understanding wins out every time."

> "Clewer is part of Windsor, and while visiting there we heard the boy choir of St. George's Chapel, Windsor Castle, sing most beautifully the anthem 'God Shall Wipe Away All Tears from their Eyes,' sung on All Saints' Day. The two Sisters were admitted by card as this was a popular service. They sat in the choir facing the screened balcony where the Royal Family sit when attending a service privately. The choir was lighted by candles stuck in holders in the parapet. The whole experience put the Americans in a medieval atmosphere. On another occasion they were privileged to go through the vaults of Windsor Castle. One of the Sisters had a friend who was custodian of this treasure. Here they saw silver and gold that filled many rooms to the ceiling, such elaborate dinner sets and center pieces and treasures worth a King's ransom" (*A Follower's Story*).

To Sister Beatrice it was a relief to see Queen Victoria's favorite tea set, a simple, unadorned silver teapot, sugar bowl and creamer as might be seen on your Grandmother's table. They could not see all of Windsor Castle as it was being prepared for a visit from the German Kaiser. Previously they had been caught in the throngs on a London street following his procession but they did not see him. Said Sr. Beatrice, "That is as near as I ever came to royalty that I know of and quite near enough for a good Yankee."

Sister Beatrice, S.S.J.B. (Sisters of St. John the Baptist) also took them to visit her aunt who was Mother Superior of the enclosed Society of the Most Holy Trinity located at Ascot Priory. When the little novice who showed them around learned that they were from Ohio, she thought they had a mission there. She really meant Hawaii. Years later the Sisters of the Transfiguration took over that Hawaiian Mission. It was St. Andrew's Priory in Honolulu.

"When we went through the dear little "Lodge" where Dr. Pusey died, I noticed the heavy growth of English ivy over the entrance. I nipped a small sprig of it as we left and showed it to the group of Sisters assembled at the door as we bade them good-bye, saying laughingly I had stolen it. "Oh no," said a shocked Sister, "you said to the Sister, 'may I have this spray of ivy?' and she consented." "Oh, no," I said, "I took care to take it when she was not looking." My memory is of a doorway full of curious, shocked Sisters bidding us queer Americans goodbye. "That ivy sprig survived many discouraging years and is now trying to cover the North side of our Chapel in Glendale."

They left with real regret after a very pleasant and profitable visit in Clewer. The Sisters of St. John the Baptist added much to our trip in England. They were told that the highest praise we could receive from these new friends both in East Grinsted and Clewer was to be told we seemed more English than American! A doubtful compliment to the ears of staunch Americans but appreciated when it was meant as true praise.

Sisters of St. Mary the Virgin, Wantage, England

Before leaving America they had been asked by a friend to visit his sister who was a Sister of a Community in Worthing (Sisters of the Holy Rood) and so their pilgrimage led them there! "How great and inexhaustible are the gifts of God and how mysterious are His Ways!"

This Sisterhood is under the direction of the Sisters of St. Mary the Virgin at Wantage. Their Mother Superior, Assistant Superior and Mistress of Novices are Sisters from Wantage. "When they learned the object of our visit to England and that Wantage was not on our itinerary they felt quite hurt. Mother Eva explained we had no letter of introduction nor invitation to visit them. The Reverend Mother promptly said she would obtain one for us at once. This she did and after our visit in Clewer we spent three days in Wantage."

Beatrice writes, "We felt much at home immediately in Wantage. We were impressed with the sense of youth and vigor and also with its wholesome growth. Imagine a Novitiate of over fifty!" (*A Follower's Story*). They left in August, 1907 and returned in November, just in time for Thanksgiving.

Since that time there, other Sisters have been able to visit several English convents and they have always had the same warm welcome. Our Community is also indebted to the Community at Wantage for their assistance to us in more recent years. Sister Morag Michael came to help us with our renewal in 1970, and Mother Winsome, their Superior led us in a renewal workshop in the fall of 2007.

Sister Beatrice and Mother Eva found the details of worship in England as varied as their Chapels. They decided on certain things to be their custom. It was not from ignorance but with deliberate decision that they planned the customs which were to be ours. For many years we used handwritten copies of the music for our Office Book. In 1970 our choir director gave us the music in a booklet printed by Wantage.

BETHANY HOME GROWS 6

By 1901, with 10 adults and 25 children, Bethany Home had become very crowded, and plans were made for a new building. The addition to the original farmhouse was still insufficient. Mother Eva planned for 60 children. The new building, which in 1928 became the Sisters' convent, adjoined the original building.

Mother Eva and Sister Beatrice formed two groups of older girls. The St. Mary's Society of confirmed girls was directed by Mother Eva, with a rule akin to our Associates' Rule. It evolved into an Altar Guild. The St. Martha's Society, directed by Sister Beatrice, was designed to train the girls in good housekeeping. Children participated with the Sisters in the Chapel services. Sister Beatrice's mother, Mrs. Henderson, had taught the children to sing the Psalms. They observed the seasons of the Church year, and they earned money for mite boxes during Lent. Hilaritas Hall, a prefab-

Addition to original convent.

ricated building, was built by the girls and the maintenance men. It was for many years used for recreation and for plays and other activities. It is now replaced by the gymnasium, also officially called Hilaritas Hall although that name is seldom used. Sister Beatrice looked back with nostalgia to those early days, but she recognized the value of adapting to new ways of child care.

✠

Building and Dedication of the Cottages

In the early 1920s, to keep with modern methods of institutional child care, Mother Eva and Sister Beatrice decided to change to the Cottage System for care of the children, and Bethany Home Village was built. Three dormitory buildings, the refectory, and infirmary buildings were dedicated on St. Nicholas' Day, December 6, 1927. Mother Eva arranged a little ceremony for each cottage. The children who were to occupy the house met Mother Eva and a delegation of Sisters, of course the house mothers were among them, on the porch where the oldest child received in trust a scroll bearing the words, which Mother Eva read with impressive earnestness:

> "In the Name of God. Amen. The Sisters and Associates of the Community of the Transfiguration hereby present to the first group of the Children of Bethany home for their own use and in trust for those who may succeed them this complete Cottage of Bethlehem and all its contents, furnishings and equipment in the hope that they will enrich this gift with many happy customs and good traditions before they pass it over to their successors. Presented this Saint Nicholas Day, Dec. 6, in the year of our Lord 1927."

Bethel was duly presented to the "second group," and Bethsaida to the "third group." There were eventually also an infirmary, Bethesda, the refectory with music rooms, and library upstairs, Beth Eva, a large well-equipped school house, St. Faith's, and the children's store, run by the Seniors. The buildings were connected with walks and roads—Irving Avenue and Paul Street.

The oldest girls were still housed in alcoves down at the Hope, the laundry building, and felt a little abused at the contrast. Then Sister Constance Anna came home from China on her furlough. Their woeful looks roused her untiring energies and promptly put her rare gifts, including her flashing dimple, to the task of raising money for a suitable cottage for them, and in short order she raised enough for the best dormitory building of them all. It is called BethAnna, the House of Grace. Each girl had her own room with running hot and cold water. Mother Eva never saw BethAnna, the school house or the Chapel, but she died happy in the thought that her dear children were adequately housed at last.

✠

The Old Convent

When the children moved into the cottages the Sisters moved into their space and renovated it into small rooms, called "cells," for the Sisters. The cells were divided by thin partitions. Each room had a bed, a cupboard for clothes, a stool and a small table for a desk. Some also had a shelf above the bed for books. The doors each had a transom window to allow for air circulation. On the ground floor there were two large rooms. The children's refectory became the Sisters' refectory. The other room became the Community Room. There was a wide hallway which led to the pantry and then to the kitchen. Beyond the kitchen were the guest dining room and then the Red Parlor, a sitting room so named because of its original decoration. A corridor led on to the oratory. There seems to have been some kind of kitchen and storehouse in the basement where Sister Hilda made marmalade.

Life in the Cottages

When the cottage system began in 1927, there were two cottage mothers in each cottage, sometimes two Sisters, or a Sister and a secular cottage parent. Each cottage had room for 20 children. There were two dormitory rooms with bunk beds upstairs for the girls, plus a room for a cottage parent. Downstairs there was one cottage mother room and a dormitory type room with four beds for the girls. A new postulant was frequently assigned to a cottage. Religious education was not neglected. Over the years the schedule no doubt changed from time to time. In the 1950s the children attended the Sunday Eucharist and one weekday Eucharist. They attended Evensong every day. The children were taught about baptism and the un-baptized were encouraged to ask for baptism. Each one who did was allowed to choose a Sister for a godmother. Some of those Sisters kept in touch with their godchildren long after they left the Home. Some children who had the same godmother called themselves "godsisters." There were special celebrations at Christmas and Easter. Each cottage had a Christmas tree which was decorated by the cottage mothers as a surprise for the children. On Christmas Eve the children hung up their stockings in the children's dining room, and found them filled in the morning. The stockings were procured in pairs and filled ahead of time and replaced by their mates on Christmas morning. The older girls came to the convent and awakened the Sisters by singing Christmas carols. When there were no longer boarders the novitiate continued the custom. On Easter morning there was an Easter egg hunt in the yard behind the convent. The Sisters kept Vigil in the Oratory from Good Friday until Easter morning. Some of the Sisters were assigned extra vigil time early Easter morning so that they might leave the vigil and hide the Easter eggs for the children. Naturally some children objected to so much church going, but coming back for a visit years after leaving Bethany Home, they remembered it with pride and affection. For many years the Christmas Midnight Mass congregation included many "old girls" who came back to visit their Sisters. Although most of those Sisters have passed on and the "old girls" have aged, there are still a few who come back on Christmas Eve.

High School

For many years Bethany Home had its own high school. At first the older girls were sent to the village high school but they found that the many disadvantages outweighed the advantages. It took the girls out of the routine life and set them apart, making them not quite one with the group at home. It brought different standards and ideals into the home atmosphere. Over time, the Sisters realized that the high school was always very small, and eventually it was decided that larger classes and more outside contacts would be of greater advantage. In the fall of 1943 the high school girls began to attend the Glendale High School.

In October, 1912, came the first issue of the Bethany Home Chronicle. It was edited by Margaret Beresford, age 14, and Pearl Robinson, age 13. At the begin-

High school aged girls.

ning it was published monthly during the school year, but later it was less often. The second issue lists a larger staff, including a printer. Everything was hand written and apparently duplicated on a hectograph or ditto machine. After nearly a year they had use of a typewriter, and perhaps a mimeograph. Each issue contained news of the home and the Sisters, including the monthly Honor Roll. There were articles, stories and poems by the girls, and sometimes there was a story by Mother Eva. Sisters went out to China in 1914, and many of the letters home from China and from other branch houses were copied into the Chronicle. Some later issues have news of Alumnae and also of Associates of the Community. During the last few years it was published bimonthly. There was a subscription price of 50 cents, later raised to one dollar. In 1945, the Sisters began publishing the Transfiguration Quarterly and the Chronicle became more specifically a school publication. The last issue is dated March and April, 1950. Copies were bound and preserved and have furnished much information about that era of the Community's life.

May Pole dance.

THE COMMUNITY AND THE DIOCESE OF SOUTHERN OHIO 7

Bishop Vincent and Mother Eva

When Bishop Vincent gave Mother Eva his permission to begin the Community, she promised to obey him faithfully and in accordance with the canons of the Episcopal Church and the American Book of Common Prayer. She kept that promise faithfully, but there was one point on which this promise was grievous to her. Her conversion to Anglicanism was in a large part due to its sacramental life. The chapel was the most important room in the house and Holy Communion was celebrated daily when possible. In the first years, before they had a resident chaplain, they had to depend upon Father Paul Matthews and sometimes other clergy, who could not come every day.

Mother Eva very much desired to have the Blessed Sacrament reserved in their chapel, but on this matter the Bishop would not give his permission. She wrote him twice a year asking for this. He always answered, sympathetically, but saying that he could not in good conscience do so. He knew that some bishops did allow it, but as long as the Church had not officially recognized it, he could not do so. The following letter shows Mother Eva's constant efforts to receive his permission. He wrote sympathetically, on Feb. 8, 1916:

> "Dear Mother Eva,
>
> I feel this is a very serious matter. It is true that with reference to most of the points made in the "Declaration" in your "Constitution," I have given you comparatively a free hand, even while I understood perfectly their doctrinal significance. But your present proposal goes, of course, to the very heart of the matter; and I cannot maintain the same attitude about it as about the other points. The opinion laid down in your "Declaration" with reference to Reservation is perfectly legitimate, of course, as an opinion and even as a purpose. That is, I believe that it is perfectly legitimate for any member of this Church to agitate and work for Church's permission to "Reserve."
>
> But actual reservation, in the present state of the law, is a very different thing. Even "Reservation for the Sick" I believe to be clearly against the Church's law, both in the rubric itself and in the distinct provision of an Office for a clinical Celebration. The House of Bishops of this Church so declared in its Pastoral letter of 1895: concerning only that a bishop might authorize such reservation only in time of plague or epidemic. Reservation for adoration is even more positively against this Church's mind and law, as expressed not only in our own rubric but also in "the black rubric" in the Communion Office of the Church of England.
>
> I don't want to forbid such reservation to the Chaplain at Bethany Home until I am compelled to. But I cannot sanction or ignore it; I must discountenance it positively as squarely in the face of the law of this Reformed Branch of

the Church Catholic; and so as being not only illegal but also disloyal. You cannot realize, dear Mother Eva, what pain it gives me to have to write to you in this way. You know how cordially I have sustained your Society and its beautiful work from the beginning.

But I feel compelled to draw the Line squarely now at this point. If your present purpose is persisted in, I feel quite sure that it will have this effect: It will forever prevent diocesan recognition and authorization of your Society to which we were once so near. It will destroy much practical sympathy, including my own, with your work. It will eventually compel me, I fear, to sever my relations with the Society as President and Visitor.

Signed Faithfully and Affectionately,

Your Bishop Boyd Vincent," (*A Follower's Story* p. 259).

Mother Eva believed devoutly that the Presence of Christ in the Blessed Sacrament in the chapel was necessary for the spiritual welfare of the Sisters. Her thinking is shown in a meditation given to the Sisters in Wuhu, China, in 1915. Wuhu is the first place where they were allowed to have the Reserved Sacrament.

"In our life Christ's Presence is of supreme importance for we have cut loose from other things that we might have that One Supreme Good—not as a future inheritance but as an immediate and present possession. If we have it not, there is an emptiness in our life which will inevitably make it as sterile and unsatisfying as any old maid's in the world."

Bishop Vincent did not change his mind.

The Sisters continued obediently until, in 1923 the Community received an invitation from their friend from Omaha, Irving Johnson, now Bishop of Colorado, to move to Denver to the Oakes Home Corporation, an institution which he thought could be continued as Bethany Home. It included not only a children's home but also a hospital. The Sisters were attracted by the fact that there the Reserved Sacrament would be allowed. The matter was discussed at length, and two Sisters visited the institution. However, they decided that as part of a larger institution they would not have sufficient freedom, and voted to reject the proposal, and to stay in Glendale.

A letter came from Dr. Frank Nelson, rector of Christ Church, Cincinnati, while they were considering the proposal:

Irving Johnson.

Jan. 7, 1925

My Dear Mother Eva,

I have just heard this morning that you are definitely considering the plan to remove the headquarters of the Sisters of the Transfiguration from Cincinnati, or rather, Glendale—to Colorado Springs—and that Bp. Johnson and Bp. Matthews are to be here this week to talk it over with you. I hope you will not consider that I am taking a liberty in writing you about it—but as one of the Clergy of the Diocese I am presuming to do so. I hope before making the final decision, you will fully take into account the whole situation here. I quite realize how great an appeal the move to Colorado makes, and yet, here is the home of the Sisterhood for many years, with the ties and roots, close and deep, that that means. The work of the Sisterhood in the Bethany Homes for Boys and Girls, is a very valuable one for us in Cincinnati; and one that we depend on. Just now a Red Cross worker came in to see if I could get a boy they are working over into the Home for Boys and I am waiting for further information, before taking the case up with you. I value deeply the work you are doing there and should be greatly disappointed if it were lessened or given up. I have been greatly interested in your plan for a home for old women in the West End, and while that is still new it offers great possibilities. And then the Sisterhood is part of our Diocesan life, and I should be very sorry to have it withdrawn. The help you have given us, in sending the Sisters from China to tell us of your work, has been a highly prized one, and I shall miss it if it is to be no more. And so, I hope that you will see the way clear to remaining here—and perhaps opening a Branch House in Denver to undertake the work that offers there.

Again, if I have intruded in writing you—please forgive me and believe me.

Very Sincerely Yours, Frank Nelson

It was after this decision to stay in Glendale that Mother Eva wrote to Bishop Vincent saying that they were going to begin Reservation. The letter from Bishop Vincent replied acknowledging their decision, but offered his resignation as Visitor and the end of any official relationship between the diocese and the Community. This was as he had warned them. In his letter he said that he had also discussed the matter with Bishop Paul Matthews, their Chaplain General, who was now Bishop of New Jersey. The Chapter accepted Bishop Vincent's resignation and proceeded to elect Bishop Irving Johnson as their new Visitor.

Reserved Sacrament in our Chapel (1925)

The Blessed Sacrament was reserved on the altar of the Chapel on January 19, 1925. In the Book of Common Prayer, 1979, Reservation is allowed, (BCP pp 96 and 406). Mother Eva died July 6, 1928. Sister Beatrice succeeded her as Superior of the Community.)

Reconciliation (1929)

Mother Beatrice wrote of the conclusion of this unhappy situation with the Diocese.

> "In 1928 Bishop Vincent was a very old man and Bishop Reese was a very sick man with no hope of recovery. Early in January the first year I was Superior, I wrote to Bishop Vincent asking him for his terms for our reinstatement into the diocese. I told him we had always wanted to be loyal and that we had been very much hurt at his disapproval of us. I reminded him that he was growing old beyond the length of years allotted to man and that he knew Bishop Reese was very ill. (Bishop Reese was the Coadjutor who would succeed Bishop Vincent upon his retirement or death.) It would be a great blessing to any incoming bishop not to be burdened with a problem which in some ways was more of a misunderstanding than any deliberate defiance of authority. I wrote to Bishop Reese, using the same arguments. In all this I had the co-operation of Bishop Matthews who was our Chaplain General. On Feb. 25, 1929 Bishop Reese wrote that he would take steps towards our reinstatement. In April Bishop Matthews called on him and brought back a message from the Bishop that

he planned to re-instate us in the diocese unconditionally. We sang a solemn Te Deum on hearing this. Father Lewis, our chaplain, then called on the Bishop and reported the conference was very promising. Dr. Frank Nelson, acting for Bishop Reese, gave permission for Bishop Matthews to confirm our girls on June 11 in the newly consecrated chapel, our first confirmation service in our chapel for four years. Bishop Reese was a very sick man. Bishop Vincent came for the consecration of our chapel."

As Mother Beatrice describes it:

"He was a most saintly character but very feeble and bent, nearing his nineties. Those who saw, say they witnessed a most touching and beautiful sight as handsome Bishop Matthews in his vestments met dear old Bishop Vincent in the entryway of the chapel, knelt and kissed Bishop Vincent's ring and received the Bishop's spontaneous blessing. Bishop Vincent said, as I took him over to the chapel, that he was coming to represent Bishop Reese, but after the marvelous service as I took him over to the Community Room to sign the necessary documents he said, 'I want you to know that I came also for my own sake.' He told me to invite him to come and preach in our new chapel, which of course I did right then and there. He came out one Sunday afternoon for Evensong and preached a beautiful sermon. I know he loved doing it. Thus our wounds were completely healed through the grace and blessing of God."

Mother Beatrice continued with the story of the Chapel:

"This was the year of the building of our chapel and plans for the consecration and the placing of the body of our Rev. Mother Foundress under the high altar was taking much of our time and thought. On August 6, our Feast Day, Bishop Reese called me over the telephone and arranged for Bishop Matthews to go in to receive the official permission or notification of our reinstatement and the assurance that Father Lewis was to be given canonical standing in the Diocese of Southern Ohio. Bishop Reese had made the effort to have this announcement come to us on our Feast Day and he wrote a beautiful letter stating the fact of this re-instatement. We sang the doxology on hearing the success of Bishop Matthew's mission. This letter is now in our archives. Since then our connection with the diocese has been without incident."

Bishops of Southern Ohio after Bishop Vincent

Bishop Hobson, their successor was a wise and sympathetic Father-in God. He was also President of the Society of the Transfiguration. Although no longer president of the Society, succeeding Bishops: Robert W. Blanchard, John M. Krumm, William G. Black, Herbert Thompson, Kenneth L. Price, and Thomas Breidenthal have been our good friends. Bishop Price, who was suffragan under Bishop Thompson and then acting Diocesan until Bishop Breidenthal's election, has paid an annual visit to Bethany School on December 6, St. Nicholas Day, to represent St. Nicholas. Newly consecrated (2008) Bishop Breidenthal has also shown great friendship for the Community.

THE COMMUNITY GROWS 8

The first two Sisters, of course, were Mother Eva Mary and Sister Beatrice Martha. Sister Ellis Victoria came in 1903. She looked old and feeble but she was very able and a good example to others. She had been with them in the "House of Women" in Omaha for a year because her own Order was breaking up. Having been released from her allegiance to the Order of St. Monica by her Superior, Mother Caroline, then in charge of the Orphanage of the Holy Family in Springfield, Illinois, Sister Ellis became affiliated with us. She ranked second in our Order for the three short years she lived. She died in 1906. It is said that before she died Sister Ellis had said that in Paradise she would pray for the growth of the Community and that a series of postulants who came soon afterwards were called Sister Ellis's postulants. Then came Sister Ethel Bertha, Ethel Lee who had helped in the Mission House, but whose profession was delayed until 1907 when she was old enough to make vows.

The Community did not grow until after both Mother Eva and Sister Beatrice had taken their life vows. Many unsuitable women came and went but few stayed long. Sister Beatrice wrote, "Mother

Eva never wavered; she was always hopeful. She remembered Father Huntington, and the Order of the Holy Cross, that they were slow in their first healthy growth." Some aspirants came who were quite unsuitable and really did not understand the meaning of the Religious Life. After Sister Ethel Bertha's life profession in 1907, there were no others until 1910.

Sister Beatrice told of these first Sisters from personal knowledge of them. They were especially exciting to her because they were the first at a time when growth was uncertain. She describes the next four quite fully. Her description indicates the character of those who applied and also of some of the obstacles they had to deal with in their personal religious beliefs.

> "Miss Edith Holliday—now our Sister Edith Constance, certainly had the double vocation to the Religious Life and to the Mission Field. She arrived on the day of a funeral of a Bethany Home girl who had died from an accident! We considered her a great acquisition. Educated, refined, gentle and spiritual, with a very fine mind, she has proved to be a leader always. She had been a secular teacher in the St. John Baptist School, New York, and so was very familiar with the Religious Life."

She was professed on September 28, 1909. She was principal of St. Mary's school in Burlington, New Jersey, was one of the first two Sisters sent to China, and at various times served as Novice Mistress, and as Assistant Superior. She died July 26, 1962.

> "Miss Julia Austin, a dainty little lady all in grey, grey hair, grey furs, pallid complexion, came to us from Brooklyn though she was a Southerner from Charleston, South

Carolina. She had been a member of the Sisterhood at the Church Charity Foundation in Brooklyn but wanted a stricter rule of life and so came to us. She was nearly sixty years old when she came to us but showed herself very adaptable. She became our Sister Irene Augustine. She lived to be nearly ninety-three years old. She was always the most patient, uncomplaining, gentle Sister—dearly loved by everyone, old and young alike. During her aging years she refused to be more of a burden than could possibly be helped. She had a keen sense of humor and a remarkable memory of the most extraordinary experiences which she related well. Sister Irene was always giving us fresh air, opening windows in Refectory, Oratory or Community room, and this in spite of shivering, thin-blooded Sisters who watched with beseeching eyes. Dear Sister Irene died quietly in her chair early one morning, just as she reached to open the window. May her soul rest in peace. She was professed on December 28, 1910 and died Nov. 14, 1943.

"Sister Clara Elizabeth was also professed on December 28, 1910. Sister Clara had come from Switzerland as governess to the Cleveland family in Glendale (Mother Eva's sister) and to teach their children French. Sr. Clara told of a dream she had before coming to America. When she came to Evensong at the convent and saw the chapel, she saw it as the chapel of her dream.... and the Community of the Transfiguration gained a new member. This was the original Chapel, now called the Oratory. Sister Clara was trained as a wood carver and the small Oratory was beautified by her work. A Sister checked her claim that every pew end was different, and so it was. Sister Clara was responsible for bringing Fritz Abplanalp from Switzerland to work on the furnishings of the new Chapel. Sister Clara was also in charge of the Boys' Home connected with Bethany Home. Soon afterwards her health made it impossible for her to continue. Sister Clara was elected Mother Superior in 1938, at the close of Mother Beatrice's term of office. The rest of her story is in Chapter 16.

"Miss Margaret Cherry was from the deep South, with a delightful Alabama accent. She is a Southerner of few but poignant words. She is our Sister Margaret Dolores. Sister Margaret was an artist and she illuminates beautifully."

There is an Altar Book, now in the Archives, which was beautifully illuminated by her. She was professed in August 6, 1910 and died December 27, 1950.

"Miss Ada Banyard—also an artist—was an older woman than we now like to receive. We made no mistake in receiving her though. She became our Sister Ada Francis. She was an Easterner who had lived in the West. She was competent along with her artistic ability. Her delight was to serve meals daintily, to make dainty articles with her needle—lace and other pretty things—and to make children happy. After she had been a postulant six months she had conscientious objections about signing our required declaration. She did not like to consider herself Catholic. She disapproved of what she thought [to be] compulsory confession, Reservation of the Blessed Sacrament and other Catholic practices. She left us to try her vocation with a small order in Washington. As she lived there her objections melted and it was not long before she asked to come back. Sister Ada had to bear the worst persecution for the

Catholic faith of any of us, except possibly Sister Edith in Wuhu, which will come out in the Chapter on China. Sister Ada was called upon to defend the use of Confession, of Reservation, of the practice of the Catholic Faith in general. She was in charge of St. John's Orphanage in Cleveland at the time. She stood her ground valiantly, ably supported by her Bishop, Bishop Leonard. We have to smile to think that she of all of us had to take the near-persecution that she did and we thank God that she came out so victoriously. She lived an active life in spite of a serious heart condition for many years. She died May 30, 1933. May her soul rest in peace."

Sister Beatrice goes on to say,

"We have much for which to thank the Holy Spirit, especially in his protection of us in this matter. He had kept us from making any fatal mistakes. We never yielded to the temptation to add to the Community for the sake of numbers, even when we were so 'young and few' and were in such need of helpers. The Community was not to be sacrificed for the work."

But some really had a vocation. Some came first as helpers in Bethany Home or in the Boys' Home. Others felt the call in other ways and asked to become members of the Community.

Of some of those who have followed there is little known other than dates of birth, of profession and of death. Of them there is no material remembrance but only in the hearts of those who knew them and loved them but are themselves no longer among the living. Ministry includes ministry to the welfare of the Sisters as well as their guests, to work in the kitchen or laundry, sacristy or library. Some had a great influence on the Community, not because of their obvious leadership, but by their faithfulness, their humility, their perseverance in the face of difficulties and their cheerfulness when suffering from infirmity. "There were some of them who have left a name and people declare their praise. And there are some who have no memorial, who have perished as though they had not lived," (Ecclesiasticus 44: 9-14). All their names are included in Appendix I.

The profession dates were often at the convenience of the Bishop Visitor or the Chaplain General who officiated at the ceremony. Sisters Margaret Dolores, Irene Augustine, Clara Elizabeth and Ada Francis were all professed on December 28, Holy Innocents Day, 1910. Sisters Deborah Ruth and Eleanor Mary on June 11, 1914.

Between 1910 and 1928, the year of Mother Eva's death, there were 28 Life Professions. Six lived to celebrate 50 years of Profession.

THE RULE IN THE DEVELOPMENT OF COMMUNITY LIFE 9

Purpose of the Rule

As her plans developed Mother Eva thought more deeply about what her life and the lives of her future Sisters would be in terms of her vision of an American Community. As Religious, we take the Vows of Poverty, Chastity and Obedience, which are the mark of monastic communities. We live in Community. "A common life presupposes a common standard for all who are to live it. Not arbitrary, but set and fixed and accepted by all who are to live it," (Rule, 1945, p. 17). Women come to the Community from many different places, and varying backgrounds. Living by the Rule helps each one learn to respect the differences in one another and to appreciate each others' gifts.

Sisters in the Chapel.

A Rule embodies the spirit of the Community. Our current Rule begins with the words, "The object of our Community as a whole and of each member is the praise, the glory, and the love of God manifested in a life wholly dedicated to prayer and service."

We live in community under the vows of Poverty, Chastity and Obedience. Poverty means giving up personal ownership of goods and property. All Christians are called to chastity by the promises made in Holy Baptism, but for the Religious, it also means Celibacy, giving up marriage and family. Obedience is to God, but is channeled through the Community and by obedience to those set in authority through the Rule.

Forming the Rule

Their first Rule, Sister Beatrice says, was written by Mother Eva and her brother Father Paul Matthews, based on a model rule by the Rev. R. F. Littledale, published in the periodical Church Work. A copy of this is in our archives. Father Littledale, an English priest, was instrumental in promoting the establishment of Religious Orders in the Church of England. He was a colleague of John Mason Neale who founded the Sisters of St. Margaret and also translated many of the hymns in our office book. Neale is in *Lesser Feasts and Fasts.*

Each chapter of the Rule describes some aspect of the Religious Life as lived in our Community. Each chapter begins with an appropriate quotation from the Scriptures and ends with a quotation from Mother Eva.

Two ways in particular show Mother Eva's willingness to be different. Unlike most Communities, her Sisters were encouraged to keep a close relationship with their families. Whereas members of the novitiate were allowed to speak only to their novice mistress or to their work supervisor in most Communities; our novices were incorporated into the total life of the Community, except for

Chapter meetings. (In this context Chapter means the governing body of the Community.)

The words 'religious' and 'community' were both very important to her. In this context the word Religious means a member of a Religious Community. Apparently it was suggested to her that she become a Deaconess, but she questioned this:

> "The question in my mind is, have our Deaconesses the spiritual background necessary to make the interests of others as dear to them as their own?...but the sisterhood can only be properly regarded as a life. Its main object is the life, the work being rather a means to an end. The Sister must go where she is sent, obedience being the main principle upon which the life is wrought," (Cleveland, p. 78).

The first Chapter meeting of the Community was held on September 12, 1898, with Mother Eva, Sister Beatrice, and Fr. Mathews presiding. The Rule was considered at succeeding meetings, (Old Chapter minutes). While respecting the wisdom of the older Communities, Mother Eva felt free to adapt older customs to the needs of an American community in the present day.

The Vows and the Motto

The vows involve sacrifice, but this is more than made up for by the joy of serving God. The Rule provides for the prayer life of the Sister, both personal and corporate even before its active work. The idea of family life is exemplified by our motto: "Benignitas, Simplicitas, Hilaritas," (Kindness, Simplicity, Joy). Benignitas matches the vow of chastity in that we give kindness to all, not just to one person as in marriage. Simplicitas matches Poverty; to everyone according to his need. We have enough for ourselves and to help other people. Hilaritas is described in the Rule as, "Joy is the expression of the Religious Life in its upward tendency to God. It is woven of kindness and simplicity. It is the intrusion of self that is the kill-joy." Mother Eva said, "Exact obedience to Christ is an essential precedent to joy." Obedience means to follow the will of God as we do what the Community sends us to do. At life profession the Sister commits herself to God through the Community for the remainder of her life. Regretfully, there have been some Sisters who, for various reasons, have asked to be released. The Community can release such a Sister from her commitment to the Community, but only the Bishop Visitor may release her from her vows to God. It should be recognized that many Sisters who have been released have made valuable contributions during their time of membership and have gone on to serve God in other ways.

Living by the Rule

In the early years the Chapter met monthly. There was usually a report on new children admitted to Bethany Home, of many deaths of the children, of applications to join the community, but always further discussion of the "constitutions."

On January 26, 1899, Mother Eva announced that she had completed copying the "constitutions," as the Rule was then called. When the Sisters first made their vows, they knew the meaning of the vows, but Mother Eva, with her brother Father Matthews and with Sister Beatrice, were still working on the Rule. A copy of the original Rule, in Sister Beatrice's handwriting has been found in the Archives, with notes as to changes which were made during the process of writing. It is probable that each Sister made her own hand-written copy. As far as is known the first printed copy was printed in 1918 after it had been revised and adopted by the Chapter. This, done while Mother Eva was still in reasonably good health, probably is a good picture of her ideal of community life as it had developed over 20 years. It shows that our emphasis is definitely upon life in community. In regard to ministry, the most certain thing was that Mother Eva wanted to do God's Will. I do not think she had any hard and fast ideas about the type of ministry. Her vision was not of forming new institutions, but it has happened that almost all of our ministries have been connected with institutions. She once had a dream in which she was holding the Christ Child in her arms, and she visualized her Sisters as ministering to mothers and children, but I do not think that a home for children was part of her original vision. But there was a need, and in Sister Beatrice was a person able and eager to fill it. And so Bethany Home began almost simultaneously with the Community.

That Rule described Mother Eva's idea of "intentional" ministry, that is, planned ministry. Her description of her plans for the House of Women in Omaha, and the similarity of that House to the Bethany Mission House and also to some aspects of Bethany Home, indicate a ministry to others which she many not have thought of as ministry, but rather as providing opportunity for other women to do ministry, (Cleveland, p. 85).

The Rule was revised in 1945 and again in 1978. In each case the revision was a result of lengthy discussion and planning by the Community, with every Sister given a chance to contribute. Work began on a revision in 1971 after the renewal. The 1918 Rule includes Duties toward God, Duties Toward the Community, and Duties Toward Work. The following sections are the Use of Recreation, Duties Toward Outsiders, and Personal Duties.

Unlike the 1945 Rule, in the 1978 edition each chapter has two parts, one of principles and one of directives. The final draft was written by an appointed member of the committee, and it was approved by vote at a General Chapter in 1978. Since then there have been amendments in keeping with changes in the Episcopal Church and with society in general. Although the format has changed the Sisters have always sought to continue Mother Eva's vision of Mary and Martha.

The Rule of Prayer

Although much of the Rule focuses on ministry, the life of prayer is the basis of the total life of the Community. The Eucharist is the heart of that life. The Eucharist and the Divine Office are the essential parts of our life together. Each Sister is required to spend at least a half an hour daily in meditation or contemplation, and half an hour in spiritual reading including Bible reading. The Sisters have a monthly weekend retreat and a yearly retreat of five days.

As our Rule calls us to live a life both active and contemplative, it has been from the beginning a real challenge to keep the proper balance between the life of prayer and the life of service. Mother Eva said, "A Rule well kept is the Religious' best defense in time of temptation."

In addition to the liturgical prayer, *The Angelus*, a commemoration of the Incarnation, is said three times a day.

The Angelus

The angel of the Lord announced unto Mary,
And she conceived by the Holy Spirit
Hail Mary, full of grace, the Lord is with you,
Blessed are you among women,
And blessed is the fruit of your womb, Jesus.
Holy Mary, Mother of God,

>Pray for us sinners, now, and at the hour of our death
>Behold, the handmaid of the Lord,
>Be it unto me according to Your Word.
>Hail Mary...
>And the Word was Flesh,
>And dwelt among us.
>Hail Mary...
>We beseech you O Lord, pour your grace into our hearts, that as we have known the Incarnation of your Son Jesus Christ, by the message of an angel, so by his Cross and Passion, we may be brought unto the glory of his Resurrection, through the same Jesus Christ our Lord. Amen.

Because times and places of silence are essential for a life of prayer the Rule provides for silence at certain times and places, including most meals. In the Rule as revised in 1948, the silent times are from Compline until after breakfast, and from after the Noon Office until 3:00 p.m. Breakfast and the noon meal were eaten in silence except on Sundays and major feast days. One Sister was appointed to read a passage from the Bible. A chapter of the Rule is read at breakfast. Another book may be chosen by the Mother Superior or the librarian for reading during some silent meals.

Mother Eva also realized the need we have for rest. The Rule provides that a Sister have an hour of rest every day, and a month's vacation every year, either with family or friends or in a house belonging to the Community. The Rule also provides that the Superior would be elected for a five year term and might not serve more than two consecutive terms. This also provided for rest, maybe for the one who needs it the most.

Sister Beatrice tells the story of the election in 1918 when the Sisters, in Chapter, modified this rule:

"It was fifteen years since Mother Eva made her Life Profession. We numbered 16 professed Sisters. Mother Eva had transferred most of her property, real and personal, to the Society of the Transfiguration in February of that year. I do remember the day we assembled in our little Chapel for the election. Dean Matthews was there to conduct the proceedings. He held the ballots of the absent Sisters, placing them on the Altar at the proper time. I think he alone was deputed to count the votes. The dramatic moment came when he came out of the little Sacristy, with consternation on his face and in his voice, as he announced there was no election. One vote was lacking to make the required two-thirds majority. We were all dumb-founded. It had never occurred to any of us that Mother Eva would not be elected Mother Superior on this our first election. An impromptu conference took place then and there. It seems that when writing to China and Honolulu for the absent Sisters' votes, Mother did not make herself clear, and they thought she was not willing to serve longer and that she did not want them to vote for her. Sister Edith Constance assures me this was the case. So five votes were not for her. She lacked but one vote to make the required majority.

Someone had a sudden inspiration. Newly professed (April 25, 1918), Sister Olivia Mary was on sick leave living with her family at 'Opekasit,' the family home in Glendale, Ohio. We were held in Chapel while some one was sent to Sister Olivia who had been overlooked when the ballots were distributed. Her ballot, with apologies and explanations, was given to her and she promptly furnished the necessary ballot to make Mother Eva Mary our constitutionally elected Superior. As I remember, the question of electing a new

Superior never came up again. Sister Clara reminds me we changed our Constitution then to make the exception that the Mother Foundress is elected for life. So we lived happily under her jurisdiction until her death in July 1928."

The Habit

A habit is a kind of uniform which shows that the Sister is in the service of Jesus Christ, just as the soldier's uniform shows that the soldier is in the service of our country. "Our habit is a symbol of our commitment to our Lord Jesus Christ within the Community of the Transfiguration. We strive to transfigure the habit by our inner life of Poverty, Chastity and Obedience united into love," (Rule, 1978, p. 55).

The traditional habit is a long blue dress worn with a cincture which symbolizes that we are bound to Christ in the vow of obedience. The three knots on the cincture worn by the Professed Sisters, symbolize the three vows. The crucifix, hung from the cincture, is an expression of our willingness to share in the sufferings of Christ through membership in his body as well as being a mark of the vow of poverty, which makes us completely dependent on him. The white veil symbolizes the vow of chastity. It is fastened with the blue and white Jerusalem cross. Sisters originally wore an outer blue veil when away from the Convent. At the time of the renewal in 1970 Sisters who so desired were permitted to change to a street length habit and an off-the face veil. The outer blue veil was no longer used. The modified habit continues the

Shows changes in the habit.

symbolism of the vows. As time has passed a majority of Sisters have adopted the new veil, but few have chosen the shorter skirt.

Mother Eva chose the Jerusalem Cross as the emblem of the Community, and also the color blue, while on pilgrimage to the Holy Land in 1896. The gold ring with the Jerusalem cross, received by each Sister in the service of life profession symbolizes the life vow.

Their first habits were designed by Mother Eva, based on the dress of the women of Bethlehem, and were made by a dressmaker from Paris, commissioned by Mother Eva's sister, Jane Grey. They were of French serge, not suited to the Cincinnati climate. After one summer they went out and purchased Calico. The lighter weight material has remained the norm except for Sundays and special occasions when a 'dress habit' made of heavier material is worn.

The postulant wears a distinctive dress, not much different from her secular clothing, a short veil and a silver Jerusalem Cross. The novice is clothed in a habit dress and a longer veil. She may choose either the traditional veil which covers the head or the modern off-the-face veil. The novices wear the Community pin. At first profession she receives the scapular, the badge of Christ's service, as well as a cincture and crucifix. At life profession she receives the ring, symbolizing the life vow, and her crucifix is engraved with her name.

The Society of the Transfiguration

The Community is legally incorporated as the Society of the Transfiguration. The Constitutions of the Society, which are an essential part of the Rule, give the necessary legal provisions for admission to membership in the Community. A woman who aspires to join first spends at least a month at the convent as a candidate. If she wishes to continue and is accepted by the Superior and Council she is admitted as a postulant. At the end of a year she may apply to become a novice. If elected by Chapter, she is clothed as a novice, and given her name in Religion. Until 1968 at the close of three years, the novice might apply for life profession. In 1968, at a General Chapter meeting, the step of "first vows" was added, and the novitiate time was reduced to 1½ years and the first profession for an equal length of time. This was because several Sisters under life profession had asked for release.

At the end of a total of at least four years and not more than five, she may apply for life profession. A postulant or novice may choose to leave at any time, but at first profession she commits herself for a set time, and at life profession she commits herself for life. A Sister may ask for an extension of any stage of her Novitiate or first vows.

Canon Law of the Episcopal Church requires that every Community have a Bishop Visitor whose duty is a least once a year to make official enquiries into the temporal affairs of the Community. He, or his deputy, shall officiate at the life Professions of Sisters in the Community, and he alone has the authority to release from her vows any Sister who asks to be released from the Community. The Visitor is elected by the Community and serves for five years or until his successor is elected. The Chapter also elects a Chaplain General, who also serves for a term of five years or until his successor is elected. He shall watch over the spiritual life of the Community, assisting the Superior with counsel and advice over the observance of the Rule and Constitution, and may give advice on any important changes in the works of the Community.

Bishop Irving Johnson of Colorado, who had been associated with the Community since its beginning, became Visitor in 1926. It was remembered by older Sisters that he and Bishop Paul Matthews of New Jersey alternated between the two positions until 1947. The Rt. Rev. Charles Colmore, Bishop of Puerto Rico served as Visitor 1947–1950, The Rt. Rev. Edward Welles, Bishop of West Missouri, 1951–1972; the Rt. Rev. Samuel Wylie of Northern Michigan, 1973 until his very sudden death in 1974; the Rt. Rev. William G. Weinhauer, of Western North Carolina, 1975–1991. Bishop Weinhauer also served as Chaplain General after retiring as Visitor because of his age. The Rt. Rev. C Christopher Epting (our Bishop Visitor from 1991 to present) was Bishop of Iowa when he was elected and now serves at the National Church Ecumenical Office in New York.

Our Chaplains General have been the Rev. Vivan Peterson, rector of St. James Church, Columbus, Ohio, 1947–1966; the Rev. Anthony Damron, O.S.B. 1967–1974; the Rev. James Carrol, then rector of St. James Church, Chicago, 1975–85; the Rt. Rev. John Allin, the Bishop of Mississippi, 1986–1998. The present Chaplain General is the Rev. Johannes van den Blink.

THE NOVITIATE 10

Purpose of the Novitiate

The novitiate is the training step before a woman becomes a Professed Sister, making the vows of poverty, chastity, and obedience for life. As our Rule (1978) says, "The training of the novitiate lays the foundation for the future of the community."

The requirements for admission to the Community are found in the Rule of the Community and are given in the chapter on the Rule in this book. The postulants and novices are under the direction of the Novice Guardian, who is appointed by the Superior. (In the beginning she was called the Novice Mistress; then the Novice Director, and now she is called the Novice Guardian.) Following the example of some other communities, for sometimes the novice has to be protected from her own enthusiasm as well as requests from other Sisters. Sister Beatrice wrote, "Mother Eva Mary was her own Novice Mistress for our first twenty years. After all, everyone was a beginner, a novice. She was anxious to train her Sisters herself. She wanted them to understand her vision for the Community, and in the beginning she knew the responsibility for imparting this, rested on her. She had felt the call so clearly to establish a purely American Community and recognized the responsibility was on her."

Her spiritual advisor, Bishop Johnson, expressed it in his foreword to Grace Cleveland's book, Mother Eva Mary, C.T.:

> "It was during the period of 1891–1896, when she worked out the problem of her vocation to the Religious Life. It was a perplexing question she faced. Her humility called her to accept obedience to existing Orders; while her convictions and her love of adventure prompted her to pioneer in creating an order that should preserve that which was excellent in medieval tradition but should add certain elements."

Mother Eva's vision for the Community was that it allow for personal freedom with Community unity in the love of Christ and reflect more particularly than the older institutions, the peculiar genius of the Anglican Church and its passion for personal liberty, which is both its glory and its danger. The Christian life calls for self-sacrifice and discipline, but not regimentation to a mechanical standard, and, according to Mother Eva:

> "First and foremost the one living thing needful in vocation is devotion to our Blessed Lord. Second, submission to a necessary and reasonable discipline which should be more closely related to Anglican standards, than to those of medieval character."

Sister Beatrice wrote,

> "Mother Eva was a born pioneer and unafraid of public opinion even when it came from her own devoted person-

al family. As an instance of her spirit as pioneer, we were the first Religious to drive our own automobile, which we did in 1917. She foresaw that motoring would become an important means of transportation. She never learned to drive a car herself but she was in the first group of Sisters who drove down to our North Carolina mountain house over roads through Kentucky on which our more modern drivers would hesitate to drive. I am sure she would be reconciled to air travel, if she were living today, using the same good arguments. We were also the first American Community to undertake mission work overseas when we went to China in 1915."

Mother Eva was anxious to train her novices particularly in the interior life. She once said that a Sister full of grace was a graceful Sister. She was often surprised at the almost total ignorance of the Bible of many candidates. She, having been a good Presbyterian was very familiar both with the Old and New Testament Scriptures. At one time our novices were required to read the Bible through in their first year as part of their training. Their Bible reading was to take the place of almost all other religious reading.

Mother Eva prepared and dictated to her class many wonderful courses of meditations. She also compiled lessons on Theology and courses in Church History. Her classes in meditation were daily, her other courses were weekly. The Community has a great treasure in her manuscript writings, written principally for her novices' classes.

As the Community grew in numbers Mother Eva began to feel the need for the novices to have a little more supervision and detailed training. The distinction between the novices and the Professed Sisters seemed to be too slight at times. Mother Eva was not a disciplinarian in the exact sense of the word. Sister Beatrice remembered that one time, a good novice felt compelled to call Mother Eva to task for some lack in management with suggestions of how certain things should be corrected. Mother Eva then went to Sister Beatrice and said she felt the novitiate, now numbering eight, should be more closely organized and given more direction and that, "She, herself, was no good at that sort of thing." To Sister Beatrice's horror Mother Eva appointed her as first Novice Mistress.

Sister Beatrice as first Novice Director

Sister Beatrice was dismayed at the assignment. She felt her inadequacy, and seems to have been rather in awe of some of the novices. She prepared very carefully for her first meeting with that group of novices. They had been instructed to bring all of their reading matter with them to the lecture. Some came laden, others had very little. In the meeting Sister Beatrice explained her plan, gave them the rules about reading matter, and presented them with revised schedules which included both the convent daily schedule and the time given to their work assignments. She taught them the importance of humility as well as proper manners and respect for authority. She also arranged to have individual meetings with each one. They accepted their revised schedules and all of them felt they had come through the ordeal more easily than she had feared. They never had any disagreeable times after that. The anticipation had proved much worse than the actual experience.

Sister Beatrice had frequent consultation and sympathy from Mother Eva. This was their plan: Mother Eva was to keep her meditation and instruction classes; Sister Beatrice was to be responsible for all else. The novice mistress must note and remind each novice of their failure in keeping the rules and that will give ample opportunity for each to show her humility and patience.

The first rule was to pray daily for the Novice Mistress, that she may be given wisdom, and good judgment and humility in dealing with the novices and that she may not lose her own soul nor develop a terribly critical disposition. In *A Follower's Story* there is a long list of instructions which Sister Beatrice and future novice directors gave to the novices. Some of those instructions are still pertinent, but not consistent with behavior in modern society. Many of the instructions are what would have been expected of a well brought up lady in that era. And years later when *A Follower's Story* was read aloud as table reading, they caused much amusement. Many pertain especially to conduct in Chapel, which included punctuality, posture, and recitation of the Offices. They also included respect for senior Sisters, and many aspects of obedience, which involved getting permission from the Novice Mistress about reading materials, correspondence with others, use of private property, privacy regarding community affairs and behavior away from the Community. At one time all Sisters were to stand when the Superior entered a room, and the novices stood also for the Novice Mistress. In 1953 Mother Louise always motioned for everyone to sit down. Novice Mistress Sister Olivia followed her example, and from then on, that has ceased to be a custom.

After the long list of rules for conduct, Sister Beatrice ends,

"A great help in the keeping of these rules and the right spirit in the keeping of them, would be the practice of recollection, the practice of the Presence of God. If we could but be conscious of the Presence of our Lord and God and of the fact that 'there is an Eye which sees all things, an Ear which hears all things' and be conscious of "an unheard Sharer" in all our conversations, it would not be hard to keep the rule, and to be humble, lowly and obedient," (*A Follower's Story*).

The Novices and Their Training

For most novices the structure of convent life and living under a Rule was new, and many were surprised to find that living in community can be difficult. It required adjustment to dealing companionably with a group of Sisters varying in age and background. It was hard to remember times and places of silence. About four hours daily were devoted to attendance at the Eucharist and the Divine Office: Lauds, Prime, Morning Prayer, Terce, Sext and None (now combined as the Noon Office) Evening Prayer at 5:00, and Compline, the last Office of the day. In more recent years many women have not been accustomed to communal meals three times a day with no choice of menu. Customs have changed somewhat, but the general customs remain. In our large refectory, everyone, upon entering, makes a slight bow to the large Crucifix on the wall, as to Christ the unseen Guest at every meal. They enter in order of seniority. Talking is allowed at supper except on retreat days. The Novice Guardian helps each novice plan her schedule for the day which included time for private prayer and meditation and for spiritual reading as well as work assignments.

During the school year the novitiate had five hours of classes each week. The structure of the Novice classes (which also included the postulants) varied over the years according to the abilities of the Novice Director and also of the novices. There has been no educational

Refectory at meal time.

Novice class.

requirement and the novices vary greatly in their backgrounds of knowledge.

The most important class was that of the Rule of the Community. It was usually taught by the Novice Director herself. Other classes were taught by the Novice Director, other Sisters, the chaplain, or other capable teachers locally available. The subjects included the Bible, both Old and New Testaments, Church history, especially the history of the Community, Theology, Prayer and Worship, including Liturgy. The novices kept the monthly retreat schedule of the Sisters. The Novice Director had weekly conferences with each novice.

For many years, at least until the 1960s, the Sisters had a form of accountability called Chapter of Faults after the Noon Office. Each Sister reported infractions of the Rule such as missing Offices, tardiness at meals, etc. This was to impress upon the Sisters the importance of careful observance of the Rule. Mother Eva said, "A Rule well kept is the Christian's first defense in time of temptation." The novices had their own Chapter of Faults with the Novice Mistress. Faults are often due to carelessness and are not considered sins. Until the last revision of the Rule of the Community, auricular confession of sins to a priest was required four times a year. Sins were reported to the priest. In the present Rule it is recommended, but not required.

✠

The Novitiate is Organized

After the arrangement had proved satisfactory, the Novitiate was formally organized May 29, 1917, with eight novices and postulants. Sister Beatrice said with satisfaction that that particular group of Novices came through the training and each eventually became a Sister in charge of a Branch House sometime during their life.

Since then appointment of the Novice Director has been a responsibility of the Superior, and she ranks next after the Assistant Superior. Over the years Sisters Ruth Magdalene, Edith Constance, Rose Marie, Helen Veronica, Olivia Mary, Alice Lorraine, Monica Mary, Althea Augustine, and Hilary Mary have served as Novice Directors. Sister Mary Elizabeth became Novice Guardian in 1993 and is still serving.

THE ASSOCIATES AND OBLATES 11

Associates

Associates of the Community are women and men who wish to have ties with the Community's life of prayer. One might say that the Associates are older than the Community. The first Associates were received on the Eve of the Feast of the Transfiguration, August 5, 1898. Mother Eva and Sister Beatrice made their first vows the next day.

Our first Associates were friends and relatives of Mother Eva. In every ministry the Sisters have carried on, there are persons who asked for closer ties with the Sisters and who aid them by their prayer and their service. The Associates' Rule provides for prayer and worship, study, and service. Each Associate formulates her personal Rule in consultation with a Sister or a priest. An annual retreat is recommended. The Community provides two Associates' retreats every year at the Mother House, and

Associates cross.

each Branch House tries to provide at least one retreat for Associates every year. The Sisters pray for the Associates regularly and for each Associate on his or her birthday. There has always been one Sister who is appointed to be especially responsible for keeping in touch with Associates. Sister Louise Magdalene did so for many years after she retired from being Mother Superior. She was succeeded by Sister Jacqueline Marie. She keeps in touch by correspondence and sometimes telephone, and receives their annual reports. In some places where there are or have been Branch Houses there are groups of Associates who meet regularly. Many people have become acquainted with the Sisters through their Branch House ministries, and then asked to become Associates. In 2008 there were more than 500 Associates in the United States, Canada, Europe and South America.

Originally the priests were the only men Associates, but around 1970 it was decided that laymen could become Associates, and there are now a number of husbands and wives who are both Associates as well as some single men.

The Associates' emblem is the Jerusalem cross, the same design as the Sisters' cross, but in red and white instead of blue and white.

Associates pay annual dues; all receive the *Transfiguration Quarterly*. They are always welcome guests at the Convent, and Sisters when traveling have often received hospitality from them. At the Consecration of the Chapel and at similar occasions the Associates helped the Sisters by organizing and preparing meals for the guests. They have generously contributed to many special projects of the Community such as the carillon in the Chapel tower, the new Convent, our ministries at Bethany Home and School, St. Mary's Home, and our ministries in Puerto Rico and the Dominican Republic.

Oblates

After many years of deliberation, the Community decided to also have Oblates. Oblates are persons who feel called to a commitment fuller than that of an Associate. One reason for the long time of deliberation was the need of the Sisters to define the differences between Associates, Oblates and Sisters. The first four Oblates were admitted on the Eve of the Transfiguration, 2004, and two others a year later. In 2008 there were seven Oblates and more inquirers. The Oblates undergo a period of training for at least six months which is akin to that of the Novitiate and keep a special Rule. A Sister is appointed as Director. It is of interest that three of the seven are former Bethany Home or Bethany School girls, LaVone Walter-Perry, Barbara Sahs, and Toni Thomas-Faren. Another, Eve Morrow, is a great niece of Mother Eva. When at the Convent, Oblates wear a special medallion with the Jerusalem cross, and a blue scapular over their regular clothes.

The Oblates are not obliged to live at the Convent although they are expected to make regular visits, but as it developed, as of 2008, five of them do live here or nearby. They participate with the Sisters in the Divine Office and the Eucharist; they are assigned places in choir. In 2009 they were included with the Sisters as Readers in the Offices and as Servers in the Eucharist.

Some of the Oblates who live nearby have asked to be assigned regular tasks in the Convent. Others help as they can when they visit. All are cheerful and willing helpers. The Oblates are a great blessing to the Community.

12 OUTREACH FOR MINISTRY

Mother Eva's Policies for Mission

As the Sisterhood began to grow, Mother Eva felt it possible for her Sisters to undertake additional work through branch houses. Bat Cave had begun as a rest and vacation house, but a ministry had also developed there. They were beginning to receive requests from Bishops who hoped for help in their dioceses. Mother Eva had been told when visiting the English Orders, in 1907, that from their long experience they had found that a periodic change of Sisters was good for all Branch Works. These Superiors said that when a Sister hung on too long to her work as "her" work, she in time lost much of her own spiritual life. Her tenacious, possessive hold on the work, did that work more harm than good, cramping its development and hindering its best progress. Mother Eva hoped to avoid some of the failures the English had experienced or were experiencing. For that reason she had adopted a written policy "that no Sister should remain in a Branch Work more than five consecutive years except in the Mission Field where a new language had to be learned. The limit there was ten years. After five years, she required a Sister to spend a year at the convent in order to restore her loyalty, renew her religious fervor, become acquainted with their new Sisters and any gradual change of custom or policy," (*A Follower's Story* p. 158).

Sister Beatrice added, "This policy is a very definite one but not always easy to enforce."

Northern Ohio

The first call from outside the community came in 1911, just after we had accepted responsibility of the Boys' Home in Glendale. Bishop William A. Leonard of Ohio asked the Community to take charge of St. John's Orphanage in Cleveland, Ohio, which had been started in 1909. The Bishop had the hope of developing it very much like Bethany Home. About two years later, the Sisters also accepted the charge of Holy Cross Home for Crippled Children in Cleveland. In 1923 they also accepted the Church Home for elderly women, in Cleveland, our first branch work not connected with children. In 1929 St. John's Home was moved to Painesville, Ohio. These were all diocesan institutions accepted at the invitation of Bishop Leonard.

Burlington, New Jersey

In 1925 Paul Matthews, then Bishop of New Jersey, invited the Sisters to take charge of a girl's school, Saint Mary's Hall. Burlington, New Jersey. Sister Edith Constance, Sister Ethel Bertha, Sister Ada Francis and Sister Mabel Lioba taught there. We remained there for only two years, 1926 to 1928. Miss Esther Fifield, a teacher in that school, came to the Community a few years later, and became Sister Esther Mary.

China

Another invitation came in a letter from Bishop Huntington of the Missionary District of Wuhu in China, just before General Convention of 1910. In his letter the Bishop said he had had a long-time interest in religious orders. He described the situation in Wuhu and the need for persons to staff the work, especially for women and girls. He explained that Deaconess Hart had suggested that he write to her and ask if she would be able to send Sisters to take up the work in Wuhu. He would be leaving for General Convention in July, 1910, and hoped to stop in Cincinnati to talk with Mother Eva. In his letter, Bishop Huntington explained that he was not a high churchman, and neither were most of the clergy in his diocese in China. He did not understand that the monastic life and sacramental life were necessarily connected but he was sure that the clergy in Wuhu, or any place wherever they might be stationed, would be happy to do anything which Mother Eva might desire for the help of the Sisters. This work is for the Glory of God and for the Salvation of Souls.

This letter, as Mother Eva said, came as a "bolt from the blue." It was discussed at length. The Sisters had given $1,000 to a fund for famine relief in China in 1912. They took the money from the Chapel Fund saying that this was more important. Interest in China was not a new idea to Mother Eva. A letter to her sister from Omaha tells of her Sunday School class having a Lenten study of the missionary work in China. After they had voted to give the money, Mother Eva is quoted as saying, "We must be ready to follow with ourselves if a call should ever come," (Harton, p.117).

Her Policy for Foreign Missions

While pondering the Bishop's request, Mother Eva Mary

worked out her definite policy for any work which would be undertaken in the foreign field in the future. It was to be under the Board of Missions. They were to be regularly appointed by the Mission Board, not asking for any exceptions to its rules and requirements. They were to be regular appointees, having been requested by the Bishop of the Diocese to which they were going. The Sisters were to be volunteers, for every Religious vocation does not necessarily include a missionary vocation. The one exception she made to the rules of the Board of Missions was that two Sisters were to go out on the salary of one missionary. This she provided in order that our Sisters should not be asked to work in separate fields, and that they would not be required to go on speaking tours when home on furlough. And when an exception was made to this, the Sisters were to speak only to the women's or children's groups and if possible, never in the church proper. Of course there were exceptions to this rule when charity demanded it. Her Sisters were to own the house in which they were to live. Mother Eva thought owning the property on which the convent stood the possibility of any capricious removal would be avoided and this wise provision proved the salvation of our work in Wuhu later. The story of China continues in Appendix II.

The Sisters all felt that a call to the Mission field could not lightly be refused. A call to the foreign field could only come from God. After prayer and much discussion they made the following decision. They were at that time, the youngest and smallest of the Sisterhoods in the Church. They felt very inexperienced and untrained. They were few in numbers and still fewer of them had any call for missionary service. So Mother Eva wrote to Bishop Huntington and asked him to make his appeal to three other Communities first, and if they did not respond favorably, to come back in three years and repeat his call to us. The Community had at that time, eight Professed Sisters, three Novices and three postulants, and their work at home was large and expanding constantly. Yet, China's call was appealing and tempting to the Community.

In August 1913, when General Convention met in New York. Bishop Huntington came again and repeated his request in person, saying he had done as Mother Eva had asked, and no Sisterhood felt they could accept his call. One may wonder if the Bishop really made the request to other communities, but in 1913 he repeated his request and the Sisters accepted it. This new venture received acclaim from the National Church.

Hawaii

Sisters en route to China in 1915 stopped in Honolulu, Hawaii, and were entertained by the Rt. Rev. Henry B. Restarick, first American Bishop of Honolulu. In 1918 he asked the Sisters to undertake the administration of St. Andrew's Priory School for Girls in Honolulu. This school had been started in 1867 by an English Sisterhood, but Hawaii had just become American territory. The Sisters served in Hawaii through the Centennial of the School in 1967 and until 1970, when they were needed at home. In September, 1980, ten years after they had withdrawn from the Priory, the Sisters were invited to another celebration there, the dedication of another new building, by Bishop Harry Sherbourne Kennedy (retired) and Katherine Kittle Kennedy Hall. Sister Evelyn went, accompanied by a nurse from the Convent infirmary, and was greeted joyously by many friends, former teachers and students. Sister Eva Dorothea and Sister Monica accompanied her and took part in the service of dedication. The story of Hawaii is in Appendix II.

In 1926, after their experience in Northern Ohio, in China and in Hawaii, the Chapter approved a list of certain provisions for the guidance of Sisters in Branch Houses. They would keep the Rule as at home. In Houses which were supported by a Diocese there was usually a stipend from the Diocese which was put into the common fund. In accordance with our vow of poverty, salaries were not to be paid to individual Sisters, but put into a common fund for the use of all the Sisters employed there. A Treasurer was appointed by the head of the House to keep account of this money and to give it out when needed. Each House was required to make an annual report to the Community including a Financial Report.

Outreach after Mother Eva's Lifetime

The stories of the individual Branch Houses which lasted beyond her lifetime will show that for various reasons the policy was not always followed. Very often the Branch House staff included novices and Sisters under first vows, assigned there to give them Branch House experience before life profession. This made for frequent changes of staff in the House, which sometimes caused problems because of lack of training for new situations. This was a challenge to all, both to the regular staff, especially the Sister in charge, and to the temporary appointees, but they obediently persevered.

In 1931 the Sisters began a new ministry in Lincoln Heights, Ohio, not far from the Convent. In 1943 they accepted the call to manage St. Dorothy's Rest, near Camp Meeker, California. In 1945 they responded to a request from the Bishop of Puerto Rico. They later responded to requests from Bishops in Texas, Western North Carolina and the Dominican Republic. It seems as if under each Superior a new Branch Work was begun. Of course some were relinquished because the need no longer existed, or because we had an insufficient number of Sisters able to staff them.

Appendix II of this book contains a fuller account of each Ministry in which we have served for ten or more years.

Short Term Ministries
St. Phillip's School, Dallas, Texas

While vacationing in Yonkers, New York with her family, Sister Althea received an urgent request from the Rector of St. Phillip's Church in Dallas, the Rev. Jon Stasney, and a prominent board member of St. Phillip's Recreation Center, Mrs. Hilda Cooper, to come to Dallas and start a Pre-School there where they had a nursery established. After consideration and permission from the Superior, Sister Althea agreed to do so. This became an outgrowth of our mission work in McKinney, Texas. Mrs. Cooper provided Sister Althea with a car which was necessary for the daily trip to the city from McKinney.

Father Stasney and Sister Althea worked together and had a pre-fab building erected to house a pre-school classroom, a first and second grade classroom, and staff lounge, in anticipation of the growth and development of the school.

Since it has always been Sister Althea's philosophy to work in the mission field to help others to help themselves, she urged Father to find a person in the community to take over the school for its future growth. After two years, Sister Althea left Dallas and returned to McKinney. Then shortly after, she returned to the Convent for reassignment to St. John's Home in Painesville, Ohio.

Open Door Ministry, Cincinnati, Ohio

After closing St. John's Home in Painesville, Ohio, in 1978, Sister Althea went to the Church of the Advent in Cincinnati, to offer her services at the Open Door Ministry. There they were ministering to the homeless, drug addicts, prostitutes, psychologically disturbed individuals, and senior citizens who could not administer their financial responsibilities without help, families whose income was insufficient for supplying adequate food supplies, clothing, school supplies and other necessities of life. There she helped persons to budget their income in order to pay their rent, their electric bills and other important bills that would allow them to have a roof over their heads. They packed bags of food for the needy, offered soup and sandwiches for any walk-ins who were hungry, supplied clothing for others and distributed bags of school supplies for the children. At Christmas time gifts which were donated were distributed to those in most need. Sister Althea spent two days a week for some five years at this ministry. It was while she was there that she was interviewed by a board member of the Roman Catholic Franciscan Health Center in the Over-the-Rhine area in Cincinnati. She was invited to join the staff of the St. John's Social Service Center, a branch of the Franciscan Health Center (FHC).

St. John's Social Service Center, Cincinnati, Ohio

Because she wanted to offer her services without pay, Sister Althea was supplied with a brand new car, every two years and a small monthly honorarium. While there she was asked to become a member of the board, and then was asked to administer the Senior Center, which she did for six and a half years.

Ranfurly Home, Bahamas

An Associate of ours in the Bahamas, who was President of the Board of Directors for the Ranfurly Home for Children in Nassau, visited our St. John's Home for Children in Painesville, Ohio in 1978, and was duly impressed. Sister Althea Augustine was at that time in charge of the Home in Painesville, and was invited to come to the Ranfurly Home as a consultant to help them reorganize their Home. Ranfurly Home had been established as a home for homeless children by the Church of England in 1956 when England ruled the islands.

Sister Althea, having completed work on a B.S. degree in education at Lake Erie College, gave the plan some consideration. The Superior gave permission for her to accept the invitation if there was some way she could meet her daily spiritual obligations. Since the Order of the Holy Cross was well established in the Bahamas and lived only ten minutes away from Ranfurly Home, it was the perfect solution and wonderful experience to join with the Brothers for Daily Offices. The agreement was that Sister Althea would spend one year there but due to great need and work that needed to be done, she stayed two years at Ranfurly, from 1980-1982.

St. James Church, Oneonta, New York

Sister Priscilla Jean and Sister Johanna Laura took a "sabbatical year," 1995-1996, helping at St. James Church, Oneonta, New York. The Sisters in the Dominican Republic bought a building which had been intended for a funeral home. Since the electrical power in the area was rather sporadic, that business had failed and the owner sold it at a reasonable price. A group from St. James Church in Oneonta came for a visit and gave the Sisters money to refurnish the building as a chapel and a clinic. Fr. Mark Cole brought a medical team down and they had a free clinic for a week.

In October of that year, Sister Johanna Laura and Sister Priscilla Jean took time off from the Dominican Republic and worked for six months at St. James in Oneonta, New York. They lived in the old vicarage and helped in the church. Sister Priscilla served as Deacon and preached several times. Both Sisters took communion to the sick and shut-ins and helped with various projects. A little boy, Oliver, and his mother, Josefina from San Pedro, stayed with them while Oliver had an operation for a kidney problem. Sister Johanna returned with the medical and construction team to the Dominican Republic. It was a great experience for both Sisters.

Rosebud Reservation, North Dakota

Every summer from 1992 to 1997 Sister Mary Elizabeth spent a month at the Native American Reservation at Rosebud, North Dakota. Each year she was accompanied by another Sister. They conducted Vacation Bible Schools and ministered in various ways as were needed. Some members of the Sioux tribe hosted a Pow-wow at Bethany in honor of the Sisters who had taught during the summers. Sister Mary Elizabeth and Sister Stephanie were adopted into the tribe and given the names Running Antelope and Big Buffalo Woman.

Ministry to Prisoners

Visits to prisoners are a work of mercy. In the Community this has been carried out in various ways, often by individual Sisters beginning with visiting the jails when the community started. The first one now remembered is that Sister Helen Veronica was in correspondence with a man in an Ohio prison. The ministry in Puerto Rico began with a ministry to prisoners. When Sister Evelyn Ancilla returned from St. Andrew's Priory in Hawaii, she followed Sister Helen's example. To spread knowledge and understanding of conditions in prisons she began and edited a periodical which was published quarterly until her death. It acquired a large circulation in prisons all over the United States. A few other Sisters also corresponded with prisoners. A Kairos program began in Ohio prisons in 1994. Kairos is an ecumenical program developed among people who have experienced a Cursillo or Cursillo type program within their own denomination designed to bring the message of God's love to persons in prison, and to give them experience of a Christian lifestyle. The Volunteers spend a three day weekend of talks, sharing and song in an atmosphere of love and self forgiveness, a new thing to many prisoners. As a token of that love they are given home baked cookies provided by volunteers in the churches. After having attended a weekend, those who have attended gather in weekly groups to support each other, and once a month some of the team members join with them for two hours to continue the support. Sister Eleanor Grace has served on a number of teams at the Ohio Reformatory for Women in Marysville, Ohio. She has gone back to their monthly reunion meetings.

There is also a pamphlet entitled Prisoner to Prisoner, modeled after Forward Movement, which is prepared at an Ohio prison. It is written by the prisoners themselves and circulated to prisons all over the country.

From the Rule of 1978, in the Chapter on Ministry,

"The goal of our entire ministry must be to bring our Lord and His claims before each person that we serve. In order to do this effectively it is essential that we be attentive to the guidance of the Holy Spirit and corporately seek the will of God. Our work should never become an excuse for neglecting our life of prayer and worship or for avoiding our Christian responsibility of building up each other within the Body of Christ as manifested in our Community."

The directives for this Chapter add,

"In the case of work in a foreign country or in work with people of a different culture the Sisters should be prepared by study of the language and culture either before they begin their assignment or provision should be made for such study where the work is located…. In Branch Ministries the members of each house shall work out a method of making decisions and sharing knowledge of how money in the common fund is received and expended."

The Rule goes on to say:

"In order to make our ministry a reflection of God's love and not of ourselves, it must be an extension of our life of prayer. We must each strive to maintain a balance between our life of devotion and our service. Each of us has a share in each ministry whether near or far, and we must never forget our obligation to support each other by prayer and encouragement. Our corporate worship upholds each Sister, wherever she may be, as she serves in the spirit of Christ and in the name of the Community."

13 MOTHER EVA'S LAST YEARS

Mother Eva had always been very frail physically. She frequently suffered from bronchitis and pleurisy. The trying winters in southern Ohio were always hard on her. It seemed to be God's Will that her great spiritual gifts and literary talents were much more important in accomplishing his work than any manual labor she wanted to do. Her evident desire to do this physical work was an inspiration and stimulant to the rest of the Sisters and no member of our Community ever felt that Mother Eva was shirking. They were glad to spare her in every way.

Happily the whole Community wanted to save her as much as they could and Sister Beatrice was frequently sent for to take her away from the busy Sisters. Mother Eva was patient about this and submissive but inwardly hurt at not having the pleasure of washing dishes or working in the cannery or preparing rooms for guests or other such work. To her this deprivation was against her spiritual convictions as shown in the following quotation from her series of meditations on the Life of Our Lord. In the meditation on the Life of Labor she says, "No rule of life is complete that does not have a place in it for regular manual labor." There was a quotation from Mother Eva in our old Rule which one Sister found very amusing. "Our labor should sometimes be mental." When they were setting tables for 20 or more Sisters, that Sister found a good deal of mental labor in getting every Sister's napkin ring at the right place. The Sisters did not allow Mother Eva to set tables.

In Sister Beatrice's opinion the beginning of the end for Mother Eva occurred in 1913. That year, returning home from General Convention in New York City, she was half sick with a cold, but she responded to a call for help from the Holy Cross Home for Crippled Children in Cleveland. Shortly after her arrival she came down with a nearly fatal case of septic pneumonia. The doctors pronounced her case hopeless. Sister Beatrice wrote, "To medical science it was, but to faith nothing is impossible." Sister Edith Constance had been appointed to take charge of Holy Cross House. She telegraphed for Sister Beatrice who then telegraphed her condition to her brother. Her brother Paul and sister Mrs. Jane Gray came to Cleveland at once. They engaged two nurses, day and night, which meant twelve-hour duty in those days. One of Mother Eva's nurses there, Miss Anna Hayes, later became Sister Constance Anna and spent 28 years in St. Lioba's Compound, Wuhu, China.

Mother Eva received careful nursing. At the Convent, Sisters and children kept vigil for her in the Chapel. Bishop Leonard anointed her. With the careful nursing and all the prayers, Mother Eva recovered slowly. She had another near fatal illness in China in 1922, where she was again nursed by Sister Constance Anna. Still, in 1926 she was well enough to go to China with Sister Beatrice, accompanied by two Sisters who were returning to China and Honolulu, to make a pilgrimage to the Holy Land.

In the fall of 1927 Mother Eva began to show signs of weakness and had a distressing cough. Beatrice wrote to the Sisters.

"In January 1928 Mother Eva, Sister Clara and I with Alan Neale as driver went to Florida for a short stay. Later Mother Eva, Sister Martha and I went back to Sanibel Island where I left them to return to the Convent and works in Glendale. Mother Eva had rooms in the hotel where she was neither happy nor comfortable and suffered from homesickness and weakness. I made three trips down to see what could be done. Her family made trips and cheered her very much, Bishop Matthews surprising her one day. Her sisters Jane and Grace visited her. She mentioned several times that this was her "fifteenth year." When she had been seriously ill in Cleveland a few years earlier she had said that she had asked the Lord for 15 years. Her explanation was, "That was enough for Hezekiah. It is enough for me," (Isa. 38:5). The doctors would not allow her to get back into Ohio before the end of April so we moved her to the mountain house in N.C. where she was happier but conscious that she was not gaining strength."

Mother Eva was taken to Denver, Colorado, where it was hoped that the climate there would help her. The doctor in Denver gave the first real diagnosis. Sister Beatrice quotes the report the doctor gave to Bishop Johnson. "A tumor mass is compressing the trachea to such a degree that respiration is at all times most difficult. The slightest exertion may precipitate a sudden edema of the trachea, causing her death."

Mother Eva died on July 6, 1928. Her body was taken to Glendale and placed in a vault in Spring Grove cemetery. Interment was postponed until the Chapel was completed and consecrated. Although she did not live to see the cornerstone of the Chapel laid, she did see the foundations begun before her death. The Chapel was consecrated on June 11, 1929, and on the following day Mother Eva's body was translated to this Chapel of her dreams where it lies beneath the high Altar.

Bishop Matthews has written of his sister, Mother Eva:

"And there she lies where she longed to be—who was the mother of many children in the Faith, the Sister of many virgins that be her fellows and bore her company. Gladly she lived—she met life joyously, for her vital faith so illumined her mind with visions of wonderful things, that she lived in a world fertile and beautiful as a fairyland, in which lovely fancies played about her like attendant sprites. Struggle there was, and sacrifice, and not seldom agony, but in all of it, and through it all, yea even in the valley of the shadow of death, the consciousness of a Power and a Presence that was a staff to support and to comfort her soul, though it were a rod to correct and smite her; the rod was God's, and when she felt it she felt His touch, and though that touch might hurt, it was the one supreme help and healing that her human weakness craved.

An eager and ardent spirit, a naturally impetuous will, and intelligence and comprehension that was like the quick flashing of the light, she learned to live as the sailor learns who in communion with the great deep has learned to feel:

> "The virtues of the starlit heaven,
> The glorious sun's life giving ray
> The whiteness of the moon at even,
> The flashing of the lightning free;
> The whirling wind's tempestuous shocks,
> The stable earth, the deep salt sea
> Around the old eternal rocks."
> (St. Patrick's Breastplate)

14 THE STORY OF THE CHAPEL

The story of the Chapel of the Transfiguration of our Lord begins in 1898, the first year of the Community and of Bethany Home. The first chapel was the ballroom of the original house. During 1899 they had the chapel windows put in, at a cost of $6.50 a window. The windows with the blue Jerusalem cross were in what was then the Sisters' choir; the windows with the red Associates' cross were given by the Associates for the nave. This first Chapel had a bay window at the west end of the room which served as a vestry immediately behind the altar. A red curtain separated this little vestry from the sanctuary and formed the dossal for the altar. The organ and choir stall pews were brought from the house in Freeman Street.

In 1905 the chapel was enlarged by the addition of a choir and sanctuary. The windows in the sanctuary were made in Cincinnati. Mother Eva and Sister Beatrice selected the designs. The Good Shepherd window was given by the children at a very reasonable cost. Little Lillian Sears thought she could see her pennies in the small circles in the design at the bottom of the window! The

Purification window was a memorial to Sister Ellis Victoria, the first of our Sisters to enter Paradise. For a short time the room felt quite spacious.

For forty years it held the entire family of Sisters and children until they spilled out into the hall and up the stairway. It is incredible the number of people it held, boys, girls, ladies, and Sisters. It was soon realized that no corner of the house, nor its extension, would be permanently adequate for the Sisters whom God would send and the children for whom they would care. So, though they loved the little chapel they hoped for a building made especially for God's glory and for His worship alone.

The Dream of a New Chapel

In 1906, Eleanor Meyers, a Bethany Home child, who later became Sister Eleanor Mary gave the first dollar she earned to start a Chapel fund. This was followed by a gift of twenty-five dollars from a friend. With these gifts as incentive they began to work definitely for the building of the Chapel. Sisters and children made anything for which they could get a sale: marmalade, embroidered garments, articles of tooled leather and carved wood. Many beautiful necklaces were made from exquisite Venetian beads given to us, and these sold at a very good price. Any undesignated gifts of money received by the Community were added to the fund and also the offerings given at the Midnight Mass at Christmas.

It was hardest to raise the first one thousand dollars. After that, the money came in steadily. Two gifts of five thousand dollars each helped greatly, but so did each smaller gift and the continued earnings. The largest gift was for the organ, given by Mrs. William Cooper Procter in memory of her sister, Miss Mary Johnson. All were works of love blessed by God. The funds received were wisely invested and by 1927 we felt assured we had enough money in sight to really plan the Chapel.

Meanwhile the altar had been acquired. Arthur Nieb of the American Expeditionary Force, WWI, son of our chaplain the Rev. Charles Brookins, spent the year 1919, after the first World War, in Paris, France. There he carved this altar as a surprise for his adopted father. Father Brookins had, unfortunately, no way of using the altar himself and was greatly rejoiced that Mother Eva did.

Picture of the High Altar.

Mother Eva Mary and Sister Beatrice Martha felt it had truly been made for our Chapel-to-be. The carvings which ornamented it are of Christ blessing little children, Mary and Martha with our Lord at Bethany, and Mary washing Christ's feet with ointment. What could be more appropriate for Bethany Home and for our Sisters, especially as the figures of a monk and a nun are carved on the left and right corners? So, with the help of our Associates, the altar was purchased, and for ten years it was stored in our attic awaiting the Chapel which should house it.

✠

The Dream is Materialized

In 1927, in Boston, Mr. Ralph Adams Cram, the well known church architect, was invited to tea by Mother Eva's sister, Jane Gray, to meet Mother Eva and Sister Beatrice and to hear of their hoped-for building. Mother Eva told Mr. Cram that she wanted the Chapel to be of English village-Gothic type, and gave him a suggestion of a floor arrangement together with pictures of the Altar. Mr. Cram was delighted with the idea and said gleefully, "This will be fun!" A few days later, at his office, Mr. Cram showed them his tentative plans which were admired and approved. Mr. Cram gave his services for the planning of this Chapel. The Associate Architects were Matthews and Dennison.

So, after about thirty years of prayer, hope, visions and hard work, the Sisters' dreams began to materialize. The Chapel is built of water-worn stone from the Miami River. Interior beams are of Douglas fir from Washington State. The pews in the nave and choir stalls are of black walnut.

The cornerstone was laid on September 29, 1928, almost three months after Mother Eva's death. The total cost of the building materials amounted to about one hundred fifty thousand dollars. Beyond that there were many gifts for the furnishing and beautifying of the Chapel and for providing all things needful for its use.

Dedication of the Chapel

The first service in the new Chapel was held on June 8, 1929. The first chords of the new organ resounded forth, "Praise God From Whom All Blessings Flow." The dedication took place a few days later on St. Barnabas Day, June 11, 1929.

At 10:00 Bishop Matthews said Morning Prayer in the new Chapel and then proceeded to the Children's Corner with the babies in the procession and only a few Sisters and Mrs. Gray. There he unveiled the very beautiful window by the great artist Coniche, given by Mrs. Grey. The subject of the window is the hymn of Saint Francis. A little Bethany Home girl, in her red cape, is shown in the corner on her knees, looking up at the figure of our Lord as a boy of about fourteen among his creatures: Father Sun, Sister Moon, Brother Wind, Sister Water and the little things of creation. A verse in the window reads, "All Thy works praise Thee O Lord."

As 11:00 drew near, the people came in crowds. The children formed a line in front of their cottages and the Sisters formed in line in front of Bethesda Cottage. The eight Bishops, the servers and nearly thirteen clergy vested in the two Sacristies, the Children's Corner, and in the large Chapter Room under the Chapel. They were all resplendent in vestments, cloth of gold copes and mitres and hoods of gorgeous colors. As Sister Beatrice later wrote, "We surely did things right and brilliantly for once in our lives!"

Mr. Prower Symons had designed the wonderful three manual organ especially for the children's and Sisters' voices. He had been training the children all winter in chorus work. They were all prepared for the great service. He was at the organ and played for some time as the people came into the church.

The procession marched to the Chapel door and parted ranks. The Consecrator came through with his attendants to the closed door and gave three loud knocks. Mr. James Cleveland, assisted by the Trustees, Mrs. Mortimer Matthews, Sister Edith Constance, Sister Clara Elizabeth, Sister Paula Harriet, Sister Martha Mary, and Sister Beatrice, opened the door.

The procession entered, the younger ones first, as always in Bethany Home, but the very little ones did not stay; they kept right on processing out of the side door. For the first part of our three hour service they stayed on the lawn until after the grand procession around the Chapel between the service of Consecration and the Eucharist. Then they were slipped back into the Chapel through the side door and stayed in the crossing in front of the pews, all of which they did very inconspicuously and yet had a real part in the service and memories for the rest of their lives.

When the whole long procession had entered, Bishop Matthews began Psalm 24 which continued until all were in their places. The choir held fifty-eight chairs in two tiers. The two back tiers were full of blue Sisters, and the front tier was full of vested clergy on both sides. The sanctuary was full of Bishops and their assistants. Bishop Johnson and Deacon John Cleveland sat outside of the altar rail on the north side of the Chapel, and Mr. Frank Hamer and a marble mason sat on the south side, the mason in his overalls. In fact, every available spot was used for the crowd.

After the opening hymn Bishop Matthews took his seat, and Mr. Hamer came forward and read his testimony that he was the Master Builder and that he certified the church was well and conscientiously built. He then delivered to the Bishop a large wooden key, a pure piece of ritual, for the key is for nothing but ornament and only symbolizes the turning over of the responsibility of the building to the Consecrator. Then Mr. James Cleveland, as Trustee of the Society of the Transfiguration, read the Instrument of Donation certifying that the building was free from debt. There had been a thrilling meeting of the Trustees the night before when they found that in almost a miraculous way, the funds had come in until there was enough to pay for the Chapel. They had closed that meeting with the Doxology and a prayer of Thanksgiving.

The service then went on as Bishop Matthews, his Chaplain carrying his crosier, the Master of Ceremonies, and the thurifer formed a little procession and went from Font to Rood Screen, to altar, to altar rail, to the lectern, to the nave, blessing each spot in order and then returned to the sanctuary. Just after the words consecrating the building, the marble mason came forward and chiseled a Maltese cross in the platform directly in front of the altar while Bishop Matthews, robed in cloth of gold and wearing a most gorgeous mitre, stood watching him.

Then followed the grand procession. Three hymns were sung; "Blessed City, Heavenly Salem," "Lights Abode Celestial Salem," and "Oh Son of God, Our Captain of Salvation."

They went out at the end quietly without any special procession, just in order and the children went out the side doors as the aisles had been filled with chairs as soon as the great procession had passed.

Immediately after the service, the Bishops came over and signed the important "Sentence of Consecration." Both the Instrument of Donation written by Sister Clara and the Sentence of Consecration written by Sister Paula are hand-printed and hand-illuminated; they were framed and hung in the narthex of the Chapel.

The service of Confirmation took place at three in the afternoon. Bishop Matthews confirmed ten little girls and the mother of two of the children.

Mother Eva Mary's Burial

Mother Eva had died on July 6, 1928. In the afternoon of the dedication, her body was brought out from the cemetery and placed over the prepared vault under the high altar. It was covered with a beautiful blue and white pall. A large floral cross from Bishop Matthews and a wreath from Mrs. Grey were place upon it. Then the temporary altar was put in place. The altar had been moved to one side of the Sanctuary. Vigil started at once and was kept up all night, three Sisters to a vigil of two hours length.

Bishop Matthews celebrated the Requiem Mass at 7:30 the next morning. Bishop Leonard, one of eight Bishops who were present, came down from the seminary at Gambier, Ohio, for the service. Bishop Leonard read the Gospel and Bishop Vincent read the Epistle. Bishop Johnson preached his sermon to the children. Sister Ruth Magdalene was organist for this service. Then Bishop Mathews had the committal service, and all the Sisters and relatives who were sitting in the Choir drew close to the open vault, as if before an open grave, while the body was lowered. At the completion of the service the high altar was placed again in position. In the marble over her vault is carved:

THE REVEREND MOTHER FOUNDRESS EVA MARY
1898—1928
THE VIRGINS THAT BE HER FELLOWS
SHALL BEAR HER COMPANY
AND SHALL BE BROUGHT UNTO THEE

The Sisters wanted a memorial to Mother Eva Mary, but not just in wood and stone. During her lifetime, her birthday had always been joyously celebrated by her Sisters. They now decided to continue to celebrate her birthday through their liturgical calendar. So February 9th became Mother Foundress Day, a major feast with its own proper use for the Divine Office and the Eucharist.

The old Chapel, now called the Oratory, continued to be used by the Sisters for their daily Offices. It contained beautiful carvings by Sister Clara Elizabeth. This Oratory was burned in the fire of 1958. A small Oratory, designed to be temporary, was built in the Convent for the benefit of the older Sisters, but for a number of years, until a permanent Oratory was built as part of the new Convent, the Sisters had all their Offices in the Chapel.

The Carvings

The furnishings of the Chapel were by no means complete when it was dedicated. It was in 1929 that Fritz Abplanalp, a young Swiss woodcarver, arrived. He spent six years carving the figures on the Rood Screen, the angels in the reredos, and the choir stalls including the misericords under the seats in the back row of each side. (In medieval monasteries the monks and nuns stood for the Office, which was always sung; but for the older and infirm members, seats called misericords, were provided against which they could lean.) In the back row of each side of our Chapel there is a carving of a an event in Our Lord's life above each seat; on the Misericord underneath, there is an Old Testament subject which corresponds to the New Testament one above. For example, the carving above the Superior's stall is of our Lord reigning in glory. The corresponding Old Testament subject below is of King David on his throne. The three panels behind the organ, where there are no seats, show the Crucifixion, the Resurrection, and Christ's Commission to his Apostles. Sister Beatrice, who planned the subjects, said there were no corresponding Old Testament subjects for these.

Sister Clara was responsible for the carvings on the ends of the pews in the nave. No two are identical. To better accommodate small children the front two pews are lower then the others and the parapet is open rather than solid so that very small children can see through.

The Chapel Windows

Stained glass windows were part of their vision for this Chapel. Sister Beatrice planned the subjects for the windows. They were installed at various times over the years as the money became available. Most are memorials or thank offerings. The Rose window, also called the "Children's Window," shows the Christ Child surrounded by the Holy Innocents and the youthful saints, Timothy, Agnes, Tarsicius, Cecilia. It was dedicated by Bishop Matthews on St. Luke's Day, 1948, the 57th anniversary of his ordination to the priesthood. It was made by Charles J. Connick Associates of Boston.

The windows in the sanctuary are of women of the New Testament: the Blessed Virgin, St. Elizabeth, St. Anne with the Blessed Virgin as a child, and Mary and Martha. Today we understand Mary of Bethany and Mary Magdalene to have been two distinct parsons, but at that time it was believed that the two were the same person. So the window for Mary is entitled Mary Magdalene.

On the north side of the nave are double lancet windows depicting Anglo-Saxon Religious founders and on the south side modern Anglican founders. Each lancet window has, in addition to the principal figure, two medallions representing some aspect of the person's life.

The principal figure of Mother Eva shows her dream of holding the Christ Child in her arms. In the first smaller medallion she is shown writing stories for the children. The lower medallion represents a Chinese Sister. Another small one represents the mission at St. Simon's Church in Lincoln Heights. This window was given by the girls and boys who had known Mother Eva. This window and the one of Harriet Starr Cannon, foundress of the Community of St. Mary, were dedicated at the time of our Golden Jubilee, August 6, 1948.

Next on the south side are the windows in memory of John Mason Neale, founder of the Society of St. Margaret, and of Mother Harriet Monsell, foundress of the Sisters of St. John the Baptist. These windows were dedicated to Bishop and Mrs. Matthews on May 11, 1956. Representatives of both these Communities were here for that service.

On the opposite wall, the window of St. Boniface is dedicated to the memory of Bishop Irving Peake Johnson. The window of St. Lioba, for whom our work in China was named, was dedicated in honor of Marianna Matthews, sister-in-law of Mother Eva and mother of Sisters Mary Catherine and Olivia Mary, on May 10, 1959.

Last on the south side are the windows dedicated in honor of Mother Priscilla Lydia Sellon and Marion Rebecca Hughes. In 1845 Mother Sellon established the first Sisterhood in the Anglican Communion since the Reformation and hers was the first group of Sisters to undertake work in the foreign mission field. They started work in Hawaii in 1867. The Sisters of the Transfiguration carried on their work from 1918 to 1970. The coral cross in the medallion is on the grounds of St. Andrew's Priory. In the window Mother Sellon carries the crozier of an Abbess. A procession of Priory girls is shown in the medallion. Marion Rebecca Hughes was the first woman of the Anglican Communion to make religious vows, in 1841, but she was unable to found a community until several years later.

On the north side are the windows of St. Bride of Ireland and St. Hilda of Whitby, which were blessed on the Feast of the Annunciation in 1949. Those of St. Frideswide and St. Ethelburga were blessed at the First Evensong of Advent IV in 1937. St. Frideswide was a Mercian princess who founded a nunnery in Oxford. St. Ethelburga was the daughter of King Ethelbert of Kent. Ethelburga, after the death of her husband, founded a nunnery in Kent.

The last window to be installed was the St. Clare window outside the St. Francis Chapel, which was dedicated on Mother Foundress Day, 1960, in memory of Mother Clara Elizabeth. It is opposite the St. Francis window which was the first one.

The statue of St. Michael, made of white Cararra marble, above the door on the north walk, was given by two Associates, Miss Florence Roberts and Miss Laura Roberts. A bas-relief of singing cherubs was presented by the Associates in 1907 as a memorial to Mrs. Henderson, Sister Beatrice's mother. It was moved to the Chapel in 1929. The statue of the Good Shepherd now in the niche of the tower was originally near the entrance to the Oratory. The children liked to pat the little lamb as they came in for Evensong.

The Chapel Bells

In the tower of the Chapel there is a carillon. A carillon is a set of fixed bells tuned to play chromatic tones as on an organ or piano. There would be no bells in our tower had it not been the desire of our dear friend Mr. John Prower Symons. He installed a carillon in the tower at the time that the Chapel was built. The making of a carillon was a labor of love of Mr. Symons, but his facilities were inadequate for the proper casting of bells. When these bells were made the making of carillons in this country was very young, and no one is to blame that they did not turn out as had been hoped. The bells were used but it did not take long for the Sisters to realize they were not in good tune. The day was long awaited when they could have them rebuilt.

Then the Community was contacted by a representative of the Petit and Fritsen Company which had been making bells in the Netherlands for nearly three hundred years. They had made several single bells for the United States, but now they wished to make a carillon. Mr. Boyd Jordan, carilloneur of the Singing Tower at Mariemont, Ohio, brought a young man, Mr. Fritsen, who represented the firm of Petit and Fritsen. Petit and Fritsen made us a very generous offer and we began to raises the necessary funds, with the enthusiastic help of Sister Constance. Articles by Sister Ruth Magdalene in the Quarterly helped make friends aware of the Sisters' hope.

Sister Ruth Magdalene wrote in the Transfiguration Quarterly, "A carillon is a lovely thing and would greatly add to the Chapel and to Bethany Home Village." In a later article she wrote, "The beautiful Chapel of the Transfiguration is even more beautiful because of the carillon of thirty-six bells housed in the upper level of its sturdy square tower, making it indeed a Singing Tower worthy to take its place among the other Singing Towers of our country. And now that we have the bells we can forget the waiting and agree with Mr. Price, the Carilloneur of the Burton Tower of the University of Michigan in Ann Arbor." Mr. Price had written her, "After all when one is installing an instrument that will last hundreds of years, what is a wait of a few months?" Mr. Price made the drawings for the installation and it was executed by the I. T. Verdin Co. of Cincinnati. It is considered, by those who know, to be a very fine piece of work. The frame is of steel, but the bells all hang on great wooden beams which makes the tone sweeter and softer. The countless rods and wires connect the beautiful bells with the clavier, and the action is simpler than that of a piano.

After the first two octaves of the bells came, but before they were actually installed, Sister Ruth raised enough money to purchase one more octave. When the third octave came, the bells were installed in time for the dedication. The bell that plays the lowest C was named for our Mother Foundress. A lower bell, which was added later, was named John Prower Symons, for it was in his mind and heart that the bells came into being. This bell plays B-flat below Mother Eva's C. Sister Ruth wrote,

The Carillon in the Singing Tower of the Chapel of the Transfiguration, Glendale, Ohio is dedicated to sing always to the Praise of God the most glorious, holy and undivided Trinity the Father, the Son and the Holy Ghost.

885 lbs Bartholomew 105 lbs Ben
185 lbs Matthew 80 lbs F.
ths James 70 lb

List of the Carillon Bells.

> "On Trinity Sunday, May 20th, 1951, Mr. Percival Price played the Dedication Recital of the bells. It was a glorious day and literally hundreds of people came to hear and no one was disappointed. Mr. Price is one of our foremost carilloneurs and under his skilled touch the bells sang and rippled and shouted for joy. It was indeed a joyous occa-

Sister Ruth Magdalene.

sion. He began with the glorious old hymn tune 'Nicea Holy, Holy, Holy,' of course one of the special hymns for Trinity Sunday. He played it first on the upper bells very simply and then the second and third times more and more of the bells rang out in happy variations until all the Apostles and other saints for whom the bells are named were taking their part and the melody rang out with Christus, Maria, Raphael, Gabriel, Michael and Uriel–and to finish the octave of pedals, Peter, James, John, Andrew, Philip and Thomas. We really had never heard the bells do their very best before. Mendelssohn's Spring Song was very lovely as it floated down from the tower and "Jesu, Joy of Man's Desiring" showed how the music of bells lends itself to such classic compositions."

Sister Ruth Magdalene was the principal convent organist for many years until her sight and hearing failed. She learned to play the bells and in 1952 she was admitted as a carillonneur member of the Guild of Carillonneurs. Other Sisters may have also occasionally played the bells, but their names have not been remembered. Mr. Albert Meyer, carillonneur at the carillon in Mariemont, came every Monday night for almost 40 years. The Rev. Ralph Spinner, who became our chaplain in 1952, learned to play the bells and played almost every Sunday afternoon as long as his health permitted. It should

Mr. Meyer playing the carillon.

be noted that access to the bell chamber and the clavier (the keyboard for playing the bells) is by means of a steep ladder which not everyone is brave enough to climb. It is like going up three step ladders. Father Spinner and Mr. Meyer taught Sister Monica to play the carillon. A few novices were interested but there was not often time to practice and not all of them became Sisters. Sister Monica spent many years in branch houses away from the Convent and is now physically unable to go up the tower. Sister Priscilla was also interested, but she was transferred to Puerto Rico. As of 2007 there is no Sister playing the carillon, but it is to be hoped that this will change. A bequest to Sister Margaret made possible a renovation of the clavier in 1970. Some time in 2007 Richard Frye, a friend who is carillonneur at the Episcopal Church of the Ascension in Middletown, Ohio, began to play our carillon regularly once a week until he could not longer do so.

In the tower there is another bell not attached to the carillon's clavier, which is rung by a rope from the St. Francis Chapel as a summoning bell before the time of a service. The bell at the start of the service is the Christus bell of the carillon, which can be rung from the choir and the clavier. The bell before Mass is rung 33 times. The Lord was 33 years of age when he was crucified. Some of the older Sisters remembered that Mother Eva was 33 years old when she began the Religious Life and it was 33 years more when she died. Sister Ruth hoped that the Christus bell would always be rung in multiples of three in honor of the Holy Trinity.

Visitors to this day experience a special spirit of reverence in the Chapel. Sister Beatrice, now Mother Beatrice, wrote in 1940:

> "....there is something like awe, their consciousness of the presence of God there. Some have thought that this was as the spirit of the early monasteries, where the work

was done by the monks themselves. It was suggested that Fritz Abplanalp, loving his work as he lived here creating and carving his designs, made his contribution to this spirit, as did the love and devotion of Sister Clara Elizabeth in doing her beautiful carvings for the ends of the pews in the nave...."

Many thanks have been given to God there, praises sung; sins have been confessed and forgiven, and petitions for such things as are requisite and necessary as well for the body as for the soul have been made with steadfastness and seriousness, with affection and devotion of mind. God has accepted our bounden duty and service and has vouchsafed to give whatever His Wisdom saw was expedient for each one. Besides the blessings of the Daily Eucharist, there came the time when it was possible to have the Blessed Sacrament reserved on the Chapel Altar, for the Communion of the sick and the devotion of the faithful. This, His House, has long been the place of His Sacramental Presence, filling our hearts with joy. There have been many miracles of grace performed in our dear Chapel and many hours have been spent in meditation and prayer in this atmosphere of peace. May God grant a continual flow of His grace to all who seek it earnestly in this Chapel of the Transfiguration."

This thought has continued in the mind of the Sisters of the Transfiguration.

View from the back of the chapel full of guests.

15 LITURGY AND MUSIC

From the beginning, in accordance with Mother Eva's promise of loyalty to the Episcopal Church, the Book of Common Prayer was used for the Eucharist and Daily Morning and Evening Prayer. In the early days the children of Bethany Home attended both Morning and Evening Prayer, although later they attended only Evening Prayer. In the 1950s the children attended Evensong daily, and the Eucharist one weekday, usually a Thursday unless a Saint's Day occurred during the week. On Sundays they attended the choral Morning Prayer and Eucharist as well as Evensong. In the early years Mrs. Henderson, Sister Beatrice's mother, taught them to sing the Psalms. Since Bethany Home became Bethany School, without a boarding department, the School has its Eucharists in the Chapel. Since the School is much larger than Bethany Home, there are two Celebrations of the Eucharist, one for the Lower School and one for the Upper School. The Sisters have a daily Eucharist.

Although the services were strictly according to the Prayer Book, the Sisters did adopt an enriched Calendar. Some of the additional Feast Days which they observed are now in the official church Calendar, such as the Feasts of St. Joseph, Mary Magdalene, and the Visitation of the Blessed Virgin. A number of Lesser Saints were commemorated, most of them being "black letter days" in the Calendar of the Church of England. In the 1960s we further enriched the Calendar by adding a fuller observance of what seemed to be the more important feast days, such as the Visitation, St. Joseph, and Mary Magdalene, which are now in the official Calendar. We continued to keep a few, such as the Nativity of the Blessed Virgin and St. Francis of Assisi even though are not in the official Calendar. The Sisters keep one Feast that is not in any other Calendar which is Mother Eva's birthday, in celebration of her life. Sister Beatrice chose the special prayers and Lessons for Mother Foundress Day, February 9, 1929, which became a Major Feast in the Sisters' calendar. The Episcopal Church has added a few minor feasts at every General Convention since 1967, most of which the Community has added to its Calendar as commemorations.

We used the Prayer Book of 1892 until the 'new' Prayer Book came out in 1928. In 1967 the Standing Committee of the Episcopal Church published "The Liturgy of the Lord's Supper," the first of a series of trial uses including the "green book," the "zebra book," and finally the Proposed Book which was finally adopted by General Convention in 1979. The Community obediently made use of these proposed services, some Sisters considering them a trial in more ways than one. When the Proposed Book came out in 1976 we tried various alternations between Rite I and Rite II, continuing for a time to do this when the 1979 Book of Common Prayer was approved by General Convention. We finally adopted the use of Rite II as a normal thing, although permitting use of Rite I if desired for any special reason. As a matter of fact at the time of our Centennial, for historical experience, we used the Prayer Book of 1892 for one service.

The 1979 Book of Common Prayer includes many rites and customs which the Sisters had adopted long before, such as the special rites for Holy Week and the Easter Vigil. It was in comparatively recent years that the Community adopted the Maundy Thursday rite of foot washing. From the beginning the Sisters have kept one liturgical observance in Holy Week that they have not found in any other place; they keep vigil before the tomb from the close of the 3-hour service on Good Friday until the first Eucharist on Easter morning. This was started by Mother Eva.

In 2008, as directed by the General Convention of 2007, the Sisters began using the Revised Common Lectionary.

The Divine Office

In addition to Morning and Evening Prayer, the Sisters recite the Divine Office, the traditional corporate prayer of monastic houses. It consists principally of the Psalms, with the addition of hymns, and short portions of Scripture and a Collect. There were seven: Lauds, Prime, Terce, Sext, None, Vespers, Compline. These are the Latin names for the times of day at which they were originally said.

Sister Beatrice did not remember the details of transition in the use of the Office Book. In the beginning they said Prime, Sext and Compline from Dr. Pusey's little Office Book, (No copy of this book has been found.) and Morning Prayer and Evening Prayer from the Book of Common Prayer. About 1910, after the trip to England, they began using a Breviary printed for the Sisters of St. Margaret, "The Day Hours of the Church of England", adding Lauds, Terce, and None. They said Evening Prayer in place of the monastic Office of Vespers. This book was translated and arranged from the Sarum book, the Breviary commonly used in England before the

Reformation. After some years of using this book, in 1928, they changed to "Hours of Prayer," edited by Fr. E. C. Trenholme, SSJE. It was also based on the Sarum use and was very similar to the one they had been using. One reason for the change was that this Breviary had a service for the Feast of the Transfiguration which the "Day Hours" lacked.

The books were getting old. "Hours of Prayer" was not reprinted after 1949, and liturgical changes in the Church made it out of date. The Sisters began to realize they would have to make their own edition of the breviary.

Revised Office Book and Book of Common Prayer 1979

On the advice of Dom Anthony Damron, our Chaplain General, in 1968 we had already begun to shorten the Office, making it five-fold instead of seven-fold. The Office of Prime was dropped, a single Noon Office replaced combined Terce, Sext and None, dividing the 178 verses of Psalm 119 into six parts divided among the six weekdays instead of the entire Psalm divided among six Offices in one day. For many years Lauds had been said in the evening after Compline, in anticipation of the coming day. It was now moved to its more logical place in the morning, preceding Morning Prayer and the Eucharist. Memorials of saints at the close of Lauds are now said after Compline. Offices were compiled for some of the new Feasts. We continued to recite Lauds and Compline from the Breviary and Morning and Evening Prayer from the Book of Common Prayer. For a long time we continued to recite Lauds from "Hours of Prayer" with new Antiphons to the Benedictus based on the new Lectionary and the Revised Standard Version of the Bible.

After the Proposed Book was approved by General Convention in 1976, the Sisters began to work on the Noon Office following the pattern of "Hours of Prayer" with the new translation of the Psalter and new Antiphons. Compline was completed in 1979. The full revision of Lauds was completed in 1995, most of the work being done by Sister Monica Mary. The Office book was loose-leaf to allow for further revision.

Because it was done in sections in a loose-leaf notebook, this book did not have consecutive page numbers and each Office was identified by a letter. These pages also began to wear out. So it was revised again by Sister Rachel Margaret, with consecutive page numbers, and including some Community services which had not been in the first book. This new edition was edited and printed in a better format in 2005. It is still in a loose-leaf binder. Further revision may occur.

Healing Ministry

The charismatic movement in the Church for a time had a divisive effect upon the Community, as in so many parishes. One of the positive things which came out of the charismatic movement was a renewal of the healing ministry and the presence on the grounds of Emily Gardiner Neal, who lived with us until her death. She served at our altar as Deacon and held a healing service for us once a week. Since her death our Chaplain has had a short healing service after Evensong once a week.

Music

Mother Eva and Sister Beatrice first heard plainsong in the choir of St. Mary the Virgin at Wantage, in England. It was most elaborately sung by well trained voices. Sister Beatrice wrote that she lost count of the notes one syllable went through during a festal Vespers. In spite of the fact they brought home the latest publications on plainsong, they decided to wait until they had especially trained voices with true ear before they attempted the impossible in our choir! Plainsong was sung in the various Convents they visited and they grew quite used to it but never were enthusiastic over it. Since both the 1940 Hymnal and the 1982 Hymnal have a good many plainsong tunes, the Sisters have used them as a matter of course, though perhaps not as beautifully as at Wantage. We have always used the Anglican chant from the Hymnal as well as the plainsong chants. The plainsong tunes for the Office Hymns are from a booklet published by the Wantage Sisters. The tunes are numbered in accordance with the numbers given in Hours of Prayer. They have been copied into our new Office Book. For the Prayer Book services we use the Hymnal 1980 and several supplementary books which have been published.

We say the Daily Office without music except for the hymns, which are sung without accompaniment. The exception is Evening Prayer, which is called 'Evensong' because the hymns, the canticles and the responses are sung, whether in the Chapel or in the Oratory. It may be remembered that in the early days of the Community and Bethany Home, the children were taught to sing the Psalms. Now we sing the Psalms on certain days, accompanied by the organ. The Eucharist on Sundays and Feast Days is always in the Chapel and we are accompanied by the organ. The musical pointing for the new translations of the Psalms was arranged by our then Choir Director, Richard Silbereis, using the familiar tunes. In 1970, after a visit to England, he gave us new printed booklets with the traditional tunes.

The Organ

At the beginning, Mr. John Prower Symons played the organ for many services. Another organist friend was Miss Mabel Moore. The original organ was designed by Mr. Symons with women's and children's voices especially in mind. It was made by the Moeller Organ Company at Hagerstown, Maryland. It was beginning to wear out. The music committee visited several churches with pipe organs before deciding how to proceed in planning the new organ. The present organ was designed by Mr. Roger Heather and was installed in 1977 by the Schantz Organ Company in Orrville, Ohio. The last service with the old organ was the Life Profession of Sister Mary Elizabeth on St. Stephen's Day, 1976. The next day that organ was dismantled. Every Sister worked on cleaning the Chapel in preparation for the new organ, and it was used for the first time on Easter Day, 1977. In the meantime all of the Sisters' services were held in the Oratory. By this time Bethany Home had become Bethany School with many more children, and the school services were held in the gymnasium until the Chapel was again ready for use.

There have been many Sister organists. Sister Ruth Magdalene played the organ for many years. Others have included Sister Leinaala Josephine, Sister Esther Mary, Sister Angela Hannah, Sister Virginia Cecilia, Sister Paula Irene, Sister Hilary Mary, Sister Elizabeth Anne, Sister Marcia Francis, Sister Monica Mary, and Sister Diana Dorothea. There have been other organists, not members of the Community, who have also served as choir directors.

Dr. John Deaver, organist and choir director for over 30 years.

Dr. John Deaver is the present organist and choir director. He plays for services three times a week, leads choir rehearsal, and usually teaches one of the Sister organists.

PART TWO
The Community Continues

16 DEPRESSION AND WORLD WAR II

MOTHER BEATRICE MARTHA, SUPERIOR, (1928–1938)
MOTHER CLARA ELIZABETH (1938–1943)

As early as 1923 Mother Eva had shown signs of deteriorating health, and much of the responsibility of the Mother Superior fell upon Sister Beatrice. The decision to reserve the Blessed Sacrament had given Mother Eva new energy. At a Chapter meeting early in 1925 Mother Eva had proposed the employment of a resident Chaplain, the building of a house for the Chaplain, and improvements in Bethany Home. These were accepted and accomplished before her death in 1928. The first resident Chaplain was Stanley Cleveland, the son of Mother Eva's sister Grace Cleveland. Until then they had had to depend upon the services of the Rev. Paul Matthews or some other clergyman to celebrate the Eucharist, and it was not always possible. They now built a house for the

Mother Beatrice Martha.

Chaplain, called Orchard Corners. In 2008 it became the residence of the Bethany School Chaplain. 1925 was also the year in which they decided to go ahead with the building of the Chapel and with the building of the Bethany Home cottages.

Sister Beatrice was elected Superior immediately after Mother Eva's death. She accepted reluctantly but she knew that was what Mother Eva had desired. Mother Beatrice's first priority after her election was to restore the good relationship between the Community and the Diocese of Southern Ohio. Her role in that has already been told as well as her part in the completion and beautification of the new Chapel.

The Community was now 25 years old. It had two Bethany Homes in Glendale, one for boys and one for girls; in Cleveland there were St. John's Orphanage, Holy Cross House, and the Church Home for old ladies; St. Andrew's Priory in Honolulu, Hawaii and the overseas work at Wuhu in China. Although the Community had grown slowly there were Sisters at each of the Branch Works, and twelve stationed at the local houses, who were present at the election Chapter meeting.

Her journal mentions correspondence with the Branch Houses. There were often requests for advice from Sisters appointed to be in charge of these houses. She also visited each of the Branch Houses including Wuhu in China. There were sometimes requests from Bishops and others asking for Sisters to undertake a new work.

Head of Bethany Home

In addition to being Mother Superior, Mother Beatrice was still head of Bethany Home. The cottage system was just beginning and she had to deal with the exigencies of the new system. Sister Edith Constance was the principal of the school. Mother

Beatrice's office was on the top floor of the old building, called Mount Tabor. It has been said that children sent to her office for disciplinary reasons were told to "sit on Mt. Tabor steps and think about it." Anyone passing by knew why she was there. Apparently that was usually sufficient. The Bethany Home Chronicle reports her periodic visits to the schools to meet with the children and sign report cards. It is probable that many of the customs connected with Bethany Home and its school were developed during her term of office.

✠

Mary Jane Beekley's Letter

A letter from Mary Jane Beekley, then a freshman at Bethany Home School, written in 1937, describes the Home. It was printed in the "Bethany Home Chronicle."

Aerial view of the grounds.

"Ten years may be a long time for some people, but not for me. The happenings that far back are almost as vivid as a year ago. As I remember there were only six buildings at Bethany Home. The largest building was the Convent, where the Sisters and bigger girls slept. Also the kitchen, guest rooms, dining-rooms and even our Chapel were in it. Our Chapel was very small; we called it the Oratory. The other buildings were old St. Faith's, the Lodge, the Hope, Hilaritas Hall and the garage. St. Faith's was the residence of the smaller children. We ate at Hilaritas Hall. The laundry was in the lower floor of the Hope, and upstairs were the bedrooms for the rest of the older girls. The Lodge was the residence of our priest and of the men who worked for us.

The grounds were very large. In one large corner was a vegetable garden, which helped to provide food through the winter. Only a few long pavements connected the buildings. There were two large orchards; apple trees were in one and peach, plum, cherry and quince trees in the other. There was a lovely front yard by the Convent, cool, quiet and shady. School classes were held in rooms at St. Faith's, a portion of the Hall and a few other places. The population was not very large, but more children were~ pouring in and, therefore, more room was required.

St. Faith's.

Now the little village of Bethany Home has greatly increased in buildings and population. In the place of St. Faith's stands a grand schoolhouse named after the old building. Four cottages have been constructed, each with a name and dedicated for the girls' homes. A large dining-room for the girls and an infirmary for the sick have been built. All are well furnished and comfortable, but none of them can compare with the new Chapel. It is the most sacred and the most beautiful building on the grounds. It is gray stone outside and has hand-carved woodwork inside. In the middle of the campus is a small building. It is "Ye Bethany Shoppe" run by the Seniors. They use the profits for their clothes to wear after graduation. The Hope is used for the same purpose as before, but the laundry is much improved by modern machinery. The Lodge has been made over and changed somewhat, but is still used by our men. As for the Hall, we don't eat there any more. It is used for a gymnasium, auditorium, play-house and other things, because of its large size and the fact that it has a stage. Instead of a garden, we have a baseball diamond and a court. The orchard and front yard are unchanged. Many cement pavements are laid from the cottages to other buildings. There are now about eighty girls from two to eighteen years old, healthy and happy, living in separate cottages according to age and grade, which maintains contentment and training." (Chronicle, 1937).

1928 New Book of Common Prayer

The 1928 Book of Common Prayer had just been published and there were liturgical decisions to be made. While very capable of making decisions herself, Mother Beatrice's first question was likely to be, "What would Mother Eva do?" In many matters she asked advice of Rev. Paul Matthews, their Chaplain General, now Bishop of New Jersey.

Lincoln Heights, Ohio St. Simon's Mission

In 1930 the Sisters, with the permission of the Bishop, began a new mission at St. Simon of Cyrene Church. As the beginning was told to me, the Sisters had been invited to work in Africa. Sister Beatrice happened to have been driven through a nearby area, now called Lincoln Heights. It was at the worst of the depression, and the people there, all African-Americans, were living in the utmost poverty. Sister Beatrice is quoted as having said, "If you want to help Africans, why not come here?" And so the Mission of St. Simon of Cyrene began. The rest of the story is told in Appendix II.

Sisters of the Tabernacle

During these years, The Sisters of the Tabernacle were a very small Community in Chattanooga, Tennessee. It had begun in 1918, and its purpose is described as working for adoration and intercession; promotion of retreats and quiet days, (Call of the Cloister, Anson, 1951, p. 575). It had not grown and in 1931 their Chaplain, the Rev. Arthur G. Wilson, contacted the Community of the Transfiguration suggesting that the remaining Sisters of the Tabernacle be received by us. We responded favorably. The necessary legal and financial matters were arranged. One of the Tabernacle Sisters, Sister Mary Joseph, who had been Life Professed in 1918, was received by us on All Saints' Day in 1931 and died in December, 1934. The other four Tabernacle Sisters are remembered by us in our monthly requiems. Their one Novice returned to her family but later returned, was received into our novitiate, and became our Sister Mary Agnes. She was professed June 8, 1935 and died in 1960 at the age of 89.

General Convention, 1937

In 1937 there was great excitement among both Sisters and girls at Bethany Home. The General Convention was going to meet in the city of Cincinnati, October 6-19. General Convention is the legislative body of the Episcopal Church. It meets every three years and is always accompanied by the Triennial meeting of the Women of the Church, then called the Women's Auxiliary. There are over 1,000 delegates, Bishops, priests and lay people, plus exhibits by many Church organizations and by suppliers of Church furnishings. The Bethany Home Chronicle reported that preparation was being made for 35 guests who would be coming to stay at Bethany Home. The high school girls were moved into temporary quarters in the school library, leaving Beth-Anna for the guests. The older girls were allowed to miss classes for a week to help as pages at the Convention. (The principal's report stated that they made up the work later.) The guest list included several Bishops, Priests, Sisters of other Communities, Church Army Sisters and missionaries.

Three Life Professed Sisters with Bishop and Superior in front of the Chapel.

Three Life Professions

On St. Luke's Day, October 18, 1937, Sister Evelyn Ancilla, Sister Grace Elizabeth and Sister Helena Miriam made their life vows in the Community of the Transfiguration. Bishop Paul Matthews of New Jersey was the Celebrant. Bishop Irving P. Johnson of Colorado preached the sermon and conducted the Profession Service. They were assisted by Bishop Thomas Jenkins of Nevada and Bishop Wallace J. Gardner of New Jersey and Father Gerald Lewis, the Sisters' Chaplain. A number of delegates to the Convention came out especially for the service. Sister Evelyn in later years said that it was planned for that day partly to show those attending the Convention that there were Sisters in the Episcopal Church.

Mother Beatrice retires to Bat Cave

At the completion of her two terms as Superior in 1938, Mother Beatrice retired to our vacation house at Bat Cave, North Carolina, where she wrote *A Follower's Story*, an account of the beginnings of the Community. The title illustrates how she thought of herself as simply a follower of Mother Eva, but the book itself also shows how the young fifteen year old girl developed into a mature, capable woman, well able to follow in Mother Eva's footsteps. She can rightly be called the co-foundress of the Community. The book exists only in manuscript, and it is the best source we have for the history of the Community prior to Mother Eva's death in July, 1928.

Sister Beatrice did not live alone at Bat Cave. Of course there were occasional visits home to the Convent. Another Sister was always there to be her companion; sometimes she would be a Sister who was in special need of rest, sometimes a person in need of a temporary home or a place of refuge, and there were always a couple of dogs. Sisters visiting in Bat Cave in the 1970s met a priest who remembered attending a retreat for clergy organized by Sister Beatrice. Sister Beatrice died in 1963. She is still fondly remembered by the people at Bat Cave to this day. She is remembered by her Sisters as co-foundress of the Community of the Transfiguration.

Mother Clara Elizabeth, 1938-1943

Sister Clara Elizabeth was born March 13, 1873, in Switzerland and came to the United States to be governess to the children of the Cleveland family in Glendale. She was one of the early Sisters in the Community. Chapter 8 tells of her coming. With her great gift of wood carving she beautified the little Oratory in the Convent. Although there were no side aisles, she carved both ends of the pews, saying that God could see them if we could not. She was appointed Sister-in-charge of Bethany Home for Boys, located near the Convent. The wood work in the little chapel at St. Edmund's is her work, along with the work of the boys to whom she taught the art of woodcarving. (The chapel now stands in the Glendale village square.)

Sister Clara was in charge of Bethany Home for Boys for fifteen years until a serious heart condition caused her to retire from that place. She was given a Sabbatical year to rest and a trip to visit her family in Switzerland.

Sister Clara was responsible, in 1929, for bringing to this country a young Swiss woodcarver whom she had taught in Switzerland, Fritz Abplanalp, who did most of the carving in the new Chapel choir and the sanctuary.

In 1928 Sister Clara was sent to St. Andrew's Priory, Honolulu, for a year. She returned, but a year later was appointed Sister-in-charge of the Priory where she remained until she was elected Superior of the Community in 1938.

Mother Clara Elizabeth.

First African-American Sister, 1938

It was after Mother Clara had been in office only a short time that an important matter for the life of the Community was brought up. In October, 1938 Sister Olivia presented a motion in Chapter that African-American women might be received as candidates. Mother Clara had visited two women in Raleigh, North Carolina who were interested. One was Sister Anna Mary who had been professed in 1910 in a Community for African-American women which had been started in Baltimore, called the Sisters of St. Mary and All Saints. When that Community dissolved, some of the Sisters entered a Canadian Community. Segregation was part of the United States' social culture at that time and we had not accepted her. Some Sisters felt that such a proposal was too radical, and at first there was not a majority in favor of it. But other Sisters kept the proposal on the agenda and the Sisters went through a time of discernment. In 1938, Sister Anna Mary was asking again, along with a young woman named Myrtle Deane. Bishop Johnson, their Bishop Visitor, and Bishop Matthews, their Chaplain General, both spoke to the Community about the importance of this proposal. There was also a letter from Bishop Hobson, the Diocesan Bishop. All urged the Sisters to vote in favor of accepting African-American candidates into the Novitiate. This time the motion passed unanimously. Miss Myrtle Dean was then elected. It was decided that she would be clothed as a Novice in September, 1939. She was professed on St. Luke's Day, October 18, 1942. She later asked to be released from the Community. Sister Anna Mary was professed in this Community in 1956. She died in 1967.

Ministry in California: St. Dorothy's Rest and San Mateo

Although Sister Clara seemed to have recovered from her heart attack, she was still not strong. Chapter minutes of her term of office indicate that at times Sister Edith Constance, the Assistant Superior, presided. However, in 1940, during Sister Clara's time in office, the Community accepted the invitation of Bishop Karl Block of California to operate a summer camp for children, St. Dorothy's Rest, near Camp Meeker, California. The camp had been started by Mrs. Nellie Lincoln as a memorial to her daughter, Dorothy. It is said that she was attracted to

Four Mothers Superior (Beatrice Martha, Clara Elizabeth, Olivia Mary, Louise Magdalene).

the Sisters of the Transfiguration by their blue habits, which she thought were more joyful than the black habits she had seen worn by other Orders. Mrs. Lincoln died in 1953. The story of St. Dorothy's Rest is in Appendix II.

Mother Clara's Retirement

Mother Clara's health was still uncertain. Eventually she broke down and she resigned a few months before the end of her first term. Her health had improved sufficiently so that she was able to be assigned as the first Sister-in-charge of St. Dorothy's Rest, the new work in California, which had been accepted while she was Superior. Sister Madeleine Mary and Sister Marjorie Hope accompanied her.

Sister Clara returned to the Convent in Glendale, in 1952. She was there when the old Oratory burned in 1957. She saw it burn and was reported to have said, "If only I were 20 years younger." She died about six months after the fire, some said from a broken heart. Her death occurred April, 1958. She was 85 years old and had been professed for 48 years.

END OF THE WAR AND TRANSITION 17

MOTHER OLIVIA MARY (1943-1953)
MOTHER LOUISE MAGDALENE (1953-1963)
MOTHER ESTHER MARY (1963-1973)
MOTHER LOUISE MAGDALENE (2nd Term 1973-1983)

On Mother Foundress Day, February 9, 1943, Sister Olivia Mary was elected to succeed Mother Clara. Sister Olivia was the niece of Mother Eva, (Quarterly, Fall, 1993, 49:2), and the daughter of Mortimer and Marianne Matthews. She entered the Community in 1914 and was professed in 1918. Shortly afterwards she was sent to be the first American Sister in charge of St. Andrew's Priory School for Girls in Honolulu, Hawaii, and was there for eleven years. In 1931 she was appointed to be Sister-in-charge of the new work which the Community had begun at St. Simon's Mission, Lincoln Heights, Ohio, which she led for twelve years.

Mother Olivia's ten years of leadership in the Community were a time of growth and development. We were still in the midst of World War II when her term began. Gas rationing and food rationing no doubt affected the daily life of the Community. One change, still being mentioned in the Community ten years later was that of the Lenten diet. Because the meat ration for the following period was based on the amount used on the preceding period, the Sisters changed from no meat on weekdays in Lent to meat only once a day and Wednesdays as well as Fridays were days of abstinence. It was also said that the doctors who served the Community were pleased by the change and that fewer Sisters needed to take vitamins.

End of World War II (1945) and Community Growth

The end of the war brought new life to the Community. During Mother Olivia's years in office there were thirteen life professions. An unknown number came to test their vocation. At that time the Community had adopted a policy of accepting no one over the age of forty unless they had been in the mission field. Under that provision three women who had been missionaries in Japan came shortly after the war: Elizabeth Rogers, who became Sister Ursula Elizabeth, was a registered nurse; she had taught physical education at a girls' school in Tokyo. Margaret Hester, Sister Mariya Margaret, had taught kindergarten in Japan, including for a short time at Sendai. During the war she taught kindergarten in an internment camp for Japanese in Montana. Miss Helen Shipps, a medical social worker with St. Luke's Hospital in Tokyo, became Sister Lioba Catherine. Although they had met each other in Japan, each came without the knowledge of the others' decision to come to the Community.

Another one who came at that time was Althea King, Sister Althea Augustine, the third African-American to be professed in the Community. (She was professed after Sister Olivia's term as Mother Superior.) Sister Althea has served in St. Simon's School, as principal of Holy Trinity School, Ponce, Puerto Rico, at St. Philip's School in Dallas, Texas, and was for several years in charge of St. John's Home in Painesville, Ohio. She was Novice Director for five years under Mother Ann. She spent two years from 1980 to 1982 in the Bahamas restoring the Ranfurly Children's Home. Here at home she also worked for several years in the Open Door Ministry at the Church of the Advent, and at St. John's, a social service agency in Over-the-Rhine, in Cincinnati. In 2005 she celebrated the 50th Anniversary of her Profession.

In 1945, under Mother Olivia's leadership, the Rule of the Community was revised and reprinted. It was also in that year that "The Transfiguration Quarterly" began, and from this time the history of the Community can be traced through its pages. The second issue, Spring, 1945, gave the news that the Sisters had accepted the invitation of the Rt. Rev. Charles Colmore, Bishop of the Missionary District of Puerto Rico, and his Coadjutor, the Rt. Rev. Charles F. Boynton, to work in Ponce, Puerto Rico.

Caroa

The Community had become a member of CAROA, Conference of Anglican Religious in the Americas. Since 1943 the traditional communities have worked together to try to make the Religious Communities better known by whole Church. They always have a booth at General Convention There is a Council which meets at least every year, and is attended by representatives of all the major Communities, usually the Superior and at least one other Sister, often the Novice Director. It is a consultative rather than a legislative body.

Community photo taken at 50th anniversary.

They consider matters of concern to all the members. We have always sent representatives.

At the celebration of our Golden Anniversary our guests included Sisters from seven other Episcopal Religious Communities and representatives of two men's Communities.

Our Golden Anniversary, celebrating fifty years in 1948, was a happy occasion. Other guests included Bishop Paul Matthews, who preached at the principal Eucharist, our Visitor, the Bishop Colmoe of Puerto Rico, and the Rev. Vivan Peterson, our Chaplain General. At a Solemn Evensong the Eve of the great day the windows of Mother Eva Mary and Harriet Starr Cannon, Foundress of the Community of St. Mary, were installed and blessed in our Chapel.

Mother Louise Magdalene 1953–63

Sister Louise Magdalene succeeded Sister Olivia as Superior in 1953. Sister Louise had entered the Community in 1930. She was professed in 1934, and was assigned to the work in China. She spent the war years in free China and returned home on a "delayed furlough" in 1946. She returned to China the next year, but in December 1948 when the Communists came, she and the other Sisters there had to return to the Mother House. Afterwards she served in almost every branch house.

Another Large Novitiate

Mother Louise appointed Sister Olivia as Novice Director. Sister Olivia served in this capacity as long as her health permitted. She died in 1969. During this time the Novi-

Novice Director, (seated at right) with three Novices.

tiate became quite large and eleven of them continued on to Life Profession. Two were former missionaries: Sister Frances Helen who had served in Alaska and Sister Paula Irene who had served the Navajo in Nevada. Sister Rebecca Louise, from China and Sister Naomi Mercedes, from Spain via Puerto Rico, also came and continued to life profession, but both later asked to be released. Of those who stayed, six are still alive and active in 2008. Three have celebrated their 50th anniversary of profession. One, Sister Alice has served as Superior. She, Sister Monica Mary, Sister Althea Augustine, and Sister Hilary Mary have served as Novice Directors.

Japan

Soon after her election the first time Mother Louise, accompanied by Sister Lioba who had been a missionary in Japan, traveled to Japan to investigate new requests for work there. After her return the Community voted to accept the request of the Rt. Rev. Timothy Nakamura, Bishop of the Diocese of Tohoku, in Sendai, to open a diocesan school for women Church workers. Sisters Mariya Margaret and Ursula Elizabeth, who also had served in Japan before the war, were appointed to go. Sister Jeanette Clare was also appointed, but due to an accident while they were attending language school in Tokyo, she had to return home. The story of Sendai continues in Appendix II.

Care for the Elderly

Aid to elderly people has been a small but continuing part of the total work of the Community. In the very early days the Sisters provided a home for poor elderly or weak women in Cincinnati. Later, they provided St. Ann's Home and for a short time St.

Elizabeth's Home for women who were old but able to take care of themselves. St. Ann's can hardly be called a Branch Work since no Sisters were in residence. St. Ann's provided individual rooms for sixteen older working women, rent free. The rooms were large, airy rooms with gas stoves for heating and cooking, and running water was near. There was a nominal charge of two dollars a month to cover electric, gas and water charges. The women provided their own maintenance either through their own efforts or through relatives or church or social agency. They felt very independent as paying the two dollar charge made them feel they were paying rent and not living on charity. When they became incapacitated, their friends took charge of them. Until then, they lived their own lives, cooked their own meals, and were content and happy. They required the oversight of a Sister only to settle minor difficulties. A Sister visited them once a month. The sixteen rooms were usually occupied as this was a popular place. The women were required to keep their own rooms in good condition and were responsible for cleaning some part of the building near their own apartment. For many years the Sisters had charge of the Church Home for elderly women in Cleveland. For a few years Sisters also visited regularly in Stanley Rowe Towers, a government housing project for Senior Citizens in Cincinnati.

St. Mary's Memorial Home

In 1956, under Mother Louise's leadership, St. Mary's Memorial Home was built on the Convent grounds to carry on the ministry to the elderly. It was dedicated in 1957.

St. Mary's was planned to serve two purposes. One was for the care of elderly relatives of the Sisters so that a Sister would not have to go away to care for them; the other was to care for

Sisters caroling at St. Mary's.

elderly Associates and friends, sometimes employees or their relatives and retired missionaries. Such persons had been cared for in various buildings on the Convent grounds from the beginning of the Community. Mother Louise thought of this way of consolidating their quarters so that they could be cared for more comfortably and efficiently. It had an excellent staff of nurses, housekeeping and maintenance people. There was no chapel although they had their own service of Morning Prayer in the living room. Originally the residents had been in better physical condition and the Convent Chaplain took them communion in their rooms when needed. Some years later an addition made room for a chapel and an activities room. Now they had their own chapel, and the Convent Chaplain celebrated the Eucharist for them once every Sunday and one weekday.

Bethany Home becomes Bethany School

In 1958 it was decided to change Bethany Home to Bethany School and to admit day students, boys as well as girls. In the following years various Sisters, including Sister Mary Grace and Sister Teresa Marie served as principal or director of instruction. The boarding department continued, using only Bethsaida and Bethanna cottages.

Sisters socializing with St. Mary's residents in the activity room.

The other cottages gradually were converted into classroom buildings. In the next few years the number of boarders decreased, and it became increasingly difficult to find satisfactory cottage parents. The boarding department was closed, June 1977, and Bethany School became a day school.

In 1974 the Rev. James Hindle became Headmaster and school Chaplain. Mr. Richard Wood was named Director of Studies, but the following year he was Associate Headmaster and Principal. Dr. Paul Dawson came as Headmaster in 1980. Fr. Hindle continued two more years as Chaplain. The present Head of the school, in 2008, is Mrs. Cheryl Pez who succeeded Dr. Dawson after he retired in 1999.

In the yearbook, begun in 1975, the photos of the students show a thoroughly racially integrated student body. Administration and faculty lists show many teachers who taught at Bethany for quite a number of years. Lack of adequate transportation kept enrollment small. Numbers began to increase when, for a few years, Fr. Hindle was able to arrange for our children to ride on the Landmark Baptist School busses which covered a much wider geographical area. Enrollment increased still more when the law permitted private school pupils to use the public school transportation.

The school goes from Kindergarten through eighth grade. For a few years there was also a pre-school for 3-4 year olds, but this was discontinued for lack of space.

Over time, changes have been necessary to accommodate the larger number of students and to modernize the facilities. St. Faith's School remained the main classroom building, but the three cottages which had housed the children of Bethany Home became classroom space for the lower school. Since the boarding department was discontinued, the fourth cottage, Bethanna, has been used by the Sisters as a guest and retreat house.

The original recreation building for Bethany Home was named Hilaritas Hall, Hilaritas being one of the words in the Sisters' motto. It was a frame building, erected by the girls, Sisters, and maintenance staff. It was the scene of many parties for the girls, dramatic productions, and movies about once a month. It was no longer adequate for the needs of Bethany School, so money was raised for the building of a gymnasium which was completed and in use for the school year of 1963-64. There was an attempt to continue the old name but it usually is simply called the Gym. In 1997 that building was enlarged to be a multipurpose building, housing not only the physical education classes and the athletic program, and also providing more space for music.

The library, above the dining room in BethEva, had been moved to the first floor of St. Faith's. More classroom space was needed, so in 1990 the old laundry, known as the Hope, was remodeled and converted into the school media center, including also a computer lab and a reading lab. The laundry facilities were moved into the new Convent building.

The New Convent

It was also during Mother Louise's first term in office that the new Convent was begun. In 1951 and again in 1957 there had been serious fires in the Convent building. There was no loss of life, but it was realized that a new building was a real necessity. The new Convent was made possible in large part to a bequest from Miss Elizabeth Matthews, Mother Eva's niece and the sister of Sister Olivia Mary and Sister Mary Catherine. Building began in 1957 and the new building was dedicated in 1970. Miss Matthews was a generous philanthropist. The total of the bequest was tithed and invested in a special fund called the Elizabeth Matthews Memorial Fund to continue helping organizations and persons outside those of our Community such as she would have helped.

The first fire began in a bedroom on the second floor of the original farm house. Sisters helped to carry out as much as was possible to save. Sister Eva Dorothea was in silent retreat before her Life Profession. She kept her silence, but helped carry things out and then retired to the Chapter Room underneath the Chapel and completed her retreat. Fortunately the library was not destroyed, but suffered much smoke and water damage. The books were salvaged and placed in temporary shelving in the other section of the Convent. They were insured, but the Sisters were made aware that if the library records had been more complete, there would have been better coverage. Sister Monica Mary, then a candidate who was a librarian, came soon after that and was assigned to help the Sister librarian!

The second fire began in the Oratory. The Chaplain rushed up to rescue the Reserved Sacrament in the Oratory and moved it to the tabernacle in the Chapel. Again Sisters helped carry out things that could be salvaged. The firemen told us that the reason the Oratory burned so fast was because of all the loving care it had received with turpentine and wax over many years.

The new Convent is on the same location as the original one. The original farmhouse was torn down to be replaced first. It was very hard, especially for the older Sisters, to see their old home be destroyed. The infirmary was the first part of the new building to be built. It had nine bedrooms plus a nursing station, a small kitchen and a dining room. It also had air conditioning.

Mother Louise foresaw that there would always be Sisters in need of long-term special care as well as temporary illnesses. Six Sisters occupied the new infirmary as soon as it was ready, (Quarterly, Autumn, 1969). 1n 2008 there were still five Sisters living there and the other rooms on that wing have in recent years been equipped for assisted living with hospital beds and call bells. The new building includes a large kitchen and refectory and large common room on the ground floor which came to be called the Recreation Room where guests could be entertained. The first and second floors, including the infirmary, were bedrooms for the Sisters, much larger than the "cells" in the old Convent. The Sisters were able to move into these rooms in January, 1960. The Novice Guardian's office is in the Novitiate wing on the second floor. When this was completed the remains of the old Convent were torn down, ready to start the completion of the convent building.

In the completed building, the bedrooms on the second floor of the new wing are designated as the Guest Wing. On the first floor there is a room set aside as the Guest Sitting room. The last areas to be completed were the Oratory, the offices of the Superior, Assistant Superior and the business offices. On the first floor is another large room, normally used only by the Sisters, called the Community Room. There is a large library of over 11,000 books, catalogued according to the Dewey Decimal System. It is a varied collection, including both religious and secular books. In the last 50 years we have been fortunate to always have had professionally trained librarians in the Community.

Oratory Tabernacle.

The new building has three elevators, which have been a great blessing. This part was completed after Mother Esther became Superior.

✠

MOTHER ESTHER MARY (1963–1973)

In 1962 Mother Louise called Sister Esther Mary home from Ponce, Puerto Rico to become Assistant Superior and in 1963, at the close of Mother Louise's second term, she was elected Superior. Mother Esther Mary entered the Community in 1931 and was immediately assigned to the newly established St. Simon's Mission and worked there until 1945 when she was one of the four Sisters assigned to begin the new ministry in Ponce, Puerto Rico. While at St. Simon's, she established St. Monica's House, a recreation center connected with St. Simon's School. St. Simon's School closed in 1971 but the social service work continued at St. Monica's Center using the St. Simon's school building.

During Mother Esther's first term she visited all of the branch houses and represented the Community at two Conferences on the Religious Life in England. It was a time of liturgical change and the Community tried the various trial use liturgies proposed by the Standing Liturgical Committee. In accordance with the new customs introduced regarding liturgical space, when we built the new Convent, the altar in the Oratory was free standing with the Celebrant facing the people.

It seems that under each Mother Superior at least one new work has been started. Mother Esther Mary succeeded Mother Louise in 1963, and in 1967 Holy Family House was opened in McKinney, Texas. The Sisters' work there was carried on in connection with Holy Family Church. The largest part of the work was a nursery school designed to prepare these Spanish speaking children for English spoken in public schools. The Sisters later moved to St. Philip's School in Dallas. The Sisters withdrew from Texas in 1983.

General Chapter, 1968–70
Withdrawal and Renewal

In 1968 at the end of her first five year term, Mother Esther was reelected as Superior. There was a General Chapter meeting in

1968 at which all the Sisters were present. In addition to some liturgical changes to shorten the Divine Office, Chapter decided to add the step of Junior, or First Profession before taking life vows.

At the same time, during Mother Esther's second term, the Community found itself reduced in numbers. The Sisters were getting older and the number of new Sisters did not equal the number lost by death. During Mother Esther's time in office there were 17 deaths in the Community, and a few more had asked for release. The Community withdrew from Hawaii and Japan and California and from St. John's Home in Painesville, Ohio. The renewal period was divided into two parts so that all the Sisters could participate without completely withdrawing from the remaining works. It was a time of recalling Mother Eva's vision and rethinking our religious commitment. Religious from other Communities were asked to help us. Sister Morag Michael of the Community of St. Mary the Virgin in Wantage, England, came for the first part of the renewal. Mother Joanna of the Deaconess Sisters of St. Andrew in London, came for the second part. There were conferences given by the various leaders on Silence, Community Living, Prayer, the Vows, and other Aspects of the Religious Life. Sister Beatrice's book, *A Follower's Story*, was read at table. The first session began on January 18, 1971, the new date for the Feast of the Confession of St. Peter, and closed with the annual long retreat of five days in Easter Week, 1971.

The second session began September 26. The renewal culminated in a Retreat given by Brother Paul of the Society of St. Francis. Then, in Christmastide, 1971, there followed another General Chapter at which every Sister was present. Work began on a revision of the Rule, which was finally adopted in 1978. It has been amended several times since then.

A Renewed Community in the New Convent

After the renewal the Community was ready to reach out again. The Sisters from the House in McKinney, Texas, which had begun in 1969, came home for the renewal and returned to continue the work. Bethany School continued to flourish. Work continued on the second phase of the new Convent. The new Oratory is very modern, circular with a free standing altar, well lighted, and has double pews instead of the benches in the old Oratory. At that time some Sisters considered air-conditioning as inconsistent with our vow of poverty. The heat in the first summer showed how hot the Oratory would be, so air-conditioning was added in the Oratory. Construction was completed, and the new building was dedicated in 1970.

When air-conditioning was installed in the Oratory the ground floor underneath became cool and habitable and now includes the Guest Dining Room and office space. Now, in 2008, almost all of the Convent is air-conditioned.

75th Anniversary

In 1973 the Community celebrated its 75th Anniversary. The new lectionary now remembered Transfiguration Sunday on the last Sunday after Epiphany, in the spring, so the Sisters decided to celebrate the anniversary beginning with the Eucharist, March 3, 1973 and to continue the celebration throughout the year until the Feast Day on August 6. At the Thanksgiving Service the Rt. Rev. John Krumm. Bishop of Southern Ohio, presided. Our Visitor, the Rt. Rev. Samuel Wylie, Bishop of Northern Michigan, was the Celebrant. The sermon was preached by the Rt. Rev. John Melville Burgess, Bishop of Massachusetts, (Quarterly, Spring, 1973). He was a long time Associate of the Community who had once been priest-in-charge of the Mission of St. Simon's of Cyrene in Lincoln Heights. The celebration was held on a Saturday to enable clergy to attend who could not have come on a Sunday. A special Office for Lauds had been prepared by our Liturgical Committee. Representatives from many other Religious Communities were present. Fr. Anthony Damron, our Chaplain General, represented the Order of St. Benedict. The Order of the Holy Cross was represented by its Superior, Fr. Connor Lynn, and the Society of St. John the Evangelist by the Fr. David Clayton, a friend of the Sisters who had been in Japan. Seven women's Communities were represented, each by its Superior and one or more Sisters: the All Saints' Sisters of the Poor, Community of St. John the Baptist, Community of St. Mary, Sisterhood of the Holy Nativity, the Order of St. Anne, the Sisterhood of St. John the Divine and the Order of St. Helena. At an open house in the afternoon the children presented a play about Mother Eva and the beginning days of the Community, Mr. Albert Meyers played a recital on the carillon. St. Mary's Home and Bethany School were both open to visitors. "The Quarterly" published a short history of the Community written by Sister Monica Mary.

At the completion of her second term of office Sister Esther returned to Ponce and remained there until 1984 when the Sisters withdrew from that work.

Large meeting of Sisters and clergy in the Community Room.

✠

MOTHER LOUISE MAGDALENE, 1973–1983

A Superior is elected for a term of five years and may not serve more than two consecutive terms. Mother Esther completed her second term in 1973. At the close of the annual long retreat in June, Sister Louise Magdalene, who had served as assistant under Mother Esther was again elected. The Feast of the Transfiguration on August 6, 1973 was celebrated with her installation as Superior.

The Sisters in Texas, who had returned to McKinney in 1971 at the close of the Renewal, moved to Dallas in 1977. They remained in Texas until 1983. Beginning in 1979 the work in California was revived by Sister Alice Lorraine and Sister Teresa Marie, first in Ferndale, then in Eureka. Appendix II has the story of the Sisters in the West.

At the suggestion of the Rt. Rev. William Weinhauer, Episcopal Visitor of the Community, a new ministry in the Diocese of Western North Carolina began in 1979 at a retreat house owned by St. Luke's Church, Lincolnton, North Carolina. Its story is also in Appendix II.

During Mother Louise's second term, many aspirants to the religious life visited the Community. For several years the Novice director organized a Vocations program designed to give them an idea of what life was like in the convent, and to show them the local branch works. She also tried to show them other types of religious vocations. Only a few came back to test their vocations. There were many other careers open to women then. However, the number of postulants grew until at one point in the late 1970s the Novice Director remembers there were twelve postulants and novices. But of that number only two are still with the Community in 2008.

At the end of Mother Louise's last term, Sister Ann Margaret was elected Superior.

Mother Louise had served as Superior from 1953 to 1963, and 1973 to 1983. She had the responsibilities of Assistant Superior under Mother Esther from 1963 to 73 which amounts to 30 years altogether.

REVIEWING THE PAST, PREPARING FOR THE FUTURE 18

SR ANN MARGARET (1983–1993)
SR ALICE LORRAINE (1993–1998)
SR ANN MARGARET (2nd Term 1998–2008)

Sister Ann Margaret was elected Superior in 1983 at the conclusion of Mother Louise's last term. Sister Ann first met the Community as a volunteer college worker to help with the ministry in Puerto Rico. At the time of the "renewal" she was a Novice, and she was sent to Puerto Rico so that the Sisters assigned there could come home for the renewal. She had also served as Sister-in-charge of the Bethany School boarding department. She had been trained and was licensed as a nursing home administrator and was assistant administrator at St. Mary's Home at the time of her election. She preferred not to be called Mother, although most Sisters kept on using that title.

During Sister Ann's first term Sister Mary Elizabeth continued her summer ministry at the Native American Reservation, Rosebud, SD (1992–1997) Another Sister always accompanied her each year.

Dominican Republic

In 1984, at the invitation of the Rt. Rev. Telesforo Isaac, Sister Priscilla and Sister Hilary began a new work in the Dominican Republic at San Pedro de Macoris. The Sisters had visited the Dominican Republic several times from Puerto Rico. Sister Esther came over at least once. Sister Priscilla had also been there. After hurricane "David" Sisters Ann, Mary Luke and Hilary came down for six weeks to stay in Santana-Bani to help with relief work and be a calming presence among the people. The rest of the story is in Appendix II.

Building Reconstruction

A good deal of reconstruction work on the Convent took place during Sister Ann's term of office. The old Bethany Home laundry was remodeled to become a library and media center for Bethany School. The Convent laundry was established on the ground floor of the Convent in what had been the Guest Dining Room; the Guest Dining Room moved into the former craft room; the business offices were expanded into what had been guest bedrooms, and an elevator was added to give access to the second floor bedrooms and to the library for guests who could not use the stairs. The library was rearranged and the workroom space was remodeled for more efficient use.

SISTER ALICE LORRAINE 1993–1998

Sister Alice Lorraine was elected Superior in 1993. She also asked not to be called "Mother." Sister Alice had served as Novice Director (1970–73) and Assistant Superior under Mother

Louise (1973-1978). She had served at Bethany Home, in Japan, and California. From 1967 to 1970 she was Executive Director of St. Dorothy's Camp and Conference Center. In 1980 she was stationed at our house in Ferndale, CA. The Community was approaching its 100th year of existence.

Sister Lydia Magdalene was sent to California to take Sister Alice's place with Sister Teresa. She was a very happy addition to the ministry there. Unfortunately she became ill and had to come home to the Mother House. She died in 2006.

Much of the activity in 1997 was related to preparing for the Centennial celebration to be held in 1998.

REMEMBERING THE PAST, APPRECIATING THE PRESENT
Home Life of the Sisters

The daily life of the Sisters centers around the prayer life as directed by the Rule.

There is always a time set for Eucharist and the Divine Office, and for communal meals three times a day. Each Sister plans her time for private devotions according to her schedule for ministry. Helping with Community activities such as housework is also considered ministry. Some tasks are assigned, but many are volunteer. Each Sister has her own work assignment. Because each Sister may have many and various activities, a Sister's day is fully occupied. As Sister Beatrice had observed years before, it is always hard to keep a balance between prayer and action. Once, Sister Olivia reported speaking to a church group about the Religious Life. She had been describing the various activities of the Sisters. She told the Sisters at home that she was asked to "describe a day in the life of a Sister." A Sister asked her, "Whose day did you pick?"

Traditionally the ministry of Hospitality is a part of monastic life, and this is certainly true of the Community of the Transfiguration. St. Mary's Home was the outgrowth of a ministry of hospitality to persons who had been given a home in one of the houses here on the Convent grounds. Families and friends have always been welcome. They, our Associates, and our other visitors are informed of our schedule so that they may observe it. They are always welcome at our services. Many guests come simply for time of quiet and rest.

We also have a ministry of intercessory prayer. We keep a record of all the requests for prayer. Often a Sister, when she has been away from the Convent, at the doctor or shopping, may receive a prayer request. That Sister then reports the name of the person who has asked for prayers. There have been Sisters who make prayer ministry one of their chief concerns. We have a prayer board for making requests known to all the Sisters.

The home life of the Sisters has also included pets, not only for the sake of the Bethany Home children, but also the Sisters. A newcomer in 1950 heard of Sister Anna Grace's lamb named Agnes, who had followed her around the Convent, and another Sister's turtle, which got lost when she took it on vacation. Sister Beatrice, in retirement at Bat Cave, North Carolina, had two dogs. "A Follower's Story" has many tales of dogs. One was Lassie, whom the children volunteered for the World War I K-9 effort. Lassie was accepted and went off to war. Fortunately she returned unharmed and was joyfully welcomed by the children. There have been many much loved pets.

Creativity

The Community has never had an educational requirement for entrance. Sisters have frequently been assisted to acquire further education which will make better use of their gifts for ministry. Several have received higher degrees. They have been encouraged to use their literary and artistic skills.

Sister Beatrice's book, *A Follower's Story* has been cited frequently in these pages. Mother Eva is remembered for her spiritual writings for the Community, her meditations, including "Little Foxes" and her many tales for children. Except for "Community Life for Women" they were not published, but they were duplicated, principally for the benefit of the branch house Sisters, and copies exist in the archives of the Mother House.

Some Sisters have written books. A collection of poems by Sister Mary Catherine, *Votive Candle and Other Poems*, was printed by the Community in 1934. Sister Julia Margaret wrote a history of the Church for the benefit of her Religious Education classes in Puerto Rico. It was in English and Spanish, in manuscript. We have a copy of each. It is not known how many copies existed. Sister Hilary Mary wrote *Caught by Glory: Some contemplative dimensions of the mystery of the Transfiguration* (1974). Sister Monica Mary's Master's thesis at the University of Hawaii, Manoa, "The History of St. Andrew's Priory, 1867–1918," was photocopied by the Associates there in 1978. The number of copies is unknown. Sister Esther wrote a history of St. Michael's House in Ponce, Puerto Rico, *Spark of Love*, printed in 1988. Sister Margaret Alice's dissertation, "A Study of Member Satisfaction. Cohesiveness, Service, and Spiritual Growth as They Impact Group Satisfaction, Maintenance in Small Groups in Episcopal Churches," was completed for a PhD from the University of Pittsburgh in 1993. *Chapel of the Transfiguration*, inspired and edited by Sister Mary Veronica, was published in 2005. These were all privately published. Sister Priscilla's pamphlet, *In the Fellowship of His Suffering* was published by the Forward Movement. In 2008 there are still copies of some of these available at the Convent.

The "Transfiguration Quarterly" has frequently had articles by Sisters. Sister Diana, who delights in making Anglican rosaries, has written an explanatory pamphlet about them. As editor of the "Transfiguration Quarterly" she has written many articles.

In the Community archives there are paintings by Sister Paula Irene which accompanied Bible talks she gave. While in Ponce, Puerto Rico, Sister Julia Margaret painted many watercolors of scenes there and at home. In various old Service and Office books there are examples of beautiful illuminated text done by various Sisters, in particular an Altar Book illuminated by Sister Margaret Dolores. Felt wall banners for the seasons of Christmas, Easter, Pentecost and Transfiguration were made by Sister Teresa Marie, and are hung on the walls of the Oratory during those seasons.

Community Room at Christmas time.

We have always needed to employ helpers from beyond the Community. Throughout the years the Sisters have been blessed by a succession of such helpers in maintenance, the kitchen and housekeeping staff, the business office and the infirmary, and some of our long-term employees have become almost like members of the family.

Mother Eva wanted us to be like a family. That can mean patience with each other even when we disagree. It also means taking care of each other in poor health, and even more with the elderly. Mother Eva herself was the recipient of much care. We have always had good medical and nursing care for the Sisters who need it. Since the Sisters come from various backgrounds and with varying talents, we learn to appreciate one another's gifts. We remember that we all share in both the work of Martha and the prayer of Mary.

1998 THE CENTENNIAL

Planning for the celebration took place over the whole year. Every Sister in the Community helped, including those in branch houses. The Sisters compiled a time-line of the Community history. Collages were prepared and framed illustrating the work the Sisters had done over the years in each branch ministry, including some short-term ones. These are still on the wall of the corridor on the ground floor near the Guest Dining Room. As we had done on our 75th Anniversary, we began the celebration the Last Sunday after Epiphany, which this year was February 22. The celebration began during Sister Alice's term of office, in 1998. The first event was Evensong on the Eve of Mother Foundress' Day. Our friend Marilyn Keiser played the organ and the Rev. Edward Payne, Priest-in-Charge of St. Simon of Cyrene's Church, Lincoln Heights, sang a solo. This was also the anniversary of the founding of St. Simon's Church by the Sisters in 1931.

The principal event was the Pontifical Eucharist on Sunday, February 22. It was a grand and glorious occasion. Unfortunately, our good friend and former Chaplain General, the Rt. Rev. John Allin, who had accepted our invitation to preach at that service became seriously ill and could not be with us. (He died less than two weeks later.) Another friend, the Rt. Rev. Frank Griswold, formerly Bishop of Chicago, who was at the time the newly installed Presiding Bishop, had accepted our invitation to attend, and now he graciously agreed to preach in Bishop Allin's stead. Our Visitor, the Rt. Rev. Christopher Epting, Bishop of Iowa was the Celebrant. The Rt. Rev. William G. Weinhauer, our Chaplain General and retired Bishop of Western North Carolina, was there. So also were the Rt. Rev. Herbert Thompson, Bishop of Southern Ohio and the Rt. Rev. Kenneth Price, his suffragan. Dr. John Deaver, our regular organist and choir director, played the organ. The organ music was enhanced by a brass quartet from Trinity Church in Covington, Kentucky, where Dr. John Deaver also plays. In the opening procession there were sixteen banners representing places where the Sisters had worked, each carried by a person in some way associated with that place.

The preceding evening we had an Ecumenical Evensong. Bishop Weinhauer was the preacher. Clergy from other denominations also participated. Dr. Deaver was again at the organ, and Cynthia Priem played the violin. She is a member of the Order of Emmaus Pilgrims, a Religious Order of the United Church of Christ. In the afternoon there was an Open House, and at 4:00 there was a carillon recital by Mr. Albert Meyers, who had been playing our carillon almost every Monday night for over thirty years. One of his selections was the Children's Suite, by Percival Price, who wrote it specifically for our Sister Ruth Magdalene and our carillon.

Our Sisters from California and the Dominican Republic all came home for the occasion. Representatives came from other Religious Communities. The Sisters of St. John the Baptist, the Community of St. Francis, the Community of St. Mary, the Society of St. Margaret, the Sisters of the Holy Nativity, The Order of St. Anne, the Community of the Holy Spirit, and the Order of St. Helena were all represented. A Brother came from the Order of St. Gregory. Friends came from far and near. Our former Chaplain General, the Rev. James Carroll, came from San Diego, California.

Sandra Parker, who was in charge of our kitchen, and her helpers did a magnificent job of preparing meals and the special recep-

Guests from other Religious Communities in the Community Room.

tions held during the weekend. Associates and friends also helped both with the meals and with transportation for the many guests.

Bethany School also celebrated its 100 years of life with an all-school Eucharist which was attended also by most of the Sisters, including Sister Ursula in a wheel chair carrying a banner.

In 1998, at the end of Sister Alice's first term of office, Sister Ann Margaret was re-elected and Sister Alice joyfully went back to the ministry in California.

✠

A NEW CENTURY: SR ANN MARGARET (2nd Term 1998–2008)

The Community was aging but still active. Sister Althea Augustine and Sister Joan Michael celebrated 50 years of life profession in 2005, Sister Monica Mary in 2007.

On the Eve of the Feast of the Transfiguration, 2004, after several years of discernment, the first four Oblates were received.

Canon Law of the Episcopal Church now requires every Religious Community to be visited by its Bishop Visitor, with consultants, to evaluate its condition both physically and spiritually. In 2001 we had a Visitation from our Visitor, the Rt. Rev. Christopher Epting, accompanied by the Rt. Rev. William G. Weinhauer, our Chaplain General and former Visitor, and the Rev. Richard Halladay from the Diocese of Indianapolis.

In 2006 we had another visitation from Bishop Epting, this time accompanied by Sister Constance Johanna, SSJD, former Superior of the Sisters of St. John the Divine, and the Rev. Johannes Van den Blink, our Chaplain General. A follow-up took place in May, 2007.

In November, 2007, in the week before Thanksgiving, we had a special week of renewal led by Mother Winsome, Superior of the Community of St. Mary the Virgin, Wantage, England. That week was preceded by much prayer and preparation by our Sisters and by Sisters in Wantage.

Preparing for the Future

Remembering that Sister Ann would not be eligible for re-election at the conclusion of her term in 2008, many Community meetings were held and much planning was done to follow the recommendations of the visitors and to make it easier for the future Superior. In particular there was much thought and prayer given to the future of St. Mary's Home. Government regulations made it much more expensive to maintain, and the number of residents was shrinking. After much prayer for discernment, in 2008 the Sisters decided to close St. Mary's as a nursing home. The next question was the future use of the property. This again required much prayer and discernment. At the close of the annual long retreat in June, 2008, Sister Teresa Marie was elected our new Superior.

Community in front of the Convent taken in 2008.

EPILOGUE 2008-2013

Holy God, we have no idea where we are going.
We do not see the road ahead of us.
We cannot know for certain where it will end.....
We believe that the desire to please you does in fact please you. And we hope we have that desire in all that we are doing. We hope that we will never do anything apart from that desire.
And we know that if we do this you will lead us by the right road, though we may know nothing about it. We will not fear, for you are ever with us, and you will never leave us....
(Thomas Merton: Thoughts in Solitude, p. 83, adapted)

This prayer seems to express very clearly where we are as members of Religious communities in the early 21st Century. As I begin to write this I am sitting in our house in the Dominican Republic typing on a iPhone and connected to the rest of the world by Internet. There is no way I could have imagined this nearly 50 years ago when I entered the Community of the Transfiguration, nor could I have imagined the changes that are taking place in in the culture, the Church and Religious Communities. We are living in a challenging time and we truly do not know where the road will lead but know that we are we are called to follow it with faith and courage wherever God leads us. As members of this amazing Community we need to always to be true to our own traditions and the vision of our Foundresses as well as true to the millennia-long ideals of the Religious Life, while at the same time being open to the currents of life in the world surrounding us and to adapt to them in order to remain open and responsive to them in order to best fulfill our vision and mission. As Mother Eva wrote, 'The Religious Life should not cut itself off from every living, loving sympathy with the world and with the age in which it lives" (The Rule, p 29). It is a delicate balance to maintain and we always need to be clear when taking any new direction or making changes in our daily life that we are true to the vision which has guided this Community since its very beginning.

Almost every dimension of the Religious life has shifted and needs to be rethought in terms of the current reality. Communities of all types are finding that the current generation of young people are drawn to some expression of community life and service and are enthusiastically experimenting with sharing life and ministry together. This is what is currently being referred to as the New Monastic Movement. This movement cuts across denominational and even faith lines, attracting men and women, single or married who wish to respond to God's call to ministry. But few of them are drawn to the traditional Religious Communities such as ours, and many of them of them have no interest in making lifetime commitments. Communities such as these that have developed some stability may be recognized in the Episcopal Church as Christian Communities by the House of Bishops. They have a Sister organization to the Conference on the Religious Life in the Americas (CAROA, which represents traditional communities) referred to as the National Association of Christian Communities (NAACC). These two groups are meeting together for the first time in 2013 as they recognize how much they can share together and support each other.

Because of new opportunities for women in ministry such as the diaconate and priesthood and because of the opportunities for different types of community life vocations to the traditional Religious Communities, especially women's communities, vocations have become much fewer, but a small stream of people continue to seek out the Traditional Communities. Some communities that are unable to adapt are dying either by choice of not accepting new members or by attrition, but those that are stable and vital as attracting new members. By the grace of God we seem to be able to do so.

When Sister Monica began this book she planned to close with the end of Sister Ann's term of office in 2008. But with the process of collecting information and photos, editing, etc., it is only now being published in 2013. A great deal happens in a community in five years. Some significant changes have occurred during this period that should be included in this history.

✠

THE TRANSFIGURATION SPIRITUALITY CENTER

I was elected as Superior of the Community in June, 2008 just at the point when the Sisters were nearing the conclusion of several years of discernment on whether or not to continue the ministry of St. Mary's Memorial Home which over the years had evolved from a residential home to a full care nursing home. We were providing excellent care and a loving environment for a very small number of people. But it had become increasingly evident that it was, for many reasons, impossible to continue its operation without sacrificing other ministries. So in the spring of 2009 with the help of a consultant, Mr. Pat Ryan of Skystone-Ryan Inc., we were able to make the very painful and difficult decision to cease the operation of St. Mary's Home with a nearly unanimous vote. God always seems to send the right people at the right time. Pat, an active Episcopalian as well as an extremely able business consultant guided us smoothly through the process of closing the home, relocating the residents and making as smooth a transition as possible for our employees. We then had a beautiful but aging building on our hands and we needed to find a new use for it in ministry. The Sisters had some brainstorming sessions in which it soon became clear that we would like to use it for some sort of hospitality center where we could host individuals and groups for retreats, workshops and spirituality events. We dreamed of having art, music and inter-faith events. We thought of needs to minister to youth, and to the underprivileged. We hoped to have it be an ecumenical center, a place where all types of church and diocesan groups could come for meetings in a quiet and beautiful place. During the summer of 2009 Pat Ryan led us through a feasibility study to see if there was a need for such a facility in our area. The result was a resounding yes! There was a need for such a facility in the Greater Cincinnati area. In September the Community voted to begin the new ministry of the Transfiguration Spirituality Center. Planning for the renovation of the building began immediately. Martha Schickel Dorf a talented interior designer who specialized in designing sacred spaces was hired to envision use of the building's spaces and provide a unified interior design and original artwork. One Sister's vision of rooms with private baths in a limited amount of space became a reality. The actual renovation work began in the spring of 2010 and was blessed and dedicated on 10/10/10 (October 10, 2010). The Center now includes the renovated St. Mary's building with 21 rooms as the centerpiece, with Bethanna Cottage adding another 19 rooms and additional guest buildings on the campus making for very flexible accommodations for various groups and uses. Its full capacity will be tested this spring with theologian Marcus Borg's weekend presentations. Pat Ryan who has been an invaluable partner and friend, is now an

Associate of the Community and a member of the Transfiguration Spirituality Center Board.

From its beginning the Spirituality Center under the very capable leadership of its director, our Oblate, Toni Thomas-Feren, has shown that it is meeting needs in this area and is a vibrant extension of the hospitality ministry of the Community. I am convinced that the quiet and prayerful atmosphere of the St. Mary's Building is a result of the prayers of its residents over decades and the presence of a Religious Community surrounding and supporting it. This endeavor was a major undertaking for the Community and has resulted in bringing a wide cross-section of people onto our campus.

One extremely important contribution of the Transfiguration Spirituality Center is the provision of retreats for homeless women in recovery under the direction of the Ignation Spirituality Project. For many of these women it is the first time they've ever had a room of their own. It is often a turning point in their lives. Two or three of these retreats take place each year.

Another outstanding program that the Center hosts is the Capacitar Program (capacitar.org). Under the direction of Dr. Patricia Cane we have become the Midwest center for this creative initiative which trains people to minister to individuals who have lived through traumatic situations of war and violence and to empower them to develop in their own recovery and to assist others.

THE TABOR MINISTRY

Under the direction of the visionary Sister Mary Luke, the ministry at St. Monica's Recreation Center grew and flourished. One of her dreams was realized in the early 1980's when she and Sister Mary Evelyne located some property in northern

Ohio which could be used as a country property to give the youngsters of Lincoln Heights a chance to experience some time away from their urban environment and have some different experiences in a rural setting. The new property they acquired near Butler, Ohio in Richmond County. It is in Amish country but away from the more busy and tourist-centered communities a few miles away in Holmes County. She soon acquired more property and built modular buildings which could house small groups of children. They began to rotate groups for a week's stay in the country each summer. That ministry continues in the summer months, but it seemed unfortunate that this lovely property with its excellent buildings was only in use for three months of the year. In June, 2011 the Chapter of the Community unanimously voted to begin a new branch ministry at the Tabor property with Sister Nadine Elizabeth and Sister Rachael Margaret living there. In August 2001 the two Sisters moved there and began to develop a new ministry there. They can accommodate a few guests overnight and larger day groups for meetings. They are active in the Ashland, Ohio parish leading a weekly Evening Prayer service and participating many ways in parish life. They are beginning to explore campus ministry in several nearby college campuses. The longtime relationship with Amish families that Sister Mary Luke developed is being renewed by working with Amish in many ways. They provide transportation for them as well as being present in some crisis situations. Both Sisters are gifted artists and their pottery studio is a source of beautiful ceramic carved wood pieces which are sold at local fairs making another opportunity to connect with local people. An extensive garden keeps them busy during the growing season providing fresh produce for themselves, the children from Lincoln Heights as well as neighbors in need. Most important they are there to welcome and to interact with the children when they arrive for their weeks in the summer. Their ministry will continue to take shape and expand as the Sisters explore and respond to emerging needs.

BETHANY SCHOOL

Our excellent K-8 Day School continues to flourish and expand. In 2012, four new classrooms were added to the present gymnasium providing much needed space for primary classes. Now in the spring of 2013 a new multi-purpose building, the Bethany Activity Center is nearing completion that will accommodate a variety of school activities and athletic tournaments as well as large groups for the Spirituality Center. The school staff and parents will soon begin an evaluation in cooperation with the National Association of Episcopal Schools to develop a long-term strategic plan for its future.

ORDINATION TO THE PRIESTHOOD

In June, 2011, the Community Chapter gave permission to Sister Diana Dorothea Doncaster to enter the discernment to seek ordination as a priest in the Diocese of Northern California. She was accepted by the Bishop and the Commission on Ministry as a Postulant for Holy Orders in October and is continuing her studies through the Episcopal Seminary in Berkeley, CA with online course and periodic residence at the Church Divinity School of the Pacific. This is a major milestone for the Community and Sister Diana will join Sister Priscilla, a deacon, as the two ordained members of our Community. Sister Diana continues to live and work in our ministry in Eureka, California.

BAT CAVE, NORTH CAROLINA

As is related earlier in this book Mother Eva and Sister Beatrice acquired property in the beautiful mountains of Western North Carolina as a rest house for the Sisters and a center of ministry to the local people of the area. Sister Beatrice spent the last years of her life there and had a very active ministry. More property was gradually acquired over the years. In the 1990s the house itself was rebuilt and Sisters continue to use it periodically, but there is much more land there than we actually use. In order to protect the land from development we are currently in negotiation with the Carolina Mountain Land Conservancy to donate some of our land to create an Educational and Research Preserve in partnership with some local institutions. This will protect the land and the rich variety of species that inhabit it, including some which are endangered. Some groups are already beginning to do research there.

IN CONCLUSION

As we look over the past five years a lot has been accomplished and we move into the future with hope and faith that we may remain both open to the future and faithful to our past in the light of the mystery of the Transfiguration. In the words of our Vision Statement: *Guided by the Holy Spirit we seek to respond courageously to God's voice in order to minister to others in a changing world.*

I want to express gratitude to Sister Monica Mary for her research skills, knowledge of Community history and diligence in preparing this book. It has truly been a labor of love for her. Also great thanks to Dr. Martha Decker, Ed. D. and Oblate of the Community for her faithful shepherding Sister Monica through to the publication of this book. Special thanks too, to Sister Eleanor Grace for her collection and preparation of photos and other editorial tasks. Thanks also to Sister Carina Elsa, Melinda Boyd, and many Sisters who have aided in the editorial process.

—Sister Teresa M. Martin, CT, Superior, April, 20, 2013

APPENDIX I

CHRONOLOGY OF COMMUNITY HISTORY

1862, FEBRUARY 9	Birth of Eva Lee Matthews
1877	Matthews family moves to Washington, D.C.
1885	Death of Mary Ann Matthews, Eva's mother
1890–1891	Eva joins Paul in Oxford, England
1891–1895	Omaha Mission and meeting Beatrice Henderson
1895	House of Women began
1895–1896	Pilgrimage to the Holy Land
1897	Bethany Mission House, Freeman Street, Postulancy
1898	Purchase of property in Glendale for Convent and Bethany Home
1898, AUGUST 6	First Vows by Eva Matthews and Beatrice Henderson
1900	Purchase of Bat Cave house
1903, AUGUST 6	Life Profession of Mother Eva
1905, MARCH 8	Life Profession of Sister Beatrice
1906–1926	Bethany Home for Boys
1907	Mother Eva and Sister Beatrice visit England
1909	Oratory in the Convent enlarged
1911–1929	St. John's Orphanage, Cleveland, Ohio

1913–1926	Holy Cross House for Crippled Children, Cleveland
1929–1978	St. John's Home, Painesville, Ohio
1913	Mother Eva's severe illness in Cleveland
1913–1948	Sisters work in Wuhu China
1914	• Outbreak of World War I •
1918–1971	Sisters work at St. Andrew's Priory, Honolulu, Hawaii
1918	• Armistice Day •
1925	Blessed Sacrament Reserved on the Alter
1927	Cottages built at Bethany Home
1928, JULY 6	Death of Mother Eva
1928, SEPTEMBER 29	Mother Beatrice elected Superior
1928	• New edition of the Book of Common Prayer •
1929, JUNE 11	Dedication of the Chapel
1929	Beginning of the Great Depression
1931	Beginning of the work in Lincoln Heights, Ohio
1938	Mother Clara Elizabeth elected Superior
1940	• New edition of the Hymnal •
1941	• Pearl Harbor was attacked •
1941–1946	• World War II •
1943–1971	Work at St. Dorothy's Rest in C.A.
1943	Mother Clara resigned because of poor health
1943, FEBRUARY 9	Mother Olivia Mary elected Superior
1945–1984	Sisters work in Ponce, Puerto Rico

1948	Golden Jubilee; Sisters in China forced to return home
1953–1963	Mother Louise Magdalene elected Superior
1935–1971	Sisters work in Sendai, Japan
1957	St. Mary's Memorial Home was built
1957–1970	New Convent was built; deadicated in 1970
1959	Bethany Home became Bethany School
1963	Mother Esther Mary elected Superior
1967–1983	Sisters work in Dallas and McKinney, Texas
1970–1971	Renewal time
1971	St. Simon's School closed; St. Monica's Recreation Center, Lincoln Heights, Ohio
1973	75th Anniversary
1973–1983	Mother Louise elected Superior and served two more terms
1979–1992	Sisters work in Diocese of Western North Carolina; St. Luke's House, Lincolnton, North Carolina
1979	• New Edition of the Book of Common Prayer •
1980	California ministry resumed
1980–1982	Ranfurly Home for Children, Nassau, Bahamas
1982	• New Edition of the Hymnal •
1983–1993	Sister Ann Margaret elected Superior and served two terms

1983	Sisters begin work in the Dominican Republic
1992–1997	Work on Rosebud Reservation, South Dakota Summer Mission
1993	Sister Alice elected Superior
1995–1996	Sisters work in St. James, Oneonta, New York
1998–2008	Sister Ann Margaret elected Superior and served two more terms
1998	Centennial
2001	Visitation by our Bishop Visitor
2006–2007	Visitation by our Bishop Visitor
2008, JUNE 24	Sister Teresa Marie elected Superior

* Denotes events outside of the Convent.

LIST OF LIFE PROFESSED SISTERS BETWEEN 1911 AND 2008

Sister Deborah Ruth Powell
She worked at a Boy's Home before coming to CT. She served in China and Hawaii. At the Convent, she is remembered for making a list of Mass intentions from daily newspapers and the Church Times.

BORN 1886-02-02
PROFESSED 1914-06-11
DIED 1960-6-19

Sister Eleanor Mary Meyers
She was a Bethany Home girl and sister of Sister Anna Grace. She served in Wuhu, China and Church Home, Cleveland. She was released and continued to serve at Church Home when the Community left.

BORN 1889-03-31
PROFESSED 1914-08-11
RELEASED 1939-09-12

Sister Caroline Mary Cochrane

BORN 1860-01-12
PROFESSED 1914-09-16
DIED 1956-10-30

Sister Helen Veronica Farrell
She served as Head of House in China, Hawaii, and Santa Rose, California. She was also a Novice Director and Assistant Superior.
She served in Cleveland, Ohio.

BORN 1889-02-10
PROFESSED 1914-09-16
DIED 1976-03-04

Sister Olive Rachel Bechtel
She served in Cleveland, Ohio.

BORN 1871-10-18
PROFESSED 1915-07-21
DIED 1963-10-16

Sister Gertrude Christine
She died while still a Novice.

BORN 1878-05-26
CLOTHED AS A NOVICE
1914-01-25
DIED 1917-02-16

Sister Constance Anna Hayes
She came to CT after nursing Mother Eva through an illness. She is remembered for her work in Wuhu, China.

BORN 1884-10-19
PROFESSED 1918-04-25
DIED 1972-04-25

Sister Amy Martha Arch
She served in Hawaii.

BORN 1876-10-19
PROFESSED 1918-04-25
DIED 1960-08-24

Sister Olivia Mary Matthews
(niece of Mother Eva)
She worked in Hawaii and Lincoln Heights. She was a Novice Director.

BORN 1888-01-22
PROFESSED 1918-04-25
DIED 1969-02-07

Sister Anna Grace
(sister of Sister Eleanor Mary)
She was a physician. She served in Cleveland, and she was a sacristan in the Cathedral.

BORN 1871-02-06
PROFESSED 1920-10-26
DIED 1966-04-02

Sister Lillian Martha Steineman
As a girl, she helped in Mission House. She later served in the Business Office and as a housekeeper. She worked in Bethany Home and in the Convent kitchens.

BORN 1893-11-19
PROFESSED 1920-10-26
DIED 1974-05-19

Sister Madeleine Mary Stansburg

BORN 1871-02-06
PROFESSED 1920-10-26
DIED 1954-12-30

Sister Mabel Lioba Snow

BORN 1891-09-02
PROFESSED 1921-09-29
RELEASED 1932-10-15

Sister Veronica Sacha Meyers

BORN 1895-09-24
PROFESSED 1921-09-29
RELEASED 1931-7-18

Sister Paula Harriet Bray
She served in Hawaii. She was a Convent librarian, and she worked at Bethany School.

BORN 1870-03-01
PROFESSED 1922-06-29
DIED 1946-11-14

Sister Hilda Cynthia Baskin
She served at Bethany Home. Her knowledge of produce and her experience from growing up on a farm was an asset to the cannery and the pantry. She made marmalade every year.

BORN 1877-08-28
PROFESSED 1923-10-18
DIED 1970-03-25

Sister Ruth Magdalene Kent
She was received as a Postulant in China. She later became the Novice Director for the Chinese Sisters. In the United States, she was an editor of the Quarterly and a musician. She played the organ and the carillon.

BORN 1883-11-24
PROFESSED 1923-10-18
DIED 1973-12-28

Sister Martha Mary Armstrong
She was a Bethany Home girl. She served in California and Hawaii.

BORN 1898-12-23
PROFESSED 1923-10-18
DIED 1963-11-26

Sister Mary Catherine Matthews (niece of Mother Eva and sister of Sister Olivia)
She had been a missionary in Japan prior to coming to CT. She taught at Bethany Home.

BORN 1890-05-16
PROFESSED 1924-06-27
DIED 1939-08-31

Sister Lydia Margaret Jensen
She taught at St. Andrew's Priory before coming to CT. She taught sewing at Bethany Home, and she made habits for the Sisters.

BORN 1895-12-11
PROFESSED 1926-08-06
DIED 1966-02-18

Sister Katherine Helen Barry
She worked in Santa Rosa, and she served as Guest Mistress.

BORN 1879-08-02
PROFESSED 1927-09-29
DIED 1974-03-05

Sister Joanna Mary Waterman
She served as Head of Bethany Home from 1953 through 1958.

BORN 1890-11-30
PROFESSED 1928-01-27
DIED 1967-08-06

Sister Emily Faith
She was a deaconess, and she worked with the Sisters in China.

BORN 1890-11-30
PROFESSED 1928-01-27
DIED 1936-04-04

Sister Josephine Martha Hanes

BORN 1904-07-21
PROFESSED 1928-09-28
DIED 1936-05-21

Hope Lorraine

BORN 1892
DIED 1929
(DIED WHILE A POSTULANT)

Sister Marion Beatrice Jones
She was a Cottage Mother, and she served as bookkeeper for the Convent. She also served in Hawaii.

BORN 1891-08-01
PROFESSED 1931-06-18
DIED 1973-06-03

Sister Rose Marie Thorn
She served at Church Home in Cleveland, Santa Rosa, and St. Dorothy's Rest. She was a Novice Guardian.

BORN 1894-01-12
PROFESSED 1931-06-18
DIED 1953-04-05

Sister Dorothy Mary Lanvermier
She taught first and second grade at Bethany Home.

BORN 1900-07-21
PROFESSED 1931-10-04
DIED 1989-01-08

Sister Mary Joseph
She was Professed as a Sister of the Tabernacle before coming to CT.

BORN 1854-06-13
PROFESSED 1918-05-30
RECEIVED 1931-11-01
DIED 1934-12-12

Sister Frances Mabels

BORN 1878-12-14
PROFESSED 1933-04-20
DIED 1934-03-18

Sister Agnes Margaret Newshem

BORN 1905-09-15
PROFESSED 1933-08-06
RELEASED 1940-06-26

Sister Theodora Eleanor
She grew up at Holy Cross House in Cleveland. She taught at Bethany and served as principal at Bethany and St. Simon's.

BORN 1905-11-20
PROFESSED 1933-08-06
DIED 1997-05-07

Sister Louise Magdalene Hoehn
She was Mother Superior from 1953-1963 and from 1973-1983.

BORN 1904-11-12
PROFESSED 1934-06-04
DIED 1996-12-01

Sister Marie Helen Bender
She was a nurse. She served as Convent Infirmarian, and she worked in the Guest Dining Room.

BORN 1892-12-07
PROFESSED 1935-02-28
DIED 1972-08-24

Sister Elizabeth Angela Cleveland

BORN 1883-09-23
PROFESSED 1935-06-06
DIED 1967-11-24

Sister Esther Mary
She was Mother Superior from 1963-1973.

BORN 1905-02-03
PROFESSED 1935-06-06
DIED 2000-11-23

Sister Barbara Margaret

BORN 1905-12-22
PROFESSED 1935-06-06
RELEASED 1939-08-06

Sister Mary Agnes
She was a Novice of the Sisters of the Tabernacle. When the Community disbanded, she went home and later came to CT.

BORN 1871-04-25
PROFESSED 1935-08-06
DIED 1960-12-08

Sister Rhoda Pearl Pignel
She served at St. Andrew's Priory.

BORN 1892-10-09
PROFESSED 1936-04-16
DIED 1939-10-10

Sister Grace Elizabeth Ludt
She served as Head of Bethany Home. She taught at St. Matthew's School in Eureka, California. She also worked for a short time in China and Japan.

BORN 1895-02-03
PROFESSED 1937-10-18
DIED 1983-07-13

Sister Helena Miriam Lambert
She served as a housekeeper.

BORN 1895-12-13
PROFESSED 1937-10-18
DIED 1970-09-24

Sister Evelyn Ancilla Hetherington
She was a teacher and Sister-in-charge at St. Andrew's Priory. She helped found St. Simon's Mission. In her retirement she carried on her prison ministry by mail, and she edited the Quarterly.

BORN 1909-05-08
PROFESSED 1937-10-18
DIED 2004-07-20

Sister Christina Margaret Ludt (sister of Sister Grace Elizabeth)
She served as a Convent librarian.

BORN 1905-08-29
PROFESSED 1938-11-23
DIED 1975-09-01

Sister Julia Margaret Hayes
She had some training as a deaconess. She painted watercolors of Puerto Rico and the Convent grounds. She wrote a history of the Church in both English and Spanish.

BORN 1899-09-19
PROFESSED 1938-11-23
DIED 1975-06-08

Sister Mary Elizabeth Ammon
She worked at Bethany Home and in Puerto Rico.

BORN 1903-12-10
PROFESSED 1940-09-28
DIED 1952-06-04

Sister Winifred Agnes Willcox
She served in Hawaii and St. John's, Painesville, Ohio. She was also a bookkeeper for the Convent.

BORN 1909-01-07
PROFESSED 1940-09-28
DIED 1973-02-17

Sister Margorie Hope Harkness
She served in California and in Puerto Rico.

BORN 1913-12-21
PROFESSED 1940-09-28
DIED 2009-09-01

Sister Lucy Caritas Burgin
She was a nurse. She served in China where she met the Sisters. She became principal of St. Andrew's Priory. She also served in Painesville, Ohio and as Convent librarian.

BORN 1902-11-30
PROFESSED 1942-01-25
DIED 1999-08-09

Sister Myrtle Catherine Dean
She was the first African-American Sister. She served at Bethany Home.

BORN 1897-08-11
PROFESSED 1942-01-18
RELEASED 1965

Sister Oriole Mary Oatman
She served in Hawaii and Puerto Rico. She worked in the Convent kitchen.

BORN 1906-07-14
PROFESSED 1943-11-30
DIED 1955-05-15

Sister Virginia Cecelia Wiley
She worked at St. Simon's School, and she served as Head of Bethany Home. She worked in the Convent business office, and she was an organist. She served in China.

BORN 1920-01-16
PROFESSED 1944-02-24
DIED 1978-07-30

Sister Faith Marguertite Isley
She served in Puerto Rico.

BORN 1890-04-19
PROFESSED 1945-09-29
DIED 1976-07-04

Sister Angela Hannah Eliot
She was a widow and a grandmother. She played the organ. She taught at Bethany Home and worked at St. John's in Painesville, Ohio.

BORN 1888-02-27
PROFESSED 1946-09-20
DIED 1972-02-06

Sister Ada Julian Walpole
She was a tailor, and she made the Sisters habits. She also served as sacristan.

BORN 1889-02-10
PROFESSED 1949-03-25
DIED 1967-11-30

Sister Stephanie Helen McNichol
She graduated from St. Andrew's Priory. She was a Cottage Mother at Bethany Home and at St. John's, Painesville. She served as a housekeeper and worked in the Convent laundry.

BORN 1912-10-10
PROFESSED 1949-03-25
DIED 2010-09-13

Sister Ursula Elizabeth Rogers
She had been a missionary in Japan before coming to CT. She served in Japan, Hawaii, Puerto Rico, and Painesville, Ohio.

BORN 1911-01-23
PROFESSED 1949-10-18
DIED 2003-04-22

Sister Mary Raphael McCoy
She was a nurse. She served at Bethany Home and in Puerto Rico.

BORN 1924-03-05
PROFESSED 1950-01-01
RELEASED 1960-08-24

Sister Lioba Katherine Shipps
She had been a missionary in Japan before coming to CT. She was a medical Social Worker, and she served at St. Dorothy's Rest.

BORN 1890-09-08
PROFESSED 1950-02-02
DIED 1976-03-28

Sister Mariya Margaret Hester
She had been a missionary in Japan before coming to CT. She taught kindergarten at Bethany and St. Simon's, and she started the kindergarten in Sendai, Japan. She compiled a book of photographs of the Convent Chapel.

BORN 1900-06-29
PROFESSED 1950-02-02
DIED 1994-06-06

Sister Jeanette Clare Abbey
She served at Bethany, St. Simon's and Texas. She worked in the Convent kitchen, and she had a rich prayer ministry.

BORN 1905-11-06
PROFESSED 1951-02-02
DIED 2011-04-02

Sister Leinaala Josephine Folk
She came to CT from Hawaii. She worked at Bethany Home and St. John's, Painesville, Ohio. She was an organist.

BORN 1924-07-28
PROFESSED 1951-02-02
DIED 1989-09-01

Sister Teresa Ruth Clark
She entered the Community in Puerto Rico. She came to the United States for very short visits.

BORN 1901-11-01
PROFESSED 1951-10-04
DIED 1957-12-14

Sister Jean Benedict Lynch
She taught kindergarten at St. Simon's. She also worked at St. John's in Painesville, Ohio.

BORN 120-10-19
PROFESSED 1951-10-04
RELEASED 1970-06-29

Sister Georgiana Faith Ellis
She was professed in the Community of St. Mary in 1938, and she was received into CT in 1954.

BORN 1912-04-06
PROFESSED 1938-10-15
RECEIVED 1984-10-04
DIED 2007-11-22

Sister Eva Dorothea Ely
She worked at Bethany, St. John's in Painesville, Ohio, and at St. Andrew's Priory. She was librarian and Novice Director.

BORN 1913-12-02
PROFESSED 1951-11-20
DIED 2006-12-06

Sister Lois Mary Sook
She served at St. John's, Painesville, Ohio. She served as Convent librarian and Novice Director.

BORN 1923-11-15
PROFESSED 1954-09-28
RELEASED 1974

Sister Althea Augustine King
She served at Bethany Home, St. Simon's School, and Puerto Rico. She was Sister-in-charge of St. John's Home in Painesville, Ohio. She served as Novice Director.

BORN 1924-07-08
PROFESSED 1955-01-25

Sister Joan Michael
She taught at Bethany Home and Bethany School. She served at St. Simon's, Japan, and Texas.

BORN 1931-01-12
PROFESSED 1955-10-18

Sister Emily Francis
She came to CT from a Roman Catholic Benedictine Community. She returned to them when she left CT.

BORN 1893-11-16
PROFESSED 1956-06-12
RECEIVED 1957-07-14
RELEASED 1960-12-02

Sister Monica Mary Heyes
Sr. Monica served at Bethany Home, St. Simon's, Lincolnton, St. Andrew's Priory, and Japan. She was a Novice Director. She serves as Convent librarian and historian.

BORN 1925-07-22
PROFESSED 1957-10-18

Sister Francis Helen
She was a missionary in Alaska before coming to CT. She served in Bethany School and St. Simon's.

BORN 1903-05-16
PROFESSED 1958-02-02
DIED 1969-02-18

Sister Victoria Elizabeth Hughes
She served at Bethany School and St. Andrew's Priory.

BORN 1932-02-16
PROFESSED 1958-11-01
RELEASED 1970

Sister Paula Irene Brown
She was a missionary to the Navajo before coming to CT. She taught at Bethany Home and St. Simon's, and she served in Santa Rosa, California. She gave retreats using watercolor illustrations that she painted.

BORN 1908-01-04
PROFESSED 1958-11-01
DIED 1995-02-14

Sister Laura Mary Wood
She taught at Bethany and St. Simon's. She also served at St. Andrew's Priory.

BORN 1921-04-09
PROFESSED 1959-03-10
RELEASED 1990-07-07

Sister Mary Evelyne Tookey
She came to know CT through St. Dorothy's Rest. She was a Cottage Mother at Bethany Home. She served in Puerto Rico at St. Simon's School in San Mateo. She has been Convent bursar.

BORN 1921-04-09
PROFESSED 1959-09-29

Sister Rebecca Louise
She was of Chinese ethnicity.

BORN 1919-02-08
PROFESSED 1959-09-29
RELEASED 1963

Sister Alice Lorraine Reid
(Niece of Sister Mary Evelyne)
She was a Cottage Mother at Bethany Home, and she was in charge of the kitchen. She revived the work in California. She was Mother Superior from 1993 to 1998.

BORN 1927-03-05
PROFESSED 1960-03-25

Sister Gabriel Katherine Cooper
She served in the Bethany School boarding department and at St. John's Painesville, Ohio.

BORN 1940-09-22
PROFESSED 1969-09-14
RELEASED 1972-06-19

Sister Marcelle Louise Meisel

BORN 1944-03-25
PROFESSED 1969-09-14
RELEASED 1986-09-30

Sister Priscilla Jean Wright
She was a missionary with the Navajo before coming to CT. She is a deacon. She has served in Bethany School, Texas, Puerto Rico, and the Dominican Republic.

BORN 1934-08-08
PROFESSED 1971-01-25

Sister Mary Luke Evans
She served in St. Monica's Center, and she did social work in Lincoln Heights.

BORN 1938-06-14
PROFESSED 1973-04-25
DIED 2009-09-13

Sister Mary Elizabeth Roll
She served in Texas and Lincolnton. She teaches at Bethany School, and she is in charge of the kitchen. She is currently Novice Director.

BORN 1946-11-02
PROFESSED 1976-12-26

Sister Ann Margaret Davis
She met the CT Sisters while working in Puerto Rico. She served as Mother Superior from 1983 to 1993 and from 1998 to 2008.

BORN 1935-05-03
PROFESSED 1977-06-26

Sister Jacqueline Marie Curtis
She served in Texas and Lincolnton. She is currently sacristan in the Chapel, and she is the Director of Associates.

BORN 1942-02-26
PROFESSED 1978-09-14

Sister Mary Grace Parkin
She served at Bethany School and in Lincolnton.

BORN 1934-02-03
PROFESSED 1978-10-30
RELEASED 1985-08

Sister Grace Marie Galluccio
She served in the Business office.

BORN 1939-10-06
PROFESSED 1978-10-30
RELEASED 2000-06

Sister Miriam Jeanne Campbell
She served in Puerto Rico.

BORN 1932-12-08
PROFESSED 1979-09-29
RELEASED 1984-05-02

Sister Sara Elizabeth Niles

BORN 1944-04-02
PROFESSED 1979-11-01
RELEASED 1983-06-17

Sister Johanna Laura Moseley
She has served in Texas and in the Dominican Republic.

BORN 1951-11-24
PROFESSED 1980-06-24

Sister Elizabeth Anne Coles
She was a gifted organist.

BORN 1921-11-06
PROFESSED 1984-02-25
DIED 2011-05-26

Sister Lydia Magdalene Mathews
She has served in Lincolnton and in California.

BORN 1935-12-17
PROFESSED 1987-11-30
DIED 2006-06-19

Sister Jean Gabriel Crothers
She serves in the Dominican Republic.

BORN 1943-11-02
PROFESSED 1987-11-30

Sister Juliana Justin Sweikert

BORN 1930-11-07
PROFESSED 1990-01-25
RELEASED 1996-09

Sister Rachel Margaret Phillips
She has served in St. Mary's and in the Convent laundry. She helped revise the Office Book.

BORN 1949-02-02
PROFESSED 1990-11-01

Sister Nadine Elizabeth Schilling
She has been administrator of St. Mary's Home. She is a gifted potter.

BORN 1954-08-17
PROFESSED 1992-04-25

Sister Elda Magdalene Smith
She was a missionary in China before coming to CT.

BORN 1908-09-28
PROFESSED 1960-09-28
DIED 1979-03-12

Sister Mary Veronica Hooten
She served in Puerto Rico, and she was an administrator of St. Mary's Memorial Home. She was a gifted gardener and flower arranger.

BORN 1925-12-05
PROFESSED 1961-03-20
DIED 2009-11-11

Sister Hilary Mary Moores
She served in Puerto Rico and the Dominican Republic. She was Secretary of the Community Chapter and Novice Director. She serves as Community archivist.

BORN 1930-01-15
PROFESSED 1962-09-21

Sister Marilyn Elizabeth Kennedy
She was Assistant Superior from 1978 to 1983.

BORN 1930-11-29
PROFESSED 1962-09-21
RELEASED 1983

Sister Clare Marie
She served in McKinney, Texas.

BORN 1938-09-03
PROFESSED 1965-01-01
RELEASED 1968-03

Sister Noemi Mercedes
She came to know the Community in Puerto Rico.

BORN 1915-12-02
PROFESSED 1965-11-01
RELEASED 1972

Sister Margaret Alice Allen
She was Assistant Superior.

BORN 1925-12-28
PROFESSED 1966-10-29
DIED 2010-03-30

Sister Teresa Marie Martin
She has served as principal of Bethany School. She has served in Eureka, California. She was elected Mother Superior in 2008.

BORN 1935-08-05
PROFESSED 1967-10-04

Sister Eleanor Grace Narkis
She has served in Linolnton. She was involved in the Kairos Prison Ministry. She is currently Convent librarian.

BORN 1930-01-08
PROFESSED 1992-07-22

Sister Marcia Francis McCauley
She is a nurse, and she serves as Assistant Superior.

BORN 1944-01-30
PROFESSED 1993-12-28

Sister Hope Mary Kunkle
She is currently sacristan in the Convent Oratory.

BORN 1953-06-04
PROFESSED 1996-09-21

Sister Diana Dorothea Doncaster
She serves in Eureka, California. She is editor of the Quarterly, and she is Director of the Oblates.

BORN 1956-05-20
PROFESSED 2003-06-11

Sister Lynn Julian Browning
She serves at Bethany School.

BORN 1948-04-24
PROFESSED 2006-09-29

Sister Marian Therese Miller

BORN 1944-01-31
PROFESSED 2012-10-03

The Chinese Sisters

Sister Feng Ai
PROFESSED 1926 05-13
DIED 1950-05-05

Sister Pei Ai
PROFESSED 1929-09-28
DIED 1960-11-25

Sister Shou Ai
PROFESSED 1935-12-13
DIED 1955-05-01

Sister Chen Ai
PROFESSED 1938-03-25
DIED 1959-07-29

Sister Teh Ai
BORN 1926-12-03
PROFESSED 1951-05-20
DIED 2007-02-04

DECLARATION BY NOVICE REGARDING COMMUNITY PRACTICES

(1918 RULE):

I solemnly declare that I believe all the Articles of the Catholic Faith as contained in the Apostles, Nicene and Athanasian Creeds, and that the Anglican Communion is a true and integral part of the Catholic Church of Christ and that the Formularies of Woship in that part of the Anglican Communion known in the United States of America as the Protestant Episcopal church are essentially Catholic in character and should be so interpreted and rendered and I believe that such an interpretation and rendering of the services should properly include:

(a) The use of lights upon the altar.
(b) The proper and traditional ecclesiastical vestments of Bishops, Priests and Deacons, and especially the Eucharistic vestments.
(c) The use of incense.
(d) Orientation, reverencing the altar, genuflection.
(e) The sign of the cross.
(f) The use of unleavened bread in the Holy Eucharist.

And I believe that the Holy Eucharist should be restored to its rightful position as the chief act of Christian worship: that it is truly sacrificial in its character: and that it should be received fasting unless a dispensation is given by competent authority; and that reserving of the Blessed Sacrament is a godly and reverent custom which should, when possible, be practiced for the consolation of the sick and the comfort of devout Christians.

And I further believe that to the Christian priesthood as ambassadors of Christ is committed the ministry of reconciliation to declare and pronounce to his people being penitent, the absolution and remission of all their sins, and that it is the right and privilege of all Christians to resort to private confession, and that it is the duty of all Novices and Professed Sisters to do so with such a degree of regularity as may be advised by their Spiritual Director and provided by the Rule. And I believe that the Apostolic rite of unction of the sick should be practiced, and that prayers should be offered for the dead.

(This has not been used since about 1970.)

BISHOP VINCENT'S SERMON
AUGUST 6, 1898

Sermon delivered by the Rt. Rev. Boyd Vincent, Bishop of Southern Ohio,
on Transfiguration Day, August 6, 1898,
at St. Luke's Church, Cincinnati, OH
"But we all, with open face, beholding as in a glass the glory of the Lord, are changed into the' same image from glory to glory, even as by the Spirit of the Lord."
2 Cor. 11.18

There is an important distinction in the matter of the Christian life which ought not to be forgotten. It is this: that as there is an ordinary Christian life, so there may be an exceptional Christian life. This exceptional life is sometimes called "the higher life" I do not like that definition; it savors of spiritual pride. It implies that ordinary Christian life is a lower life, which is not true. But however we define it, the distinction nevertheless remains. It is simply a fact that there are voluntary self-renunciations for Christ's sake, to which He encourages some Christians, but which he does not demand from all.

To the rich young man, for instance, who was already keeping all the commandments, Jesus said: "If thou wouldst be perfect, go, sell all that thou hast and give to the poor; and come, take up thy cross and follow me. This young man's life, religious as it was, was wholly selfish. Poverty was the specific remedy for that evil. Not that poverty is a virtue in itself; but it was, nevertheless, an indispensable means to the highest in his case.

Again, speaking of chastity, or the unmarried state, Jesus declared: "All men cannot receive this saying, save they to whom it is given." "Some men," he said are compulsorily single; others voluntarily so, for the kingdom of Heaven's sake. But," he concluded, "he that is able to receive it, let him receive it."

And again, in the matter of obedience, Jesus declared that there must often be a choice, not between duty to Him and duty to parents (that conflict could never arise) but between home ties or home comforts, on the one hand, and His service, on the other. Here, he insisted, the choice must be prompt and uncompromising. "Let the dead bury their dead," He said to one hesitating disciple; "follow thou Me. For," he continued, "no man hath left family and home and property for My sake and the Gospel's, but he shall receive a hundred-fold (compensation) in this world in this present time with persecutions, and in the world to come, eternal life."

When he found Martha so completely taken up with her household cares, and Mary eager rather to sit at His feet and learn of Him, he exclaimed: "Martha! Martha! thou art careful and troubled about many things; but one thing is needful, and Mary hath chosen that good part, which shall not be taken away." This was no disparagement of the active spirit in the home life, but it was a very special approval of the devotional and contemplative spirit in the religious life.

Again, St. Paul vehemently defends the moral right of Christians to all innocent happiness, even in this world; but he asserts no less vehemently that the law of love is greater even than the law of liberty, and that any Christian who voluntarily waives such rights and denies himself for the good of others, is doing a most praiseworthy thing. And the same apostle, speaking of the unmarried estate, lays down no command upon the subject for the majority of Christians; but he does give his own judgment as to what is most desirable for certain persons under certain circumstances. "There is a difference," he says, "between the wife and the virgin. She that is unmarried is careful for the things of the Lord, that she may be holy both in body and spirit; but she that is married is careful for the things of the world, how she may please her husband. So then," he continues, "he that giveth his own virgin (daughter) in marriage, doeth well; but he that giveth her not in marriage, shall do better." In other words virginity is neither a higher nor holier estate than wifehood, but it is a more desirable estate for those who wish to wait upon the Lord without distraction. But read that whole VII Chapter of 1st Corinthians for yourselves, and in the Revised Version, if you want to see St. Paul's exact meaning.

And then, above all, consider our Lord's own example. See how completely His life was one of poverty, chastity and obedience; see how, while it was a life of active sympathy with all ordinary human life and also one of constant service of his fellowmen, it was yet, in order to this very end, a life so largely separate and apart on its contemplative and devotional side. Thirty years of it, recollect, were spent in study and devotion, as well as in hard work, before his baptism; weeks then spent alone with God in the wilderness, before he would enter on His active ministry; whole nights during that ministry spent in prayer upon the mountain tops; seasons, again and again, when he called His disciples, too, apart from their busy life, to be alone with Him and let Him speak to them again of the things of the Kingdom of Heaven.

In short, dear brethren, there are souls, plainly contemplated by the Gospel itself, who feel themselves called by Christ's own voice to a life of special devotion to Him and special service to their fellowmen; and who feel called to this life, too, in terms of entire consecration and separation from the world. You may not hear that special call, you may not feel that special desire, but in Christ's own name, let us bid Godspeed to those who do. Call them "mystical souls," if you choose, "enthusiasts," "devotees;" that is exactly what they area—souls, with a different fibre or temperament, somehow, from our own prosaic make-up. But they are what God Himself made them and therefore made, we must believe, for His own special purpose, 'they are the kind of souls from which have come the artists and poets, aye and the prophets, saints, and martyrs of all times. They are the kind of women, filled with a peculiar spirit of personal devotion, who, in the Gospel story itself, sat at Christ's feet to hear Hun, and poured the precious ointment on His head, and left all to follow Him and minister to Him of their substance; the kind who were last at His cross and grave and the first at His resurrection. You cannot repress such womanly enthusiasm and devotion in the life of religion any more than you can elsewhere; you ought not to want to, and therefore you are not wise either to despise it or ignore it. It has asserted itself in every age of Christian history in one form or another, and it will continue to do so until the world's end. The rational thing, even the magnanimous, charitable thing, seems to be to accept it as one of the workings of God's spirit on human nature, and so protect it and direct it and use it for the best ends possible.

Such a life, we may say again, is no "higher" than the life of ordinary Christian duty in the world; and it is no holier. It claims no special merit in God's sight. It does not minister necessarily to greater sanctity, but it may to greater sanctification. The entireness of the self-devotion is only the measure of its capacity to know and enjoy and serve Christ better in its own way.

II.

But what, now, of that special form of this devotion called the "Sisterhood Life?"

Well, first of all, it is plain that it must have its roots originally somewhere in the religious nature itself, for other religions than ours have encouraged it. Thus the Greeks had their virgin priestesses, the Romans their vestal virgins, the Scandinavians their virgin prophetesses.

But the life has its own independent basis, too, in the Christian scriptures and Christian history from the very earliest times there have been such Orders of Women in the Christian Church. Scripture itself seems to divide them into three classes. St. Paul's Epistles to Timothy are especially concerned with them.

First, there was the Order of Deaconesses; this seems to have been made necessary by the social position of women in the East, as well as by the operations of the Church's charities. The deaconesses were really Church officers. They were present at all interviews between the clergy and the women of their flock; they instructed women for baptism, and attended them at the sacrament; they presided over the women's side of the church; they cared for the female sick and poor; they were sometimes, like Phoebe, the messenger of the apostles to the churches.

Then there was the class known as "Church Widows". St. Paul, in his Epistles to Timothy, distinguishes them from natural widows, and gives rules for their admission and registration. The holy Anna, who prophesied at our Lord's presentation hi the Temple, seems to have been a type of such "Church Widows", even in the Jewish Church. She was eighty-four years old, we are told, having had a married life of seven years, and departed not afterwards from the 'temple day or night, but spent her whole time in prayer and fasting. And then, as we have already seen, there was also a class of "Dedicated Virgins." The four daughters of the Evangelist Philip, particularly referred to in the Book of Acts as "virgins" probably belonged to this class. Such women evidently lived at home at first, and only later in community. By the 6th century this class had almost completely supplanted the Deaconess Order in the Church. Indeed, the disordered state of the times just then made the conventional life almost a necessity for young women.

In any case, such facts entirely dissipate the argument that such Orders of Christian women in our own day are either medieval or Roman in their origin. They were born in the very earliest and purest days of Christianity. And it is still further a fact that the Sisterhood was not originally a mere device of ecclesiastical economy for the better dispensing of the Church's charities, but a creation of the Holy Spirit primarily for the purposes of devotion. As has been beautifully said: "It was not the product of human pride or of a gloomy and false asceticism. It was not the outcome of the idea of the deliverance of the spirit from the bondage of matter, nor did it rise from that mistaken theology which supposes that heaven is gained by man's own merits, or self-denial is in itself a thing pleasing to God. But as a Christian marriage would bear witness to the unity of Christ and his Church, so the virgin estate was to set forth the ideas of self-consecration and self-sacrifice embodied in the Incarnation. Through its mist of grateful tears it sees shining the love of God unable to express its fullness save pouring out its life on Calvary; and so feels itself led to respond by an entire oblation of self, and give back hart for heart, life for life, and love for love."

Time proved, however, that such a spirit, exalted and worthy as it is, could not sustain itself without some outlet in the way of practical work. Forgetfulness of this fact was the error of the medieval conventual system and the source of much of its lamentable corruption. But modern Sisterhoods, adding the active life to the contemplative, have avoided those errors, and so won only gratitude and admiration for their usefulness, often from the most prejudiced.

✠

III.

In their Rule of Life the Sisters differ in certain marked respects from that of the Deaconesses. In so far as outward works of instruction and charity are connected, there is little difference; though the Deaconess, as she wears a less distinctive habit, so she works with more freedom and personal independence. For while the Deaconesses may live together or not, as they choose, the Sisters always live together under a common roof and a common Rule. Again, the Deaconesses, like the clergy, owe their first obedience to their Bishop; the Sisters, though their organization and work are subject to the Bishop's approval, are nevertheless under the more immediate direction of their own Superior. Again, the Deaconesses take no special "vows", other than those of worthy Christian living and service, and of deference to ordinary Church authority; they may resign their office and work at any tune. The Sisters, after a novitiate of a certain number of years, may take vows for a longer term or even for life. There are the special vows, of course, of poverty, chastity, and obedience - the renunciation, for sweet charity's sake, of so much which is otherwise lawful, beautiful, and blessed for women. Still there is no unnatural constraint or restraint in all this. There are the utmost freedom, care, and deliberation before any final step is allowed. The doors of the Sisterhood life open outward a good deal more readily than they open inward. There is no necessary dowry. Whatever property is given to the sisterhood is voluntarily given, or it may be given to someone else. There is a rule of common devotions and common work, of course; but, except for that, the interior life is that of a family, and the personal relations only that of mother, daughter, and sisters.

✠

IV.

I know the objections which are commonly made to this life, of course. I even shared them once myself. It is often felt and said that all such things are a "part of an ignorant and corrupt medievalism, or had only a pagan origin, or are against Scripture, or are sure to lead to Rome, or at least are useless in our day." But we have already seen how unjustified many of these objections are by the real historical facts, and the faithful and beautiful work of such Orders in our own day are sufficient witness to their worth. Or, it is asked: "Why not be a sensible Christian, and have nothing to do with this sort of Mummery? Why not be a Protestant instead of a Romanist. Why not be content with Christ and your Bible? Is there not Christian work enough to do in ordinary ways in your parish, in your home, or in society? Will you save your soul any more surely by going into a convent? Will good works make you acceptable with God? Has not Christ atoned for all sin, and have we anything more to do than just to believe? Are you not cowardly thus to turn your back upon the legitimate happiness as well as the trials and temptations of life, and are you not selfishly leaving your present duties for your own spiritual gratification?"

Well, my brethren, there is a sense, as even our Lord Himself recognized, higher even than common sense, and which makes some of His disciples able to realize Him with an exceptional faith, and long to know Him and serve Him with a devotion also out of the common. To such souls even He seems to say: "If thou wouldst be perfect, then make the sacrifice thy heart longs for. Poverty, chastity, and obedience are not necessities laid upon all, but they are my 'counsels of perfection' to thee, nevertheless. So then, he that is able to receive it, let him receive it." The spirit then, which follows such an impulse-is it Romish, or even Protestant, or only pre-eminently Christian? And what else is the keep the rule and render the service. "A strong body, a cultivated mind, good common sense, a cheerful disposition, a teachable will, some generosity of soul" - these are primary qualifications for the life. Next, comparative freedom from the claims of family duty. And next, in the case of a minor, the Christian parent's consent. These are the external signs.

The internal signs are wholly those of the Spirit of God: (1) the steadily increasing clearness and dearness of Christ to your own soul, and (2) the increasingly irresistible desire to give yourself wholly to His honor and service.

VI.

And now, finally, as to this, our own "Sisterhood of the Transfiguration." There are already many such Sisterhoods in this Church, though none with this particular name. This, Order is a new one, and so far belongs wholly to our own diocese. It is the outcome of the voluntary association of a few earnest women, a few years ago, for common devotion and active Christian work, and of their desire now to consecrate themselves fully and formally and at length finally to the life. It is made possible chiefly by the individual generosity of one of its members. Its services in mission and charitable work are absolutely without any cost to the Church itself. Most of you know of its work already in the establishment of the Bethany Mission House in connection with this parish of St.

Luke's, and what it has done in bringing the Church's ministrations to the unlearned and needy. Recently it has purchased an estate at Glendale, and opened a Foundling Home. All that its members are and have they have given to the cause, and future years will see its beneficence extended in other directions. Its Rule is entirely simple and reasonable, and its service practical and blessed beyond all question. May God bless and enlarge it more and more.

And now as for you, my daughters in the Lord:
In the Name of Christ and his Church I bid each of you a personal God-speed in what you are doing. You know how carefully and prayerfully I have watched you and have advised with you, and finally how warmly I have approved your purpose and work. You have been perfectly loyal to your Bishop and your Church, and I feel sure that my confidence in you in this respect will never be disturbed.

Let me now congratulate you especially on the name you have at last chosen for your Order, and on the day you have chosen for this service. No name could more fitly embody the essential idea of the Sisterhood Life than that of "The Transfiguration," and no words more beautifully set forth its motive than the Collect for this Feast.

As those chosen disciples of old, then, "being delivered from the disquietude of this world, were (for a moment) permitted to see the King in His Beauty"—so day by day may it be with you. As that marvelous manifestation was his reassurance and theirs (1) of the indwelling of the divine in the human and (2) of the glory to come after the humiliation here—such may it be to you. As they really, even with the bodily eye, looked upon him who is "God of God and Light of Light"—so may you be able to see with the inner eye of faith. As they with the natural ear really heard that voice from heaven, "This is my beloved Son: hear Him"—so indeed may you hear with the inner ear of faith and be always ready to obey. As He, "even while he prayed, was transfigured before them"—so may it be with you inwardly in your own life of devotion. As He, descending from the Mount, straightway delivered one possessed of the devil—such may your work be of overcoming evil as you come forth from that life of devotion.

In short, to all of us who are Christians, our Lord's Transfiguration is the incentive and promise of our own, and that in two ways: in body, at the last, when he will "fashion anew the body of our humiliation that it may be conformed to the body of his glory;" in spirit, even now since "we all, with unveiled face reflecting as a mirror the glory of the Lord, are (ourselves) transformed into the same image from glory to glory, even as from the Lord to the Spirit."

This, as I understand you, my daughters, is the special desire of your hearts. May God in his goodness grant it to you in full measure!

APPENDIX II
OUTREACH FOR MINISTRY: LONGTERM BRANCH HOUSES

BAT CAVE, NORTH CAROLINA, MINISTRY

The Community's house in Bat Cave began and has continued as a vacation house. It has also been a place of ministry to the people in the area as well as to the Sisters.

While it was still merely a vacation house the Sisters started a Sunday School and a Mother's Meeting. In 1906, Sister Beatrice and some others came down to have a Christmas tree for the children, said to be the first Christmas tree in Bat Cave. That same year they opened a school. The public schools at that time were open for only about two months a year. The first two years the teachers were graduates of the University of Cincinnati. The Sisters took over the teaching in the fall of 1908. The Sisters withdrew from the school in 1910, but the school continued for several years under a Bethany Home graduate. Several mountain girls had been sent to Bethany Home for their high school education. We see their names in articles published in the Bethany Home Chronicle. As the public schools improved the school was closed. The building had served as both school and chapel. In 1911, Father Willcox, who served several missions in the area asked for Sister Margaret Dolores to teach at the school he had started in Edneyville. In 1913 the mission church in Bat Cave, now the Church of the Transfiguration, was turned over to the Diocese. It was moved to its present higher location in the village.

When Sister Beatrice retired as Superior, she spent the rest of her life at Bat Cave except for an occasional visit to Glendale.

Beatrice did not live alone at Bat Cave. Another Sister was always there to be her companion, sometimes a Sister who was in special need of rest, sometimes a person in need of a temporary home or a place of refuge. One, Sister Faith Marguerite, acted as secretary to Sister Beatrice, typing out the manuscript for *A Follower's Story*. Sisters visiting in Bat Cave in the 1970s, met a priest who remembered attending a retreat for clergy organized by Sister Beatrice. Several Sisters remember visiting Sister Beatrice in Bat Cave while they were Novices. There were always a couple of dogs. Sister Beatrice died in 1963. In 2008 Sister Beatrice is still remembered fondly by the people there.

The Sisters had made some additions to the house, but the main part was over 100 years old and in very poor condition and some sections were falling apart. It was used every summer by some Sisters on vacation, and the Community decided that something had to be done. After much deliberation they decided to obtain a pre-fab modular two story house. To get the large building to that location on the mountain required some careful rebuilding of the road up from the highway. It was planned to accommodate a larger group of people than before as well as the Sisters. A ramp at the back makes the house handicapped accessible. The new house was joyfully dedicated on April 18, 2001. Ten Sisters went down for the occasion, including Sisters Ann, Mary Luke and others who had made frequent trips to oversee the building. As the writer for the Transfiguration Quarterly observed, "It was a creative challenge to build a house from a distance of several hundred miles."

In May, 2004, a new ministry began here. Several groups and individuals shared the house with Sisters Hilary and Priscilla. Sister Hilary conducted a Quiet Day at the Church of the Transfiguration in Bat Cave. Twelve Associates from the Hendersonville and Asheville area attended. Sister Priscilla has preached in Spanish at two missions near Hendersonville. Sisters have continued to also use it as a vacation house.

The Epilogue tells of new ideas that are envisioned for this special Place.

NORTHERN OHIO
1909-1979

Bishop William A. Leonard of Ohio, asked the Community to take charge of St. John's Orphanage in Cleveland, Ohio, which had been started in 1909. The Bishop had the hope of developing it very much like Bethany Home. About two years later, the Sisters also accepted the Church Home for elderly women, also in Cleveland, our first branch work not connected with children. These were diocesan institutions accepted at the invitation of Bishop Leonard. About two years later, the Sisters also accepted the charge of Holy Cross Home for Crippled Children in Cleveland. There was difficulty in finding a sympathetic chaplain for the Sisters in Cleveland, especially concerning the religious training of the children. The Community could spare only three Sisters for the combined work. Mother Eva's policy regarding the length of time a Sister could be away from home also made difficulties. Sisters who served there included Sister Ada Francis, who was in poor health, Sister Ethel Bertha, Sister Olive Rachel and Eleanor Mary.

In 1929 St. John's Home was moved to Painesville, Ohio, to property already owned by the diocese. St. John's Home was licensed to care for up to 26 girls, aged 6-16. The Sisters were under a Board appointed by the Diocese. The girls went to public school and did not wear uniforms as did the Bethany Home children. The Community refurbished the buildings, including a Chapel and several cottages for residents, a kitchen and refectory. The girls were assigned according to age.

Three Sisters were usually assigned to the Home. It was conveniently close to the Mother House in Glendale, so Novices were often assigned there to receive branch house experience which made for frequent changes in staff. Some of the Professed Sisters who served at St. John's were Sister Eva Dorothea, Jean Benedict, Lucy Caritas, Leinaala Josephine, and Althea Augustine. Usually one Sister or Novice from St. John's came home to the Convent in Glendale for the monthly Community retreat.

In 1956 a report from the Board states concern that the number of residents then was three-fourths of the capacity. One reason for this was the growing use of foster homes for dependent children. Over the years the Sisters became more and more aware of the financial challenges involved with the Home. The Sisters available did not all have the necessary training. They and the Board of Managers did not always work well together. The Chapter of the Community reluctantly voted to withdraw from St. John's but then voted again to continue but to keep only teenage girls. When the final decision to withdraw was made, the Superior reported that Sister Lucy Caritas, who had been scheduled to come home, volunteered to stay on to the end to help with the transition.

CHINA

In 1914 the Community accepted an invitation from Bishop Huntington to go to Wuhu, China. "A Follower's Story" reports: "When Bishop Huntington came for the final decision, Mother Eva had long and detailed talks with him about the spiritual privileges he would allow the Sisters and those associated with them. He was most sympathetic and understanding and generous in his promises. The Sisters could live and teach the full Anglo-Catholic life. An interested and well-trained Anglo-Catholic priest, the Rev. Edward Thurlow, was stationed in Wuhu and would serve as their chaplain. The Bishop said Fr. Thurlow would make a good confessor, have a daily Mass and the Blessed Sacrament could be reserved in the Sisters' private Oratory." The Sisters could teach what they practiced. This permission to have the Sacrament Reserved was of great importance to Mother Eva. This was the first place in our Community where the Blessed Sacrament was reserved.

The Sisters' mission at Wuhu would be named for St. Lioba, a cousin of St. Boniface, who was a missionary saint in Germany. St. Lioba founded a community of nuns. Her name translated into Chinese means Holy Love, and the Community which the Transfiguration Sisters hoped to establish would be the Sisters of Holy Love. St. Lioba's picture is in one of the stained glass windows in our Chapel. The Chinese Sisters are remembered as being Sisters of the Transfiguration.

It was the first year of World War I, which complicated their start. There was always some kind of conflict in China. In 1916 the last emperor was overthrown by a party under Sun Yat Sen, who founded the Republic of China in 1912. There was continual struggle between this group and the war lords. Chiang kai Shek succeeded Sun Yat Sen as leader of the Nationalist party. There was conflict between the Nationalists and the Communists. They both fought against the Japanese invasion from 1937 to 1945, but then the fight continued. This is the background on which the Sisters of the Transfiguration would be working. In October 1914, Sister Edith Constance and Sister Helen Veronica (the day after her Profession) volunteered to go.

The two Sisters filled out all the papers and questionnaires sent from the Board of Missions and supplied the required names for recommendations. They followed the suggestions of the Board as to equipment and clothing. They were duly examined by the physician, given anti-typhoid serum and were vaccinated against small-pox which was quite common in China.

Long letters home from both Sisters told of their adventures on the way. They stopped for a day in Honolulu. The Bishop of Honolulu, Bishop Restarick, met them at the dock with his car and he and his wife entertained them for the rest of the day. (Three years later the Community would send Sisters to his school there.) They arrived in Shanghai in November and took a river boat to Anking, accompanied by another missionary who reassured them that the noise at the port was not dangerous and helped them to unload their 48 boxes of luggage. At 3:00 a.m. they were carried in chairs by coolies through the streets of Anking. They were stopped at the gate and Dr. Taylor, another missionary who was escorting them, showed their papers to the soldier and they were allowed to pass. On the way to the Mission compound, at intervals an armed soldier would step out from some projection, look at them, and disappear.

The newly arrived Sisters finally reached the compound and the house of Miss Hopwood, another missionary, who welcomed them and showed them to a very comfortable room where they rested peacefully until time for Holy Communion. (In this context the word "compound" refers to a walled area with space for several buildings.) The letter goes on to tell of being settled in a house and of longing to be able to get back to the "simple life" of a Convent. They were in, to them, a new country with a new culture, and a new and difficult language. They stayed in Anking while they studied the Chinese language, which they found rather difficult. They also taught in St. Agnes School, the church school for girls in that city, until the time came for them to go on to Wuhu. They had to employ servants who eventually accompanied them to Wuhu.

The Bishop had recommended that they purchase a foreign (not Chinese) house belonging to the Foreign and Christian Missionary Society. It had beautiful grounds and ample land for future building. It was across the road from St. James Compound on Lion Hill in Wuhu. The purchase was arranged with the help of Bishop Huntington and Mr. Lund, the superintendent of the Episcopal Mission. Sister Edith wrote on June 16, 1915 that the purchase had been arranged and payment made, that all was settled. Legal ownership of the property was uncertain but eventually it was arranged that titles to the property in Wuhu and also Kuling, which they bought for use in the hot summer, were in the name of the Society of the Transfiguration. There was a delay because the previous missionaries did not want to vacate but in March, 1916 Sister Edith Constance and Sister Helen Veronica, with all their household goods and with a staff of well trained Chinese servants, moved to Wuhu. Their teacher, Mr. Ching, also came with them.

They named the house "True Light Convent". St. Lioba's Compound had beautiful grounds. Their plan was to start with a small school for girls and when it had proved a success the Bishop would obtain the money to build a large school on mission property bought for that purpose. The school was not far from St. James School for Boys and adjoining the Sisters' property. The school opened on St. Lioba's Day, September 28, 1916. On the day before the opening, nineteen girls arrived, accompanied by amahs and parents, with their bundles containing bed clothes and personal possessions. The school soon settled down to a happy routine. Physical education and mild sports made up a part of the daily program. The girls were awkward at first as this was so new to them.

It was a real challenge to live in the house where cleaning, painting, repairing, and remodeling were going on. Their plan was to arrange a building beside the Convent, and under the dome roof, dormitories for fifteen or twenty girls and their living quarters. The school rooms would be new, also the arrangements for a Chinese kitchen and laundry. The servants' quarters would be quite separate. A new house would be built for Mr. Ching and his family. The Sisters were very happy that in the room arranged as an Oratory, the Blessed Sacrament was reserved on the Altar, with the full approval of Bishop Huntington.

Before long the Mission developed into a variety of good works. A clinic was needed, also a special place for the amahs to live. Some of these were very old women whose services were very limited. A day school at the gate house was opened to take care of the poor children who lived in the mud huts close to the compound walls. From contacts with these children, calls were made among the families nearby and from these small beginnings there grew a great work of charity and evangelization.

Work went on during the summer. The school was ready by Fall. In August, 1916, Mother Eva and Sister Beatrice went to

Wuhu by ship, a six weeks' journey, for the opening of the school. During their visit in 1916 Mother Eva saw the need to send more Sisters to help with the work. Sister Deborah went out in the summer of 1917. Sister Edith came home on furlough in the spring of 1918. Sister Helen came home early in 1919 leaving Sister Deborah alone in Wuhu for three months. Sister Edith returned in March, 1919 bringing Sister Constance Anna with her.

After Sister Constance came out in 1919, there was more activity as she saw the needs of the people. She was a graduate nurse and the clinic grew by leaps and bounds. Soon she needed funds to support this work. She opened an Industrial Work by which she could give employment to needy women and sell their products to support the clinic. She never had complete mastery of the language, but she was able to communicate.

The Sisters' work was well established by then. The school house was enlarged and by 1924 there were 40 boarders including officials' daughters and daughters of Chinese church workers, and the day school at the gate house had more than 100 pupils.

On August 6, Transfiguration Day, 1919, Miss Ruth Kent, a missionary in Hankow, was received as a Postulant in the Community of the Transfiguration. She became Sister Ruth Magdalene.

The clinic's work expanded. Mrs. Mortimer Matthews, Mother Eva's sister-in-law, gave the funds for an adequate building for the clinic in memory of her grandson who had died quite young. Sister Constance had helped nurse him in a very severe illness and her loving care for little Stanley was rewarded by the beautiful Stanley Memorial Hospital. The building had large bright work rooms, a clinic, wards for sick women and children, a nursery for the babies of the women working there and bathrooms with plenty of hot water. There were rooms for the amahs and nurses, supply and packing rooms, dining rooms and a small room for the tailor, besides beautiful rooms for two Sisters connected with the work. The building was blessed on November 1, 1925.

Sister Helen wrote at length describing the condition of the coolies, how they suffered and sometimes died from the cold and lack of food. The coolies were very poor men who earned money by pulling rickshaws. In 1918 Sister Helen wrote of the coolie shelter they had started. Sister Edith had made mittens for the men and left them in the rickshaw when she left. That was the only way to give presents to poor Chinese. When Mother Eva came in 1922 she wrote to the Sisters at home in May, describing the work of the shelter. "The Shelter is answering its purpose, a hundred or so men stopping in daily for rest and refreshment. They get a cup of tea and a fan to cool off. Mrs. Keating (Sister Edith's sister who was visiting them) spends her days there playing records on the victrola which they enjoy very much." Sister Beatrice noticed that only the more prosperous among them had hats, and the five dollars given to her by a lady as they were coming to Honolulu she invested in coolie hats. She sold them for about one-third cost. She sold one last night to a delighted coolie who had brought someone home. The letter went on to tell more about the coolie hats. It told also of the prevalence of small pox and that small pox patients were allowed to walk around on the streets.

Another letter from Sister Edith told of a boy named Andrew who was studying English and helped in running the Rickshaw Coolie Shelter. Andrew also wrote a letter which he said was to be his English lesson for that day. He tells that he was to be baptized in St. Lioba's Chapel on All Saints' Day. Sister Edith's letter reports that on the day of his baptism Andrew said, "Today I am to be made God's child and my sins washed away in Holy Baptism." His face glowed as he told her.

Thanks to a check from Mrs. Mortimer Matthews, the Shelter had been enlarged. Mrs. Keating had furnished thirteen men with beds. There was a new roof, and cracks in the wall had been filled up. The Shelter did good work for many years. Eventually the Chinese government recognized the need and established shelters in many cities. The Shelter closed in 1927.

Mr. Frank Ching, the Sisters' teacher, who had been chosen for them by Bishop Huntington, accompanied them to Wuhu. The Sisters' study included the Gospel of St. Mark, which made a great impression on Mr. Ching. He was also very impressed by what Sister Edith explained to him about our prayers for the departed. He was a Confucianist, and apparently it was difficult for him to go against the customs of his elders. But, in Wuhu he was independent of his Confucianist relatives. He went through the Prayer Book as well as the Bible with the Sisters, and was very excited about what he learned. In Wuhu he attended Church every Sunday. He was baptized at Easter, April 23, 1916.

There was a serious testing, not related to the Chinese political situation, almost from the beginning in 1916, which was not resolved until 1922. There were many questions that needed answers and much planning to be done. Only a personal visit from the Mother Superior could solve the problems. It especially involved the relationship between the Sisters and the rest of the Mission in Wuhu. When Bishop Daniel T. Huntington invited the Sisters to come, he promised that they could have their own Chapel and Reservation of the Blessed Sacrament. This permission was one of the conditions under which the Sisters went to China in 1915. Mother Eva had discussed the matter of churchmanship with Bishop Huntington before they accepted his invitation. He had agreed to all her conditions, including the full sacramental life, and gave them permission to teach it in their school. He had appointed the Rev. Frank Thurlow, a priest who was in sympathy with our life, as our Chaplain. Fr. Thurlow did not return to the Mission Field after his furlough, leaving the Sisters dependent upon the Rev. F. E. Lund, who was not at all sympathetic with their beliefs or their practices. There was also the question of authority. Mr. Lund had been helpful in arranging for the purchase of the property, but he also assumed that he had authority over the Sisters except for in their Convent. There was an exchange of letters between the Bishop, Mr. Lund, Sister Edith and Mother Eva, regarding the legal status of the Community, and who had the authority over them and the whole Mission. According to the letters, Mr. Lund was turning the Chinese clergy against the Sisters. Fortunately, the Bishop allowed Father Vincent Gowen, another missionary, to be the Sisters' Chaplain, and he supported them. There was even a suggestion that the Sisters might be asked to leave the Mission. It was this situation that Sister Beatrice had referred to when she spoke of Mother Eva's wisdom in saying that the Sisters should own their own property.

Mother Eva Mary came herself to deal with the situation. She arrived in Shanghai, May 10, 1922. In a letter to her brother Paul, who was also their Chaplain General, Mother Eva expressed the thought that the Bishop was sorry he had invited them. He didn't really know what to do, and he was favoring Mr. Lund. The Sisters were concerned lest the influence of Mr. Lund would rob China of the sacramental life in the Church.

Mother Eva accomplished her mission. The Bishop consented to the original terms of the agreement and the Sisters' position was secure. They could build their own church, apart from the Mission. By this time St. Lioba's beautiful church was completed and consecrated. Mother Eva was in China long enough to see the laying of the cornerstone. The Mission became a parish with a Chinese priest trained in Catholic worship and practice by Sister Helen Veronica. The church building was large enough to hold 300 people. There was a beautiful side chapel where the Sisters said their Offices and where the Blessed Sacrament was reserved. Sister Beatrice reported the story in detail in "A Follower's Story". She herself was much involved in it. She had again accompanied Mother Eva to China. Mother Eva became seriously ill during that summer with flu and dysentery. Sister Constance nursed her as she had done in Cleveland. The doctor would allow Mother to be in Wuhu for the opening of the school on September 9, 1922, and he would not allow her to sail before then.

It was still necessary to explain the situation in person to authorities at home. Sister Beatrice sailed home alone on July 15, 1922. She hoped to be at home in time for the Feast of the Transfiguration, and then she was to go on to New Jersey and tell the whole story to Bishop Matthews in person. Sister Beatrice would also report to him on the constructive work they were doing besides the School, the Rickshaw Shelter, the clinic and the Industrial Work.

At a Chapter meeting of the Community on September 21, 1922 at the Mother House, Sister Beatrice reported having an interview with Bishop Vincent of Southern Ohio on August 7th, one with Bishop Matthews, their Chaplain General on August 11th, and, after a report to the Sisters in Cleveland, an interview with Bishop Leonard of Northern Ohio, all of whom were most sympathetic. They had promised to go into conference with Bishop Huntington at Portland, Oregon during the time of General Convention, which would meet that year. She also reported on the telegram from Bishop Matthews on September 4. "After several conferences, believe every point won. Have letter from Bishop [Huntington] making Sisters' position secure, original agreement will stand. Erection of chapel approved but canonical difficulties exist and must be arranged. Sister Eleanor's appointment is accepted."

Sister Eleanor Mary was appointed to be in charge of the Sisters' Mission in Wuhu. They were allowed to build their own

Chapel. Their work was to be separate of the rest of the Mission, but under the direction of the Bishop. The only restriction was the elimination of evangelistic work or teaching. This was partly because of increasingly dangerous travel conditions and the restriction was later removed. Sister Eleanor, with tact and patience, was able to heal any scars remaining from the difficulty. After Sister Eleanor returned to the United States in 1926, Sister Helen Veronica returned to China as Sister-in-charge.

Wuhu was filled with the invading armies and there were a great many wounded to be cared for. The Stanley Memorial Hospital was opened to the less desperate cases and accommodated about forty soldiers. More serious cases were sent up to the Methodist Hospital nearby. Sister Helen wrote of the care they were taking of the men in the hospital. There was also the fear that if there were any possibility of the other army winning again, the women and children would have to leave. The letter was signed by Sister Helen, Sister Constance and Sister Ruth Magdalene.

Mr. Ching lived with his family in the St. Lioba's Compound, and helped them in every way. He really became the head under Sister Edith in 1927 when the Sisters had to leave Wuhu for Shanghai because of the civil war in China. The Sisters had been warned and were packed and ready to go. Mr. Ching took charge of the compound. He had a lined trench under his bed on the ground floor and put in it all the valuable articles belonging to the Church and the Sisters. They were undisturbed all during the time the compound was used by the Chinese armies. Mrs. Ching would go out to meet the delegates of the advancing army who were looking for suitable quarters for the commanding officer and staff and assure them that St. Lioba's compound would be just the place. He would invite them to inspect the place, and each time his invitation was accepted, in turn by both the contesting army officers as Wuhu changed hands. Mr. Ching reasoned correctly that high ranking officers would keep order and not destroy the property. The Chinese Sisters lived unmolested in their Convent in the compound. Mr. Ching and his family lived quietly in their little house, and when our Sisters returned months later they found everything as they had left it.

The Sisters wished to reward Mr. Ching for his faithful service, his great care over more than 20 years. Mr. Ching had long had a dream of visiting the United States. When Sister Edith and Mother Beatrice returned home from their visitation to Wuhu in 1929 they brought Mr. Ching back with them. (Sister Beatrice was elected Mother Superior after Mother Eva's death in 1928.) Mr. Ching's health had suffered from the difficult years and a change, they thought, would restore him. He was filled with delight over the journey and his delight was contagious. He made friends with everybody. His visit to America was made quite complete. Bishop Matthews entertained him in Princeton, New Jersey. Sister Ruth Magdalene's sisters helped him to see the sights of New York. While he was in the East an important meeting of representative Chinese was being held in Washington, D.C. He joined them and had the honor of shaking hands with the President of the United States, Herbert Hoover. Wherever he went he was called upon to deliver addresses or talks. He was able to do so in fairly good English although sometimes Sister Edith acted as his interpreter. He was very happy until his health began to show evidence of serious trouble. He was placed in Christ Hospital, Cincinnati, for observation. He made real friends with the doctors and others on the staff there, but they could do nothing for him. The Sisters turned over the children's infirmary for his care and engaged three nurses for him. He was suffering from leukemia. He died in great peace and dignity on August 1, 1930.

In "*A Follower's Story*" Sister Beatrice includes copies of some long letters from Sister Helen regarding the work at Wuhu. The Community has also preserved letters written by Sister Louise Magdalene from 1934 until 1948 when the Sisters came home to stay. After 1945 letters from Sister Constance and others were printed in the Transfiguration Quarterly. They were written to inform the Sisters at home about their work. There is a continual undercurrent of their concern for the poverty of so many Chinese people, the frequent shortages of fuel and food, inadequate clothing and shelter, the lack of compassion people had for one another, and the continued urgent desire that they may show the people the love of God through Jesus Christ. This is demonstrated in the Coolie Shelter.

Sister Louise Magdalene, newly Professed, went out to China in 1934. After ten days spent visiting the Sisters at St. Andrew's Priory, Honolulu, she sailed on the Empress of Japan. Two Sisters of the Society of St. Anne, also going out to China, traveled with her. They landed in Shanghai on September 11, 1934. A letter from Sister Louise, written October 9, tells of her arrival. Shanghai was much like any city, "but when we boarded the riverboat that night and lay awake in our cabins as we listened to the strange sounds and disturbing noises of loading the boat we knew we were in a foreign land, or rather, foreigners in a strange land." On the boat with them were three hundred and two coolies who were going to work on the railroad in Wuhu and about one hundred more for Kiukiang. When they arrived in Wuhu that evening they waited for more than an hour while the men unloaded their equipment. When they disembarked they were met at the boat by a welcoming crowd of Sisters, teachers, nurses and friends. The Sisters of St. Anne had to go back to the boat to continue on to Hankow.

On St. Lioba's Day they had a sung Mass and a school holiday. The next day, a Saturday, there was a parish meeting and a talk by

Father Wang, the Chinese priest, followed by a party with singing and games on the lawn outside the Church.

Just before Christmas, 1935, the Sisters in Wuhu learned that just before Christmas a Communist band had captured and killed two missionaries from the China Inland Mission, which was within thirty miles of Wuhu. There were rumors that they were going to attack the city. Several foreign gunboats joined the American one on the Yangtze and the American Consul came to Wuhu to make arrangements for evacuating foreigners if it should become necessary.

Earlier that year, while Bishop and Mrs. Matthews were making a long awaited visit to China, there was what appeared to be a bandit attack. The commander of the American gunboats sent men to their rescue, but it turned out to be just a local quarrel.

Although the Chinese government had officially adopted the Western calendar, the people still kept up the old customs, which in 1935 meant the Chinese New Year started on February 4, 1935. Everybody had a feast on the Eve and firecrackers were going all night. In the morning the Sisters began to have callers, until about 11:00, and then it was their turn to call at their homes, having tea at each place. The streets and shops were decorated with red papers and very fancy paper lanterns and the children who were fortunate to have a change of clothes, wearing their very best.

Sister Louise's letters tell of other happy occasions. On Mother Foundress' Day and in honor of Sister Constance's birthday February 10, members of Bishop Huntington's family were guests, along with three other missionaries, including Miss Elda Smith who eventually became Sister Elda Magdalene. Sister Louise was invited to Anking for the China New Year holidays to come to meet the other missionaries.

Sister Edith Constance, who had helped begin the mission at Wuhu in 1914, revisited there in 1934, and wrote about it for the

Bethany Home Chronicle, February 1935, describing the changes that had taken place in 20 years.

Then the Sisters knew only a few words of Chinese. Their cook, who had been baptized, read a Chapter from the Chinese Bible, and followed it by a hymn from a collection loaned them by the China Inland Mission, and a few prayers. There was now a congregation of about two hundred Christians worshipping daily in a beautiful Chapel.

When Sister Edith Constance started the school in 1914 a Sister worked as principal, but they still did not know the language well and could not even read the girls' textbooks. Beginning in 1934 St. Lioba's had a Chinese lady principal who managed everything, and the Sister-in-charge only had to sign diplomas and reports to the government. The day school they had opened outside the compound gate with four pupils and a part-time teacher now had over one hundred pupils and five teachers. Three of the teachers had been students at St. Lioba's Boarding School. In 1914 most adults were illiterate. Now most of those around the area could read the newspaper, and the congregation could follow the services in the Prayer Book.

Means of transportation had improved. The first time they went to their holiday place in Kuling, it was a journey, first by steamer and then by sedan chairs; a two-day trip. Now they still went by steamer, then part way by automobile, a two hour trip instead of eighteen. An auto trip to Nanking took only two hours, although the driver had to watch out for herds of tiny donkeys.

There were new government buildings, for Kuling was now the summer capital. General Chiang Kai Shek made it his capital for training soldiers for mountain work in the Nationalist army.

There seemed to be a growing attempt to push out foreigners. In the past when someone had needed help, the Sisters went themselves. Now they found it better to keep in the background and send some of their Chinese helpers. They were not as welcome as they once had been in the homes of some of their Chinese friends. The foreign community in Wuhu had dwindled from several hundred to fifteen or twenty. The Sisters and women of the Mission were no longer allowed to go away from the mission station for evangelistic work as they had done until 1927. Travel to the country stations was too dangerous. Nevertheless the Sisters' Mission continued in spite of the political situation.

In April, 1936, the Bethany Home Chronicle reported that the Sisters in China had started a new work in Lo-kang. The priest at Maolin had told them of this village where there was already a group of Christians anxious to learn more about Christianity. Sister Ruth and Sister Feng Ai were there, "preaching the doctrine", and Joan Chang, a nurse, with her assistants was giving treatments. More than one hundred people came one day and over forty stayed for treatments. At that time there were only two Christians in the village. Sister Ruth was planning to go there one day a week, and there was hope that a good congregation would arise.

During her second summer in Kuling (1936) Sister Louise was invited to join three other members of the Mission on a trip to Peking (Beijing). This trip was one of the highlights of her time in China, and her only opportunity to visit Peking. They went by train via Hankow and stayed at the Peking Language School. They visited many famous buildings and scenic places around Peking, including the Great Wall. They toured the "Forbidden City", the old imperial palace. On Transfiguration Day they attended Mass at the Anglican Cathedral, a service arranged especially for them. From there they returned to Wuhu by way of Tai Shan, the birthplace of Confucius, a beautiful mountain area with many Confucian temples. And from there they went on to Nanking and Wuhu by train.

Not long after this Sister Louise's health began to deteriorate and she was suspected of having tuberculosis. It was decided that she should take an early furlough. She went with another missionary, Lucy Burgin who became Sister Lucy Caritas, to Honolulu, where she spent the summer being cared for by the Sisters at St. Andrew's Priory and then on to Glendale. She was finally diagnosed as having a parasitic infection which cleared up quickly. Her return to Wuhu was delayed until early in 1939 because of the Japanese invasion. When she returned, Sister Constance left on furlough.

The Japanese soldiers had invaded northern China, taken Nanking in 1937 and continued south, and before long they occupied the whole Yangtze valley from Shanghai west beyond Hankow. Sister Constance was the only American Sister on the compound at the time the Japanese took Wuhu, but she had the help of Janet Anderson, from a British ambulance unit, and Father Walter Morse an American missionary of the Society of St. John the Evangelist. They managed to take into the compound hundreds of Chinese refugees fleeing from the Japanese army. When Sister Louise arrived back there were still some refugees living on the compound.

Sister Constance left. The Sisters cared for several babies and tried to find good homes for them. One of these babies named Martha Kang, and was legally adopted by Sister Louise. Many years later Martha survived the Cultural Revolution and was able to join the community in America where she now resides and serves in many capacities.

A new floor was being built in the Church and they were also having the woodwork redone and the walls repainted. All the Sisters had just half day schedules that summer because they were not having vacations. Fortunately the summer was not as hot as usual.

In 1939, letters from China reported considerable suffering there, due to the shortage of fuel. Coal was $160 a ton and people raked up every blade of dry grass for fuel. Most things had gone up in price. Those who were on foreign exchange salaries would be all right, but the poor Chinese were going to suffer this winter.

In February, 1940, Sister Louise wrote, rejoicing that Sister Grace Elizabeth would be coming to Wuhu. School had reopened after the Chinese New Year holidays. They had had to turn away some girls because of lack of space, and there were 38 children in the kindergarten. Later that year she wrote again saying that Mr. Lloyd Craighill had a letter from the priest at Maolin, where they had served several years before, hoping that they would return. It was Mr. Craighill who had made their first contact with the priest at Maolin.

In 1941 Sister Louise's letter said that they had heard from the priest in Maolin and had decided to reopen the work there. After 1941, Sister Louise's letters were from the new Convent of St. Boniface on Maolin. A letter from Sister Louise written August 10, 1941 reports that an associate had purchased the property where the Sisters were at Maolin and the Rev. Arthur Wang, representing her, presented the property to the Community and turned over the deeds to the Bishop who then presented them to Sister Louise. The Sisters lived in a Chinese house, eating Chinese food, and doing most of their own housework. On Transfiguration Day, August 6, 1941, there was a special service of blessing of the new Convent. Besides the members of the Sisters' household there were three catechists, eight priests, and the Bishop in procession.

They were planning a small kindergarten, a Sunday School and some special classes. There was a good doctor in Maolin and the Mission had arranged for him to help with the clinic three times a week. They were planning regular trips to some of the neighboring villages.

Sister Louise wrote, "There is no limit to the amount of work that could be done out here."

Sister Louise reported that Sister Constance had written on December 4, 1941 that the kindergarten and nursery school were closed and that there were 25 women left at the Industrial Work finishing up orders. They were anxious about the future and were preparing to evacuate. They were delayed and on December 8 by Japanese soldiers carrying machine guns. They went to the Methodist Hospital first, tore down the American flags and hoisted Japanese flags. They then inspected our compound, and all the foreign houses were inspected and passes were taken away. Our missionaries were given permission to go across the road from one compound to another, but nowhere else. They could carry on their regular work. Letters could be sent and received, but they would be censored. The Japanese flag was raised on top of St. James' School tower. A Chinese policeman was assigned to guard the compounds. The children at St. Lioba's would have a Christmas pageant in the afternoon on Christmas Eve and the Sisters planned two services.

In April, 1942 all the foreigners in Wuhu were summoned to Military Police headquarters and told about the plans being made for their repatriation. They had to provide 100 yen for their traveling expenses and they were given permission to sell their furniture and personal effects. Sister Louise thought their compound was just about empty. The strain of this difficult time and overwork was too much for Sister Constance's heart. They were to be ready to leave for America by mid-June, but the doctors said Sister Constance would not be able to travel by that time.

Christmas 1942, was observed at Maolin with a Christmas pageant by the school children, a quiet Midnight Service, and another Service, with hymns in the morning. Christmas dinner was provided for the family and friends. Sister Constance in Wuhu had sent someone with gifts for them, mostly food. They continued to be anxious about her health.

Early in June, 1943 the Convent received an airmail letter from Sister Louise in Maolin, in Free China, dated March 24. All were well and very busy. Sister Constance was the only American Sister in Wuhu. There was worry about her health. She had two good doctors and was getting the best of care, but she had been in bed for more than a month. The doctors said she would get well faster if she would only stay in bed. Sister Louise was not aware that Sister Constance had been imprisoned in Shanghai in 1942.

Their isolation in Maolin was very trying. There was no radio or newspaper. They were allowed to send and receive mail, but it would be censored. They looked forward to letters from home and a weekly newsletter. The mail was slow, and they wondered how much of it was lost or misdirected so that they did not receive it. The Sisters did not hear about Pearl Harbor until four days afterwards. It was in May, 1943 that they received the news of the election, on February 9, of Mother Olivia Mary as Superior. They did receive some postcards from Wuhu, telling of what was happening there. The work in Maolin continued.

Sister Louise told of the work in Maolin, of the kindergarten, of the Christmas entertainments, of a conference for clergy and evangelistic workers in August, 1943. Bishop Chen conducted a retreat for them for Transfiguration Day. They had very little but they had a garden and a few chickens and could help their Chinese friends who were much worse off. They heard that the Church in Wuhu had been damaged. Their property in Kuling had also been destroyed. She exclaimed about the fact that this was their third Christmas in Maolin, much longer than they had expected. They were enlarging the Chapel. Sister Louise was also helping Bishop Chen in the Diocesan office. She explained that if she had returned to Wuhu, she would have had to go to Shanghai where there was an internment camp for foreigners. The Japanese authorities had hoped that all Americans would be in Shanghai early that spring. Most of the men had already left. There was continual concern about Sister Constance's health. In Maolin they were all quite well.

Sister Louise left Maolin on June 21, 1944, together with Martha Kang, her adopted Chinese daughter, Sister Pei Ngai, and another Chinese friend, hoping to reach Kunming. (During World War II Kunming acted as an Allied military center.) The roads were filled with refugees fleeing from the Japanese. Conditions changed for the worse and her Chinese companions had to turn back. At home, on July 28, 1944, word was received from the Church Missions House that Sister Louise Magdalene and two other women missionaries had reached Kunming safely by air and gave Sister Louise's address in Kunming, Yunnan, Free China. The Chinese Sisters were still at St. Boniface Convent, Maolin.

Sister Constance was released from being interned in Shanghai in 1945 after a peace treaty was signed between the United States and Japan. Sister Constance reported that they had been well treated, and her health had improved while she was there. The Nationalists were now in control, and a message form Chungking, the capital, said that General Chiang was asking the missionaries to return.

When Sister Constance returned to Wuhu she and other missionaries who had returned worked very hard to restore the buildings as much as possible. They moved into St. Lioba's on October 17, 1945 and had a special service of Thanksgiving the following Sunday. The altar and other church furnishings had been carefully stored and were found intact when the Sisters returned. This included the beautiful bell which had been buried deeply

St. Lioba.

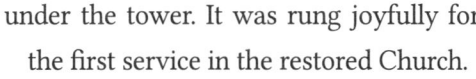

Chinese Sisters.

under the tower. It was rung joyfully for the first service in the restored Church.

The Sisters had hoped to establish the Religious Life in China. In 1921 a very devout Bible woman came to try her vocation. She became our Sister Feng Ngai. A short time later a much younger woman came, and became Sister Pei Ai. Later came Sister Chen Ngai and Sister Shou Ngai. (The name Ngai, or Ai in modern spelling, means Love.) These were all Professed Sisters before the Sisters left.

The Chinese Community which was named after St. Lioba, the Sisters of Holy Love, was expected to become an autonomous Community. A fifth woman was received as a postulant and was professed as Sister Teh Ngai in 1950 after the American Sisters had left. The Chinese Sisters, now really autonomous, stayed on in Wuhu and continued the ministry. By 1980 the Community in the United States had received word of the deaths of the first four. The plan for a Chinese Community to develop was thwarted by the political situation.

They lost trace of Sister Teh Ngai for a long time. Martha Kang, the Chinese child whom Sister Louise had adopted, had been left with a Chinese family. After many vicissitudes, Martha survived. There were still friends of the Sisters in China, and Martha was able to get in touch with the Community. She was able to come to the United States and has lived in a house on the Convent grounds since 1980. After making several trips back to China and searching for her, she found Sister Teh Ngai living with relatives. Sister Teh Ai had continued to pray and observe her Religious Rule insofar as possible. She wanted very much to join us in Cincinnati, and the Community hoped to bring her here, but because of her age and health and lack of English, she was several times refused a visa. Martha kept in touch with her by telephone. After her death, in 2007, her remains were brought to America and are buried in our cemetery. The Chinese Sisters are remembered in our monthly requiem for departed Sisters.

Sister Edith Constance and Sister Helen Veronica were the first to go to China. Sister Constance Anna came out in 1919. Others included Sister Eleanor Mary, Sister Deborah Ruth, Sister Joanna Mary, Sister Grace Elizabeth and Sister Virginia Cecelia. A life of service with an order of prayer in community attracted others. The Sisters always served in companionship and cooperation with the other members of our Mission and with Missions of other denominations. Several Sisters entered the Community after having served as missionaries in China. These included Sister Ruth Magdalene, Sister Lucy Caritas, Sister Emily Faith, and Sister Elda Magdalene.

ST. ANDREW'S PRIORY SCHOOL FOR GIRLS
HONOLULU, HAWAII

Another overseas work was added in 1918 when, at the invitation of the Rt. Rev. Henry B. Restarick, first American Bishop of Honolulu, the Sisters undertook the administration of a school for girls in Honolulu. St. Andrew's Priory was founded in 1867 by English Sisters as a school where Hawaiian girls could receive an education comparable to that traditionally received only by boys. The English Sisters were of the Order of the Most Holy Trinity, founded by Priscilla Lydia Sellon. (Her picture is in the window of our Chapel.) In their Rule a branch house is called a Priory, hence the name of the school. They came at the request of Queen Emma, widow of King Kamehameha IV. It was named in honor of St. Andrew, his Feast Day being the date of the king's death.

Hawaii was annexed by the United States in 1898 after the Spanish American War. In 1902 the Church of England turned its work there over to the American Episcopal Church. Because of the advanced age of the two English Sisters remaining, the school was then under lay administration. Bishop Restarick invited the Sisters of the Transfiguration to undertake the administration of the Priory. The American Sisters agreed to provide for the last two English Sisters, Sister Beatrice and Sister Albertina, for the rest of their lives and they retired to a little cottage on the grounds. The last one died in 1930.

Soon after Bishop Restarick's arrival in 1902 there was considerable renovation and expansion of the Diocesan property. St. Andrew's Priory, adjacent to the Cathedral, was almost 40 years old. In 1909 a new school building replaced the original building close to the original site. It was one of Honolulu's first reinforced concrete structures, two stories with an attic, and accommodated 200 girls, of whom 90 were boarders. The old building was replaced by the Bishop's House which later became the Diocesan House. Space for the new buildings was obtained by moving the Iolani campus to another location. Iolani was the boys' school of the Episcopal Church in Honolulu. It had been started by missionaries from England, even before the Priory. Many of the Priory girls had brothers at Iolani. The Priory and the other Diocesan buildings including St. Andrew's Cathedral surround a little park known as Queen Emma Square.

In 1911 the Coral Cross which had stood in the courtyard of the original Priory was moved to the front courtyard of the new one. The Cross had been hewn from the coral reef off Oahu in 1867. Mother Sellon had had it raised and set in the center of the school area. The Cross became the focus of special events at the school.

The first Sisters of the Transfiguration arrived in August, 1918. Sister Olivia Mary was the first Sister to be principal of the

The Coral Cross.

School. The others who came to Honolulu at that time were Sisters Caroline Mary and Amy Martha. Sister Caroline acted as bookkeeper and Sister Amy was in charge of the household. There were usually four or five in residence, some as teachers and some in the boarding department. The Priory became a favorite stopping place for Sisters going to and from Wuhu. Sisters who had served in China and came to the Priory, at least temporarily, when they had to leave China, included Sisters Anna Grace, Virginia Cecilia, Deborah Ruth, Helen Veronica and Lucy.

The first four year high school diplomas were awarded to four girls in 1920. It became the custom that the night before graduation the Junior class stayed all night and decorated the Coral Cross with flowers and leis to honor the Senior class. The graduation ceremony was held in the Cathedral, but afterwards there was a program at the Cross. In 1935 a wing called Restarick Hall was added to the Main Building. Sister Helen Veronica was Sister Superior from 1938 through 1948 at the Priory. During her time Sellon Hall was built, with six classrooms for elementary students. In 1940 came the Sisters' House, also called the Faculty House, and today it is known as Transfiguration Hall.

Priory Sisters c. 1960.

Students in front of St. Andrew's Priory.

The attack on Pearl Harbor, December 7, 1941 brought wartime to the Islands! All private schools were closed. Many mainland teachers were sent home to the mainland. Some Priory seniors were called upon to teach in elementary grades in the public schools. Bomb shelters were built in Queen Emma Square and the Priory playground. The boarding department was closed and has never reopened. Some of the cathedral buildings still show signs of being hit by shrapnel. The dormitory rooms were changed into classrooms. There is a story told that on the first day of school after it reopened in February, 1942, at the Chapel service of Morning Prayer, the Chaplain opened the service with the words, "I was glad when they said unto me, Let us go to the house of the Lord." A little first grader responded, "So was I." The class of 1942 walked down the aisle at graduation with gas masks hanging from their shoulders. Dorothy McNichols had graduated in June, 1941. She followed the Sisters to Glendale and was professed in 1949 as Sister Stephanie Helen. (She celebrated over 50 years as a Sister of the Transfiguration.) In 1949 a full time physical education program began for grades 2-12, and the number of students increased until in 1960 there were 600 girls in grades 1-12.

In 1959 the Territory of Hawaii became a State. A star was added to the United States flag. The people now elected their own governor. As a territory he had been appointed from Washington. It is unlikely that this changed much in the day to day life of the school, but they had a new neighbor. The school is in the heart of downtown Honolulu. The Governor's mansion, which had once been the home of Queen Liliokalani, the last reigning Queen of Hawaii, (composer of Aloha Oe) is next door to the Priory. It was reported that Queen Liliokalani used to come through the gate to have tea with the English Sisters.

Girls near staircase in Sellon Hall.

At the school new buildings were built. Sometime in the 1960's the Priory Expansion Program made possible a second story to be added to Sellon Hall for the Middle School. And just before the Centennial in 1967, a gymnasium was built named in honor of Bishop and Mrs. Kennedy. A new administration building was raised with space for a Chapel for the Sisters. As it was in the 1960's, every morning the girls walked in order by classes from their classrooms to St. Andrew's Cathedral which served as the Priory Chapel. There was a service every day.

Because so many of the girls were non-Christians, the school service was Morning Prayer rather than the Eucharist, but Christian Education was required in every grade. On Feast Days a Eucharist was provided before school for girls who had been confirmed. Parents of non-Christian students who entered the Priory were advised that Christian religious education would be required of every student, although without attempt to proselytize. The girls were encouraged to be confirmed in their parish church rather than at school, to make them part of a parish family. The Sisters believed that being connected there, would safeguard against the possibility that leaving the school would also mean leaving the Christian church. Of course some non-Christian parents asked for delay or there was delay on account of grandparents, but many girls were confirmed later and some brought their parents to Christian baptism.

On Ascension Day, which is also Founders' Day, 1967 the Priory celebrated its centennial. The beginning of the centennial celebration was Evensong the evening before followed by a reception for friends and guests. At St. Andrew's Cathedral, on Ascension Day, The Rt. Rev. Harry S. Kennedy, Bishop of Honolulu, was the Celebrant. The procession of more than 600 students, carrying banners, flags, cross and crozier was accompanied by the Iolani band. The procession made is way to the coral cross which had been decorated with Hawaiian leis and flowers. The procession was greeted by Mother Esther Mary, a Sister of the Most Holy Trinity, and Sister Olivia Mary, the first Sister-in-charge of the Priory. Dom Anthony Damron, an Episcopal Benedictine monk of St. Gregory's Priory, Three Rivers, Michigan and Chaplain General of the Community of the Transfiguration, was present. On Memorial Day, May 30, 1967, students, friends and faculty attended the centennial luau. The students presented an historical pageant celebrating Queen Emma and the founding of the Priory. A Hawaiian tradition says that a shower of rain at important events is a "blessing from heaven". Those assembled there received such a blessing, a sign of encouragement for the future.

The Priory was a Diocesan School. Bishop Restarick was succeeded in office by the Rt. Rev. John Dominique La Mothe (1921–1928), the Rt. Rev. S. Harrington Littell (1930–1942) and in 1942 by the Rt. Rev. Harry S. Kennedy. At that time Hawaii was designated as a Missionary District rather than a Diocese. In 1967 General Convention designated all Missionary Districts as Dioceses. The Missionary District of Honolulu became the Diocese of Hawaii. One difference was that a Missionary Bishop was elected by General Convention and sent out to his jurisdiction already a Bishop. Bishop Kennedy was the last one chosen in this way. He had come in 1944, in wartime conditions, and served for twenty-five years, until his retirement in 1969. The annual Diocesan meeting, formerly called Convocation, was now called Convention. This Convention chose the Rt. Rev. Lani Hanchett as the first Bishop to be elected in Hawaii. The election was held in St. Andrew's Cathedral. Bishop Hanchett was part Hawaiian. His wife was a graduate of the Priory, and his two daughters had attended the Priory. Bishop Hanchett died in 1975. By this time the Sisters were no longer at the Priory.

Other Sisters who served as principal were Sister Clara Elizabeth (1931–1938), Sister Paula Harriet (1933–34, 35–36), and 1936–1949). From 1948–51 Sister Marion Beatrice was Sister Superior. Sister Evelyn Ancilla came to the Priory as a teacher 1937–1944 and 1948–1951. In 1951 she became Sister Superior and remained until 1968 when she returned home because of her health. Sister Ursula Elizabeth was sent as a teacher to replace Sister Evelyn. Sister Lucy returned home because of age and health in 1969.

The school had grown over the years. The student body now reflected the total population of Hawaii, including not only people of Hawaiian blood, but also Chinese, Japanese, and all the immigrant groups that had come over the years, especially England and the United States. There was a large group from the American military families. Many of these preferred to send their daughters to a private school where the English was of better quality than in the public schools. A number of teachers at the Priory were alumnae who had finished their education at the University of Hawaii. Military dependents were not allowed to get paying jobs in the Islands because of the economics, but teachers were an exception if the school could show that it really needed teachers of certain subjects. So the Priory had a very good group of teachers who were military dependents. There were also experienced teachers who had retired from the public schools. The purpose remained the same, to provide Christian leaders for the people of Hawaii.

It had become chiefly a college prep school. In Hawaii of 1867, marriage was the only respectable career for girls of good family, and the Priory was founded to teach them to be good wives and mothers. By 1918 more and more women were becoming teachers, nurses and secretaries, and the school prepared students for these occupations. After 1941, with the close of the boarding department, a day school was enlarged, for that filled a greater need. Something of the old family spirit remained, however, as the Sisters endeavored to instill in their pupils and in the other teachers the ideal of "Christian community". Priory graduates have included the first medical social worker in Hawaii and the first woman elected to the State legislature. Some Priory graduates have gone on to further education and professions. In 1970, when the Sisters withdrew from the Priory, the faculty included several alumnae.

In 1969 the Sisters turned over administration of the Priory to the Diocese and the Rev. Fred Minuth became the new headmaster. Sister Eva Dorothea and Sister Monica left to return home in

August, 1971, just after Sister Monica had completed the requirements for a Master's degree in history from the University of Hawaii. Her thesis was *The History of St. Andrew's Priory*, during its first 50 years. Sister Ursula asked permission to stay another year to complete a course in counseling that she was taking at the University of Hawaii.

There was one more great celebration for the Sisters. Soon after they had left, the Main Building of the School was rebuilt and refurbished and renamed in honor of Bishop Harry Sherbourne Kennedy and Katherine Kittle Kennedy. The service of dedication was celebrated by the Rt. Rev. Edmond L. Browning, Bishop of Hawaii, successor to Bishop Hanchett.

THE SISTERS OF THE TRANSFIGURATION IN CALIFORNIA

Part I: 1943-1970

Since the founding of the Community in 1898, its works and ministries have adapted to changing needs and circumstances while adhering to its stated common purpose: the praise, the glory and the love of God manifested in a life wholly dedicated to prayer and service. The Sisters have had a ministry on the West Coast from 1943 to the present. The Sisters lived and worked in Santa Rosa from 1943—1953, in San Mateo from 1953—1970. The Sisters administered St. Dorothy's Rest from 1943 to September, 1970.

In 1942 the Sisters were invited to the Diocese of California by Bishop Karl M. Block to administer St. Dorothy's Rest as a children's camp and retreat center. The camp is located in the Coast Range mountains west of Santa Rosa. Although it is physically within the Diocese of Northern California it is owned by the Diocese of California. St. Dorothy's Rest was founded in 1901 by Mrs. James Otis Lincoln in memory of her deceased daughter, Dorothy. It was begun as a convalescent vacation home for poor children from San Francisco. She was its director until her retirement in 1943. It was her wish that 'those Sisters in the blue habits' would continue the work.

The Community responded affirmatively to Bishop Block's invitation to administer St. Dorothy's Rest. On March 15, 1943, with great excitement and joy, Sister Clara and Sister Madeline Mary left by train to begin the new ministry of the Community in California.. Sister Marjorie Hope joined them a short time later. She says, "I was thrilled because where I grew up in Kansas there weren't mountains and it was the first time I had ever seen mountains."

Sister Clara Elizabeth was the recently retired Superior of the Community. Almost immediately on her arrival in California she began building and carving an altar for the Sisters' oratory at St. Dorothy's. Sister Clara also began raising chickens and rabbits to help with wartime food shortages at the camp. Sister Madeleine wrote: "She bought 12 New Hampshire red pullets. One is on the invalid list, but from the remaining 11 we get 5 to 10 eggs a day—not bad for those so young." The Sisters also soon had a garden producing some vegetables—not an easy feat on those very steep hillsides and with competition from the deer.

The Sisters quickly plunged into summer activities as children began to arrive for the summer camp program. For the most part they were underprivileged girls from the cities. Sister Clara wrote: "Our houses are full to overflowing with children and guests. The appreciation that is being expressed continually makes us feel how very worth-while a work it is. Tired and ailing bodies find such a perfect rest."

Lydia House, a large airy building on a cliff overlooking the valley and hills, had been built in the 1920's as a vacation home for "women of small means" who needed a low cost place where they could enjoy the country. Sister Clara wrote that the women staying there are confined to indoor life in the city and they enjoy every minute up here. They love the peace and quiet of the place, the church services and the children's daily entertainments. Sister Clara was already looking forward to converting another recently acquired building to a "rest house for women who would like to do their own housekeeping and pay very little rent." After the camp season ended, the Sisters hosted conferences for clergy and lay persons from both dioceses.

Their first winter was very difficult. The Sisters had hoped to be able to establish a home for girls somewhat similar to Bethany Home, the original work of the Community in Cincinnati. Ten girls below the eighth grade who were court cases stayed on with them after camp was over and lived with them through the winter. Each day the girls had to walk down and back up the steep, narrow road to Camp Meeker to go to school. At one point during the winter there were five days and nights of rain—a total of 14 inches. The houses were damp and not winterized.

Everyone was miserable with the cold and isolation. With no care, and because of the weather, the Sisters were not able to get to church in Santa Rosa on Sundays, but they were gratified that they were able to hear the services on the radio each Sunday from the Church of the Incarnation. Sr. Clara wrote: "We joined in with the hymns, psalms and listened to the lessons and Fr. Farlander's sermon. It was a lovely service and it meant a lot to us in our isolation."

Colds and flu swept through the household. On December 2, 1943, Sister Marjorie wrote: "We finally had to send two of our girls over to the hospital in Sebastopol yesterday…I went over with them and spent the day. Last night Sister Clara tended to the children through the night, so as to let me rest…Today is the first day I have felt the effects of all this. I was extremely exhausted, but happy. The nurse at the hospital, when I went to see the children, told me I wouldn't get it, if I've gone on this long. This is the first time in my life I haven't caught something like this right at the beginning. Sister Clara still can't believe I'm up, around and on two feet and not even coughing." Everyone recovered, but the experience showed the impracticality of trying to maintain a work at St. Dorothy's the year round.

In January, 1944, Mother Olivia Mary visited the Sisters at St. Dorothy's. Together they made the decision that they could not continue to spend winters there, and that the idea of a children's home was not realistic. They would need some place else to live. Later that spring, Fr. Farlander, the rector of the Church of the Incarnation in Santa Rosa, proposed that the Sisters be given the use of a small, eight-room cottage owned by the parish at 622 Cherry Street which had been used for the Church School. The vestry agreed to repair and paint the house and see that the plumbing was in working order. The Woman's Auxiliary volunteered to furnish the house throughout and the Community of the Transfiguration supplied funds to create a chapel in one of the bedrooms. The Sisters were to take entire charge of the Religious Education of the children of the parish and do parish visiting in the environs of Santa Rosa. Santa Rosa is in the Diocese of Northern California, but Bishop Noel Porter expressed an enthusiastic invitation for the Sisters to live and work in his diocese. The house and the chapel were dedicated by Bishop Porter on December 9, 1944. So the Sisters began the pattern of spending summers at St. Dorothy's and winters in Santa Rosa.

They began a preschool in Santa Rosa as well as overseeing all of the religious education. They all did parish visiting and participated in all aspects of the congregation's life. Some friction did develop between Fr. Farlander and Bishop Block over the use of Sisters' time as the Bishop wanted them to stay at St. Dorothy's into the fall to host conferences and retreats while Fr. Farlander was anxious to have them at the parish to begin Church School in September. This was resolved between them and the Sisters divided their time between the camp and the parish during the fall.

The Sisters settled into the pattern of working in Incarnation Parish during the fall and winter with some of them returning to St. Dorothy's to administer the conference season and camp. A number of different Sisters lived and worked in Santa Rosa during the ten years. Each one contributed to the life and ministry with her own gifts. There were usually four Sisters in residence in the little house.

The war came close to St. Dorothy's in June of 1944. The Sisters were at breakfast in the St. Dorothy's House, the main building, when they were startled by the roar of an airplane motor. Sr. Clara wrote: "We were having breakfast when there was a deafening roar right above us. A moment later there was an explosion and the house shook as though there had been an earthquake, and the roar of the airplane ceased. Immediately we heard that the plane had hit the tall redwood trees between St. Dorothy's House and the Lincoln House porch and that the tops of these trees were bent over...The Air Force plane was found about 200 yards from here... smashed to pieces, and the pilot, a second lieutenant, was killed." Sister Marjorie added: "If the plane had come just a few feet closer, there is no doubt that we should all have left this unhappy world in a hurry. We certainly gave thanks for our deliverance."

After nearly three years of imprisonment, Sister Marjorie's sister, Beth, was released from the Japanese internment camp in the spring of 1945. While she was interred she had met and fallen in love with John Renning, also a prisoner of war. When the couple came to visit for a day in May, Sister Marjorie engineered an impromptu wedding in the Sisters' Chapel. What a time of thanksgiving, reunion and celebration!

In 1951, Sister Marjorie reluctantly left California to help found a new ministry in Ponce, Puerto Rico. Her sunny disposition and great gifts for working with young children were greatly missed and she was remembered with great affection.

Very soon after the Sisters began their ministry in California, a number of lay women became Associates of the Community. The women joined the Sisters by observing a rule of life which was designed to fit their situation in life. They were linked to the Sisters' life and ministry in prayer and mutual support. The Sisters' ministry would not be possible without their loyal support. Winn Osborn, Alice Havner and Dr. Lois Roberts were first among a great many Associates of the Community on the West Coast.

In 1951, Sister Lioba Katherine, a former social worker and missionary, took over the administration of St. Dorothy's Rest. Under her dynamic leadership, the camp and retreat center grew and flourished. Many people remember her with awe and fondness. She lived with the Sisters in San Mateo during the winter and spent the rest of the year at St. Dorothy's. She retired in 1967. In April 1967, Sister Alice Lorraine was appointed by Sister Esther, then the Superior of the Community, to succeed Sister Lioba.

In January of 1952, Fr. Arthur Farlander's sudden death shocked and saddened the parish. The Sisters especially felt the loss. He had been instrumental in bringing them to Santa Rosa and they had worked closely together. Following his death, some tensions arose in the parish, and in 1953, in spite of petitions signed by the vestry and members of the congregation asking them to remain, it seemed wise for the Sisters to accept an invitation to administer St. Matthew's Parish Day School in San Mateo, California. They did continue the leadership at St. Dorothy's Rest and administered the growing retreat and conference programs there until their withdrawal in September, 1970.

Part II: 1980–Present

After spending ten years in an intense period of reviewing its life and ministries, the Community wished to reach out again to areas further from Cincinnati, and particularly, to revive the ministry in California. Sister Alice and Sister Teresa were appointed by Mother Louise and the Council to begin a new ministry in the Diocese of Northern California, ministering to the spiritual needs of people on the west coast. They named the ministry the "West Coast Ministry." In September of 1980, they arrived in Ferndale, a Victorian village, some twenty miles south of the city of Eureka on the northern coast of California. From there they traveled to various parishes and missions to be with the people in their own setting, to conduct workshops, preach and teach, and meet with various groups within a parish. This also provided opportunity to be able to share in some of the joys, pains, sorrows and struggles of people in more than a cursory way. A key part of the ministry was and is with Associates. Besides the planning of two retreats a year for the Associates, there are numerous other contacts and involvements with our Associates. Serving on Diocesan commissions, the Episcopal Church Women (ECW) Board, the Cursillo group, the deanery Clericus and Diocesan Conventions are other ways that keep the Sisters abreast with life in the Church. In 1993, Sister Alice was elected Superior of the Community and returned to the Mother House. Sister Lydia Magdalene was sent to join Sister Teresa in the ministry. At the end of her term, Sister Alice joyfully returned to Ferndale, but because of the smallness of the house, the three Sisters moved to a new and larger house in Eureka. This also gave them the opportunity to make hospitality a major part of their ministry. They continued to be active in the life of the diocese and in the life of the local parish church in Eureka, serving as Eucharistic Ministers and Visitors. Sister Lydia was active with a Bible storytelling group. She was also a mentor of Education for Ministry groups. Unfortunately, Sister Lydia's health declined, and she returned to the Mother House. She died in 2006. In the very early days of the ministry, the Sisters began and hosted a meditation group. This group still gathers one Saturday a month at the Sisters' house. It celebrated its 29th year in May of 2011.

In June of 2008 came another change. Sister Teresa was elected Superior of the Community. Sister Diana Dorothea, who was and still is the editor of the Transfiguration Quarterly, came to join Sister Alice in the West Coast Ministry. The ministry continues to serve the Church and those whom we meet through our life of prayer and through the gifts of the particular Sisters involved.

In the word of our Foundress, Mother Eva Mary, "Life is the gift of God to us, full of promise and opportunities. What we make of life is our gift back to God."

ST. SIMON OF CYRENE AND ST. MONICA'S CENTER
LINCOLN HEIGHTS, OHIO

St. Simon's Mission began during what is called the "Great Depression." In the 1920s a number of African-American families had arrived from the crowded West End of Cincinnati in an area north of Lockland and east of Woodlawn. This settlement was called Woodlawn Terrace. It was later known as Lincoln Heights. Small houses were built and streets laid out. A few small stores were started. As the Depression began and deepened many persons became unemployed and many families became impoverished.

As the Sisters drove past on their way to and from Cincinnati they became conscious of the poverty and lack of churches. Mother Beatrice said, "Something ought to be done." With the help of Associates and friends they raised money to buy a small two-story frame building. The house was fitted out for mission work—a large first floor room as the Chapel and meeting room, a kitchen, and on the second floor a small room for group meetings, a good sized storeroom, and the bathroom. Underneath the house was a good sized furnace room. There were two lots in addition to the one upon which the house stood. At the back of the second lot was a small garage. The house was called "The Mission House of St. Simon of Cyrene."

A service of dedication was planned. Before the day of the service, several Sisters visited the neighborhood, telling the people of the work being planned. The first service was Solemn Evensong on the Eve of Mother Foundress' Day, February 8th, 1931. The Rev.

Gerald Lewis, Chaplain of the Mother House in Glendale, was the Celebrant. Canon Gilbert Symons preached the sermon, his topic being St. Simon of Cyrene. The first floor rooms were crowded with adults and children. It was announced that there would be a regular Sunday service and that certain activities would be started. The first Mass was on the following morning.

A church school was begun on Sunday mornings and in the afternoon there was a service of Evensong. On Saturday morning a sewing school for women and girls was held with Sister Lydia Margaret, an unusually gifted sewing teacher, in charge.

In May Sister Olivia Mary, who had returned from eleven years as head of St. Andrew's Priory in Hawaii, was placed in charge of the Mission Work. Sister Mary Catherine, her blood sister, and Miss Esther Fifield, a postulant, were appointed as her assistants. A Ford, called the 'Sibus', was given for their use in traveling between Glendale and Woodlawn Terrace. As the work increased, several other Sisters also helped.

The first large activity of the Sisters was a four week Vacation Bible School in July. Sister Mary Catherine taught the primary group in the small upstairs room, Miss Esther the intermediate group (which was the largest) in the first floor room, and Sister Olivia the seniors, in the furnace room. They were assisted by three Bethany Home girls. Sister Olivia was in charge of the "snack period". Sixty children attended the Vacation Bible School, enjoying the religious lessons, a handicraft period, and the recreation.

Following the Vacation Bible School, many of those who had attended began to come to the church services. In September, 1931, the Rev. Arthur Wilson was called by the Sisters to serve as priest at the Mission, which had been registered with the Diocese of Southern Ohio as the (unorganized) Mission of St. Simon of Cyrene. The garage was enlarged and a second story added. Father

Wilson was able to lodge in the upstairs apartment of the garage, and the building became known as the Hermitage. Later the garage section was renovated into a good-sized meeting room.

Father Wilson was a tireless and dynamic leader. Besides Sunday Eucharist he began a week-day evening meeting with a short service, community singing and religious instruction. This became very popular and soon the attendance became so large that not only the first floor rooms were filled but both children and adults sat on the stairs leading to the second floor. An instruction class was started and soon Father began a daily Mass with six to fifteen being present.

There was no good public school available at that time and the Sisters started a small primary day school with a kindergarten taught by Sister Mary Catherine, a trained kindergarten teacher. Miss Esther taught the first grade. Sister Olivia was the principal, with her office was in the kitchen. She also taught a deaf girl, aged 9, who had difficulties in the public school, and an older girl who, because of almost complete blindness, had never attended school. The Sisters served a light nutritious snack to all of the children and administered a teaspoon of cod liver oil to each child. The children liked the small lunch; they did not like the cod liver oil, even though Sister called it "liquid sunshine" and extolled its virtues.

Group of four children.

With the first grade room on the first floor being used for church services and club activities, there was a great deal of moving of furniture. Mr. George West was janitor. At the very beginning of the Mission he had asked the Sisters if he could bring his Boy Scout Troup, #277, to the Mission House, and from that time it became St. Simon's Troop. This troop and the Women's Auxiliary were the first two Church organizations to use the Mission House.

It was obvious that a church building was needed, and in 1932 Mrs. Mortimer Matthews offered $10,000 for its construction. Her son, Stanley Matthews, an architect, designed a crypt church to be built next to the Mission House. Mr. James Hunter and Mr. Walter Espy, residents of Lincoln Heights, were hired as contractors. They were assisted by Mr. Hunter's sons and a number of other residents. They all had been out of work, so to help the Church, they offered to work for pay one day and give their services the second day. Almost all of those helping to build the Church later became active Communicants.

This very attractive Church, with a fine altar and beautiful picture of Jesus behind it, together with its pews and a small pump organ, was completed by the second anniversary of the Mission. On Mother Foundress' Day, February 9, 1932, a sung Mass was celebrated, and the Church was consecrated (it being free from debt). A class of fifty, children and adults, was baptized. It was a thrilling service and the congregation filled the Church. Many of the Sisters and interested Associates and friends were present. Three days later, on February 12th, a class of 36 adults and young people received the Sacrament of Confirmation. The Rt. Rev. Henry Hobson, Bishop of Southern Ohio, performed the ceremony. The first class was named St. Mary's Class. Succeeding classes took other Saint's names.

The Crypt Church was the beginning of a series of projects Mrs. Matthews originated to help the people of Woodlawn Terrace. Property was purchased reaching from the church grounds to the corner of Independence and Chester Road, and four two-family homes were built to house families with low incomes. At the beginning a four room house rented for four dollars a week and a five room house for five dollars. On the lots on the other side of Independence Street five attractive brick houses were built to be sold at a modest price. Mr. James Watts, one of the Assistant Superintendents in the Cincinnati Schools, was one of the first to take advantage of these homes. Mr. and Mrs. Watts became active members of St. Simon's Mission in many capacities.

Another aspect of the work in these first years was that of social service. Because of the Depression, many families were without the needed income to provide food, utilities and other necessities. Sister Olivia and Father Wilson were untiring in their efforts to help. They applied to the Director of the Cincinnati Hall (the first welfare office in Cincinnati, which was in Robinson's Opera House) for aid. St. Simon's was appointed as a station for the distribution of relief commodities with Father Wilson stored supplies in the Hermitage so the families could receive food. Sister Olivia spent much time taking sick people in to the General Hospital or securing help to get children into the Episcopal Children's Hospital and some adults into Christ Hospital. There was also the need to contact various city agencies. As the day school was limited to a morning session, much of Sister Olivia's time was spent in helping families and individuals in need.

In 1933 the Rev. Charles England, an African-American priest, joined St. Simon's staff. This was fortunate because Father Wilson became ill and had to resign from the Mission. Father England carried on the work by himself until the Rev. Westwell Greenwood became Vicar in May, 1935. Father Wilson's contribution to the Mission was immense, and the majority of those he instructed for Confirmation have remained faithful to St. Simon's, providing fine leadership throughout the years. In 1938 Father England accepted a call to a church in the East, and left St. Simon's.

In 1932–33 the St. Simon's Primary Day School added a second grade, with Sister Louise Magdalene as teacher. The second grade room was in the basement, the furnace and pipes causing some difficulties. Sister Louise left for our work in China in 1934, and Sister Dorothea Mary became second grade teacher. Miss Fannie Piersawl became the first grade teacher in September, 1933, replacing Sister Esther Mary (formerly Miss Esther) who began to work with the boys and girls of the Mission. Mrs. Matthews had purchased a Lodge building, an old farmhouse, and a Young People's Recreation Center was opened there in May, 1935 This is the beginning of the work at St. Monica's House which still continues.

Father Westwell Greenwood, who succeeded Father Wilson in 1935, was especially interested in the Cooperative Movement. Soon after his arrival he began a cooperative store, having foodstuffs in his apartment in the Hermitage. As the business grew and St. Simon's people began to take advantage of it, it was moved to a small store on Adams Street.

Father Robert Dickerson, who followed Father Greenwood in 1937, had been a missionary in Africa before accepting the work at St. Simon's. He was a fine musician and raised the level of congregational music during his short tenure. His wife had been a field secretary of the National Women's Auxiliary and she aided Sister Olivia with the women's work of the Mission. One lasting contribution of the Dickersons was the beautiful statue of St. Mary and Child as a shrine in the Church. The statute had been carved in Africa with a native woman and baby as models.

When the Rev. John Burgess became resident priest in January, 1938, the Mission which had been somewhat at a standstill during the period of two short-term priests, became very active again. Father Burgess later became the Diocesan Bishop of the Diocese of Massachusetts, one of the first African-American priests to head an Episcopal diocese. He was an unusually gifted priest and pastor. Father Burgess was especially instrumental in drawing young people—teenagers and young married couples—into the Church. St. Simon's again flourished as it had in the days of Father Wilson. He revived the Sunday School, started new organizations such as the Young Churchmen, the Young Peoples' Fellowship (a lively group of young married couples) and the St. Simon's Council. The Council consisted of the officers and leaders of the Boy Scouts, the Girl Reserves, the Young Churchmen, the Young People's Fellowship, the Church School, St. Monica's Band, the Acolytes and the St. Monica's Hobby Clubs. The activities carried on were many—plays, pageants, operettas, retreats, tournaments, parties such as the Shrove Tuesday Pancake Supper, and tournaments with outside groups. Many community activities also were sponsored and Father Burgess took an active part in the life of Woodlawn Terrace.

It was also during Father Burgess' seven years at St. Simon's that the parish newspaper, "The Woodlawn Post", was started under his and Sister Esther's supervision. Franklin Shands, who later became an art teacher and football coach at Princeton High School, was the chief worker, contributing both art and contents.

Boy Scouts at St. Simon's Mission.

Sister Olivia was elected Superior of the Community of the Transfiguration in June, 1943. Sister Esther was appointed Sister-in-charge of the Sisters' work at St. Simon's and St. Monica's Houses. Her term was short, as in 1945 she was one of the Sisters chosen to start work in Puerto Rico. In 1946 Father Burgess resigned as Vicar of St. Simon's Mission to become the Episcopal Chaplain at Howard University in Washington D.C. Sister Evelyn Ancilla was appointed Sister-in-charge of the Mission work and the Rev. C. Edward Harrison became Vicar of St. Simon's. From that time the emphasis of the Sisters' work became more centered on the St. Simon's Day School, although many of the other activities were carried on.

St. Simon's Day School

On January 1, 1947, the area known as Woodlawn Terrace became incorporated as Lincoln Heights. Many of the St. Simon's members aided in the process of incorporation. It was in this year that the third grade was added to the school, using the room on the second floor of St. Monica's House, as a clubroom. Father Harrison aided the Sisters with the School, continuing the daily Service in the Church which Sister Olivia had started in 1931.

In 1948 a fourth grade was begun, in 1949 a fifth grade, and in 1950, the sixth grade. Sister Winifred Agnes became Principal in 1944 when Sister Evelyn was transferred to St. Andrew's Priory in Hawaii. The tuition of the Day School which had started with $2.00 a year in 1945 was raised to $15.00 a year. By 1950 the enrollment had increased to 157 students, and there was a faculty of four Sisters and three lay teachers.

With the increase in the size of the School and in the number of grades, almost all of St. Monica's House had to used. With the added seventh and eighth grades using the Hermitage, the need for additional space for the School became very evident. In May of 1951 a campaign was launched at the Diocesan Convention for the expansion of the school facilities. The planning and work for it was under the direction of the Diocesan Board of Missions. According to the Community of the Transfiguration's Annual Report of June, 1951, the plans for the addition to the School section of the building included erection of a first unit to include school rooms adequate for an eighth grade elementary school and a second unit to provide a gymnasium, plus rooms for home economics, a workshop and a cafeteria. The second unit was never completed.

Although by 1952 there were 188 students crowded into the existing facilities, the first unit of four new school rooms had to be postponed for another year. The cost was prohibitive and more money had to be raised in the interim. On July 6, 1953, the groundbreaking for the new addition took place, and in December, 1954, the third through sixth grade classes moved in. The new unit was blessed by the Bishop on January 17, 1954. This was an occasion of great thanksgiving. The addition of four school rooms released space for a school library. However, the seventh and eighth grades had to be housed in St. Monica's House. Various school activities to enrich the curriculum were added during the years of the school's expansion. The Bookmobile of the Cincinnati Public Library was one of the first of these and it continued to serve the school from 1947 until the school closed.

The Visiting Nursing Service provided by the County Board of Health provided a Round Up Clinic for new students, plus a physical examination by a physician or the first, fourth and seventh grade students. In the fall of 1951 season tickets for the Children's Theatre were secured. One of the school projects in which the entire student body participated was an Operetta: "Station Cloudville", in 1950. It was presented in the Wayne School Auditorium in Lockland.

In 1953 the St. Simon's School held its first Graduation Service, with twelve boys and girls graduating from the eighth grade. The Service was held on Sunday evening in St. Simon's Church.

The custom of holding a church service at the beginning of each school day was followed throughout the years. Of the 185 students in 1953-54, 102 were baptized members of the Mission and 39 had been confirmed. Daily religious instruction was carried out under the supervision of Sister Virginia Cecelia., the Sister-in-charge after Sister Winifred Agnes had been transferred to St. Andrew's Priory. In 1954—55 a Student Council was formed with representatives from each grade as members. The Council aided in planning events and improving school spirit.

By 1954—55 the Staff consisted of four Sisters and five secular teaches. The tuition was gradually increased to help pay the salaries of the secular staff. In 1954 Father James Fleming succeeded Father Harrison, who resigned to become the Assistant Rector in St. Philip's Church, New York City. Father Harrison and his wife, Ruth Chapman Harrison, continued to maintain their interest in the Mission.

In 1956—57 Sister Emily Francis became Principal of St. Simon's School. That year had a record enrollment of 204 students. Among that year's activities was a Passion Play which was presented in the Church. The Primary grades gave an operetta at the Lincoln Heights Elementary School. The School Band, under Mr. Theodore Turner, performed on several occasions. The P.T.A. participated actively, supporting the Sisters in their various activities.

During the year 1957-58 the School had its "ups and downs." This was partly due to the fact that Father Fleming left in August, 1957, and Father Carlisle Ramsharan, a Jamaican priest, did not become vicar until October of 1958. The enrollment of the school was 215. Fifteen students graduated and all entered High School in the Fall.

Due to the fire hazard in the upstairs room in St. Monica's House, a fifth room was added for the eighth grade, providing a fine, airy room and additional storeroom space. A May Festival was given in the spring of 1960; the profits were used to buy new books for the enlarged library.

In 1960 there was small drop in enrollment and only three Sisters could be assigned to the School. Sister Theodora became Principal in the fall of 1960. The kindergarten was reduced to one session for five year olds. Miss Fannie Piersawl celebrated her 25th Anniversary in 1962. A new feature of this year was the adoption of a school uniform, a navy blue pleated jumper with white blouse for the girls and blue trousers with white shirt for the boys.

In her report of 1963 Sister Theodora said that of the 224 student enrolled, the primary grades were the largest. St. Simon's kindergarten was the only one in the area, and enrollment had to be limited. Priority was given to those children having brothers and sisters in the school. In 1963—64 there were only two Sisters besides Sister Theodora in the school. Seven lay teachers aided the Sisters. It was in June of 1963 that Sister Esther became Superior of the Community. Every effort was made to keep the academic standards high. Teachers were encouraged to participate in workshops, attend lectures and visit other schools. The cultural enrichment was furthered by the children's attendance at the Cincinnati Symphony, the Children's Theatre, and participation in field trips.

The Rev. James Francis, who became Vicar of St. Simon's in 1964, served as Superintendent of the school for the year 1964-65. One third of the student population belonged to St. Simon's. Many students were members of the Baptist Church, while some were unchurched. The Diocese of Southern Ohio helped to support the school so that the tuition could be kept at a nominal amount. As in its beginning the chief objectives of the school were to train the children in Christian citizenship and to educate them in the fundamental skills of learning, with special emphasis on training them to study and do creative thinking.

The dropping of seventh and eighth grades in the year 1966—67 and the raising of the tuition, caused a loss of fifty pupils, so that the enrollment was only 135. By this time the Lincoln Heights School district had been incorporated in the Princeton School district. The seventh and eighth grade pupils attended Princeton

Junior High School, an excellent school. St. Simon's School curriculum added French in grades four through six and introduced art and handicraft classes twice a week and choral music in all of the grades.

A change in 1967—68 was the introduction of specialized classes in grades four through six with one teacher for art and religion and another for each of the classes for math, English, and social studies. The classes in the year 1968—69 ranged in size from fifteen to twenty students making specialized teaching possible. Also, through government funds, the school was able to purchase valuable visual aid equipment and materials. There was also a government Head Start School started, using the rooms in St. Monica's House, providing for needed help with pre-school children.

The next year only two Sisters could be spared to work in the day school. Sister Theodora as Sister-in-charge and fourth grade teacher, and another Sister as teacher of remedial reading; Miss Fannie Piersawl was acting Principal, and Father Francis assisted with the religious education classes.

It was during this year, 1969—70, that the Evaluating Chapter of the Community decided to close the day school, while continuing the work at St. Monica's House. Among the reasons were: 1) the difficulty of providing Sisters for teaching, 2) the fact that the Princeton District had excellent schools, 3) the increasing financial problems and 4) the necessity of maintaining the high educational standards of up-to-date equipment. When announced to the parents, there was a plea for the school to continue at least one more year. It was decided that the closing date would be 1970—71. The last year of the school proved to be a very successful one, according to Sister Laura who became Sister-in-charge in the fall of 1970. There were 100 students and nine faculty members. The educational program was many-sided: academic work, field trips, one of which was an overnight trip to the Ford Museum and plant in Detroit, and many special Services and programs. Black History Week and Martin Luther King Day were observed. The closing graduation service was a sad time for all. Marvin Stenson, a former pupil, and an outstanding community leader was the speaker at the service.

Throughout the forty years of its existence St. Simon's Day School not only helped in the education of hundreds of children but trained many for leadership in Lincoln Heights and elsewhere. John Marvin Evans, a first grade pupil in 1931, went on to college and seminary to become the first Episcopal priest from St. Simon's Mission. He served as a Chaplain in the Navy for many years, and when he retired from the Navy he was in charge of St. Barbara's Mission in California until his untimely death in 1986. Samuel Mays, another in the 1931 first grade, became a Lincoln Heights Councilman and was active in civic affairs. LaVerne Mitchell has several times served as Mayor of Lincoln Heights. Willis Hollaway and Eddie Starr were prominent in the educational field. Perhaps the best known is Nicki Giovanni, who has excelled as a poet and in other artistic accomplishments. Of course, the most important result was the forming of Christian character in the lives of many, and the providing of Christian leadership in the community and in the Church.

The St. Simon's Sunday School

Although the St. Simon's Day School had become the major work of the Sisters in the years 1946 to 1971, other mission activities were carried on during that time. The St. Simon's Sunday School was the second focus, and this fitted into the existing circumstances. The Sunday School had began during the early days of the Mission and in 1940 had a membership of over 170. Under

Father Burgess and the Sisters it continued to flourish. In 1946-47 four of the St. Simon's High School girls aided the Sisters with their classes.

Among those who directed the school after both Sister Olivia and Sister Esther were withdrawn were Sisters Evelyn, Theodora, Winifred, Virginia, Althea and Laura. Gradually the lay people were able to take over most of the classes, and by 1965 there were no Sisters helping with the Sunday School. However, in 1972 Father Golden the new Rector, asked the Sisters to help in the development of the curriculum and to serve as advisors to the teaching staff. Unfortunately during the 70's there was a rapid turnover of priests in charge of the Mission, and gradually the Sisters again lost close touch with the Sunday School and with the Mission itself.

This was true until 1983 when Father Michael Curry became Priest-in-charge. In 1984 and 1985 a Church School was started at St. Monica's House for the children of the Mission and the St. Monica's Center members. It was held one Saturday a month for four hours, including a Service, religious classes and a lunch in the St. Simon's parish hall. Father Curry was director. Three Sisters helped with the School; the remaining staff was composed of St. Simon's members. Interestingly, all but one of these were members of early St. Simon's families, whose parents had been active during the years when Father Burgess was the Mission Priest. The School began during the morning and closed with a brief meeting after lunch. After three years this plan was discontinued and a Sunday School, which was held in the Parish Hall of St. Simon's Mission, was begun for the St. Simon's children. St. Monica's Recreation Center continued to provide recreational and other kinds of activities for the youngsters in Lincoln Heights and nearby areas.

St. Monica's Recreation Center

St. Monica's Recreation Center has actually had the longest existence of any phase of the Sisters' work in Lincoln Heights, with the exception of the Church itself. From 1935 on, the Recreation Center has had a continued existence even though the use for the facilities was greatly curtailed during the growth of St. Simon's Day School. For 55 years it has been a Center for the use of the children and young people of Lincoln Heights. Miss Susie Pitts had been the Center's Hostess in the Lodge. After the move to St. Monica's House her place was taken by Mrs. Mary Reed, who remained as hostess until her death in 1957.

As an outgrowth of the work with young people begun by Sister Esther in 1933, it was first located in a Lodge building on Independence Street. Sister Esther began hobby clubs, handicrafts, folk dancing, sports and music, which met in the upstairs room of the building. The downstairs room was fitted out for informal recreation, ping pong tables, table games, as well as books for reading.

The Recreation Center's use of the Lodge was a temporary measure as Mrs. Matthews, in 1935, had purchased a large farm house surrounded by spacious grounds to be given to the Sisters to serve as a Recreation Center, facilities for the day school, and a place for the Church activities. The renovation of the house, and the addition of three cement block school rooms, the building of two tennis courts, and other facilities were in process when, on December 15th, 1935, the Lodge Recreation Building caught fire and burned to the ground. The Sisters were at a Women's Auxiliary meeting in the Mission House when the fire started at 2:30 P.M. Had it begun a half hour later, the boys and girls of the Folk Dancing Hobby Club would have been trapped in the upstairs room.

The new house had been a farmhouse before the area was settled. It was perhaps fifty years old and was a charming house with stained glass windows, a spiral staircase and beautiful woodwork. Its large grounds adjoined the St. Simon's Mission grounds. Mrs. Matthews had three schoolrooms for the small St. Simon's day school added to the rear of the building. Even though building and renovations were still going on, the Recreation Center was moved into the first floor of what was now called St. Monica's Center. The large hall served as the entrance to the Center, with equipment for the hostess, a radio, and lounging chairs. A ping pong table was placed in the sitting-room, and tables for small games in the dining room. A shuffleboard court was painted on the large porch of the house. The kitchen was used by Church groups as well as by the Center. Upstairs the double front room was prepared for parochial meeting and activities and for the Hobby Clubs. A smaller upstairs room served as an office for the Sister-in-charge. On the third floor a very attractive apartment was made, at first for the residence of Father Greenwood, a single priest, and later on as a place for Sisters working at St. Monica's.

The name "St. Monica's" was chosen by Mrs. Matthews for two reasons: first it was in memory of Mrs. Harlan Cleveland, Mother Eva's sister who had chosen the name Sister Monica when she was a Novice in the Community of the Transfiguration. She had to leave because of ill health, and died in 1933. Secondly, St. Monica was the mother of St. Augustine, Bishop of Hippo in Africa, which made her name especially appropriate for a Center for an African-American community.

As the day school began adding grades after 1946, the House was used more and more for the school, and its use for recreational activities had to be limited. The day school used the front rooms of the Center during the school day and the Center used the rooms for afternoon and evening activities, so movement of furniture and equipment was necessary every school day. When the upstairs clubroom was converted into a class room, the parish activities were cancelled. The Hobby Clubs were disbanded and the number of children using the Center became smaller.

The outdoor recreation, however, continued to flourish. In 1946 Mrs. Matthews purchased a large field adjoining St. Monica's House to be used as a baseball diamond. This added to the tennis courts and playground next to St. Simon's Church, provided a fine out door area. In 1946 under the stimulus of Sister Evelyn, a Recreation Council formed to administer the recreation program. During the succeeding summers the Council carried on an extensive program of baseball, basketball, tennis and boxing. The Council continued until 1958. In 1966 the Lincoln Heights Recreation Department, under the Anti-Poverty Program, took over the supervision of the grounds and employed seventeen young people to help in recreational activities. The addition of a Head Start Program using the indoor St. Monica's facilities, already limited by the day school uses, caused the closing of the indoor recreational program from 1969 until 1971, when the day school closed. Shortly after the closing of St. Simon's Elementary School in 1970, the Sisters decided continue to use St. Monica's building as a recreation center as it had been in the early 1930s when Sister Esther and many other Sisters ministered in Lincoln Heights. At this time the Church and its property were turned over to the Diocese of Southern Ohio while the property of St. Monica's House and its property were retained by the Sisters.

Sister Laura was assigned to be in charge of the ministry at St. Monica's House in 1971. She resumed the work of recreation, converting the downstairs school rooms into the Recreation Center. The children using this center grew from a handful to an average of 35. The furniture, materials and equipment were utilized and new recreation equipment added. The Head Start Program continued to use the front rooms while the Lincoln Heights Recreation Department continued to use the outdoor facilities. However, shortly afterwards Sister Laura left to take additional studies at Trinity School for Ministry in Ambridge, Pennsylvania. St. Monica's House then became the charge of Sister Virginia and Sister Alice. They were assisted by Mrs. Doris Thomas who had worked for several years with Sister Laura.

For a long time Sister Olivia Mary, a niece of our Mother Foundress, faithfully assisted a great many children, adults and families in Lincoln Heights with a variety of spiritual, medical, educational, housing and other significant needs as well as opportunities for employment. Sister Mary Luke, a Novice in the community at that time, often accompanied and assisted Sister Olivia.

In the late 1970s Sister Mary Luke was assigned to be in charge of the maintenance of the building and property at St. Monica's, and very soon after she was also asked to become responsible for the Recreation Center and the children. While growing up in Canada Sister Mary Luke had spent many enjoyable hours at the Boys' and Girls' Club in Montreal. This experience became invaluable as Sister assumed the responsibility of the ministry in Lincoln Heights in 1978. With the grace of God, the prayers and support of the Community, a fine staff, a myriad of friends, construction workers, benefactors, many helpers and Sister's God-given vision, gifts and spirit, the Center has become a splendid, safe and beautiful Recreation Center for "God's children." Additional rooms were built to provide for more activities for the boys and girls: a doll room in which the younger children could "play house", a resource room where youngsters could read, do homework, learn to use a computer or just be quiet; and an arts and crafts room with a variety of supplies for fun and creativity. Girls and boys, ages six to sixteen, come daily to the center on Monday through Friday afternoons. Attendance varies from thirty to more than one hundred children. They enjoyed ping pong, "foos ball," table games, pool, playing on the basketball court and much more. Time is spent with a staff who cares about them and shares the gifts of listening and encouraging them.

Since the outdoor playground could not be used periodically because of excessive heat, cold and rainy weather, it became evident to Sister Mary Luke that the playground should be located inside a building so that the boys and girls could enjoy it during all seasons of the year. She quickly planned and supervised the construction of a building large enough to house state-of-the-art playground equipment. Sister also envisioned the playground would be designed in such a way that it would "seem" to be outside! Street lights were installed inside, each named for a fruit of the Spirit. An area large enough around the playground equipment makes it possible for fourteen children of "all ages" to enjoy a trip on the "St. Monica's Express," a train built in California and brought to the Center, and of course, there is a train station to begin and end the journey. It was explained to Sister that the gazebo, located outside could not be brought inside, but, as you can imagine, it is a fine addition inside! It was a great delight to Sister Mary Luke when the youngsters began to call the playground "the park." The girls and boys truly consider St. Monica's as "their" Center. Some consider it a safe haven since serious problems with alcohol and drugs. exist in Lincoln Heights and nearby areas, but not at St. Monica's.

In addition to the various daily activities at the Center, Christmas and Easter are special occasions. With many trees beautifully decorated, bright lights, rooms filled with a great variety of all kinds of Christmas decorations and Nativity sets, the Center truly becomes a wonderland for the children. The Christmas party with

St. Mary Luke with children in front of St. Monica's.

entertainment, refreshments and gifts brings great joy to about 200 or more children each year. About the same number of girls and boys enjoy the annual Easter Egg hunt where they receive candy and gifts when they find the plastic eggs—and even if they don't find them. The youngsters who find the golden eggs receive a lovely Bible in addition to candy and gifts. Sister Mary Luke obtains the help of local residents who hide the eggs earlier in the day.

To continue Sister Mary Luke's dream for God's children, she once again followed a vision to establish a place in the country for youngsters to enjoy. "Tabor Cottage," located near an Amish community in northern Ohio, was built so that during the summer different groups of five or six youngsters from the Center can experience a "country vacation" for a week. Along with swimming, horseback riding and other recreational activities, they experience a variety of social and educational opportunities such as coming to know about the Amish people and their way of life, eating in nice restaurants, learning manners, becoming more aware of the importance of making choices, and praying and sharing with each other.

Sister Mary Luke always had an idea, a dream or a plan to make St. Monica's Recreation Center in every way the best place for God's children. It was her hope that with more recreation centers there would be less need for correctional facilities. Sister's fervent prayer and hope are best expressed in her own words:

> "What makes a recreation center is what we are trying to accomplish through this ministry. We are teaching youngsters to love God and to care for and support each other

so they become good citizens. We hope they will learn to appreciate coming to a nice place, to take care of equipment and property, enjoy flowers and landscaping and the opportunity for healthy fellowship," (Sister Mary Luke).

With all that has been and now is, the Sisters pray that with the grace of God, St. Monica's Recreation Center will continue to touch the lives of boys and girls in such a way that they may truly know they are indeed God's children.

PUERTO RICO

In 1945 the Sisters accepted the invitation of Bishop Charles Colmore and his Coadjutor, Bishop Charles Boynton, to work in Ponce, Puerto Rico.

They were asked to work in St. Luke's Episcopal Hospital, the Ponce churches, and the surrounding area. The Bishop primarily wanted the Sisters for their presence, but there was plenty to do. Sister Esther Mary, Sister Julia Margaret, Sister Faith Marguerite, and Sister Marjorie Hope were assigned to begin the work. The Sisters' activities there, mostly conducted in the Spanish language, became widely varied. One Sister did occupational therapy in San Lucas (St. Luke's) hospital. The Sisters participated in Diocesan affairs, retreats, conventions, and the Episcopal Church Women (ECW). Two played the organ and did parish work at the church of St. Mary the Virgin and at Holy Trinity Church, the oldest non-Roman church in Latin America. Holy Trinity School was started by Sister Julia Margaret, who had to return home because of her health. While there, Sister Julia wrote a history of the Church in both Spanish and English. Sister Althea Augustine came to Ponce in 1963 and served as director of Holy Trinity School for nine years.

Other Sisters assigned later to Puerto Rico include Sister Priscilla Jean, Sister Mary Evelyne, Sister Margaret Alice, Sister Mary Veronica, and Sister Ursula Elizabeth.

Dr. Jordan, a St. Luke's doctor who served at the county jail asked them to visit a detention home connected with the jail, the Galera de Menores. Sister Esther started a recreation program for boys in the jail, and it was through this they saw the need for a kind of neighborhood house, particularly for young boys. This led to the foundation of St. Michael's House. It has helped the boys as well as their families, and it developed into St. Michael's Mission. Sister Esther wrote a book about St. Michael's House, *A Spark of Love*, printed in 1988, which is available in the convent library.

Sister Ursula taught nursing at Hospital San Lucas. Sister Margaret Alice worked in the hospital laboratory. Sister Mary Veronica did occupational therapy and worked with men in the prison as did Sister Esther.

When Sister Priscilla, a Deacon, first came she taught English at Holy Trinity School for two years and pre-kindergarten at a little school by Holy Name Church. It was a lovely time and the kids were precious. While she was there she was also in charge of the chapel at St. Luke's where we had two small congregations, English speaking and Spanish speaking. She worked at the hospital as a Chaplain's assistant. She has said how she really loved that work.

From their Convent, the Sisters also helped with social service, The Community at home helped them to provide Christmas gifts for the people, and to supply food and clothing. They helped with rescue work after a flood.

They also frequently had help from volunteer workers from the United States. A volunteer summer worker, Ann Davis, entered the Community, becoming Sister Ann Margaret, and in 1973 she became Superior of the Community. Miss Ruth Clark joined them and became Sister Teresa Ruth. Except for part of her Novitiate Sister Teresa Ruth spent all of her Religious Life in Ponce. She died of cancer in 1959 at a comparatively young age. She is buried in the cemetery in a place called Quebrado Limon in the mountains.

Sister Marjorie worked in Puerto Rico for 33 years except for vacations and furloughs. Sister Esther worked there from the beginning until 1961 when she was called home by Mother Louise to become Assistant Superior. In 1963 Sister Esther was elected to be Superior. She served two five year terms, returned to Puerto Rico in 1973, and remained there until 1984 when the Community decided to withdraw from there.

In August, 1984, Sister Johanna was sent to Puerto Rico to help the two Sisters get ready to leave. They spent the Thanksgiving weekend that year in the Dominican Republic visiting Sister Hilary and Sister Priscilla who had just begun our ministry in San Pedro de Macorís. Sister Esther's eyesight had failed so that she could not longer safely continue to drive so Sister Johanna became the driver for the Sisters with Sister Marjorie as navigator. For many years after the ministry closed, as long as they were physically able, Sister Esther and Sister Marjorie traveled to Puerto Rico to visit and keep up with the Associates there who have loved the Sisters to this day.

After Sister Esther's death the Associates in Puerto Rico commissioned a local artist to carve a wooden statue of St. Michael as a memorial to Sister Esther. The memorial is placed in the Convent, near the entrance to the Oratory. Bishop Reus and several Associates came from Puerto Rico for the dedication.

JAPAN 1955-1979

Work in Japan was considered before World War II began, but in 1940 the Rt. Rev. Norman Binsted, Missionary Bishop in Japan, who had invited the Sisters, withdrew the invitation because of the political situation. The missionaries had left reluctantly but they were advised that it would be safer for their Japanese friends. By the time of Pearl Harbor all the American missionaries had left. When peace was restored a new invitation to Japan was received.

Mother Louise Magdalene visited Japan in 1954 in the company of Sister Lioba Catherine, who had been a medical social worker at St. Luke's Hospital in Tokyo before the war, to investigate the situation. After her return, the Community accepted the invitation of Bishop Nakamura of the Diocese of Tohoku to reopen a training school for women church workers in Sendai, which had closed during the war. In 1955 Sister Ursula Elizabeth and Sister Mariya Margaret were sent to Japan. They had worked in Japan as secular missionaries before the war and were already familiar with the Japanese language. The third Sister assigned, Sister Jeanette Clare, unfortunately had an accident and broke her hip. She was in St. Luke's Hospital in Tokyo for a long time and it was finally decided that she should come home. She was temporarily replaced by Sister Elda Magdalene, a novice, who had been a lay missionary in China before she entered the Community.

Chapel Room.

She could read some of the Japanese characters, but she had trouble with the spoken language. The Convent in Sendai was a western style house: two stories, with wooden floors and western style furniture, but it had some Japanese features such as sliding doors. It was heated mostly with oil stoves, one in each room. At night there was no heat except for two hibachis which were placed in the kitchen and bathroom to keep the pipes from freezing. Water came from a well. A pump sent the water to a reservoir on the roof, so the Sisters had running water.

Older student teaching younger students.

The ministry there was two-fold. The training school in Sendai for women church workers, the Aoba Jo Gakuin, was reopened with three or four students. Sister Ursula directed this school. Two who attended the school for a year were members of a Japanese Religious community, the Sisters of Divine Love. It worked in cooperation with the Society of St. John the Evangelist, a men's Community from the United States. The school lasted only a few years. While there was great need for women church workers, there was not enough money to pay their salaries. The Sisters also started a kindergarten. Sister Mariya was the principal, and there were two Japanese teachers. Most mission stations in Japan had kindergartens. It was through the children that they reached the parents. Soon the kindergarten flourished, and it became a center for missionary outreach.

Sister standing with young children.

In addition to the kindergarten a Sunday School class began, where the teaching of English was a great attraction From this there came a new mission congregation, and a church was built next to the kindergarten. It was served at first by Bishop Nakamura, the Bishop of the Diocese.

An American missionary family, the Rev. and Mrs. William Draper, stationed in Sendai, also helped the Sisters. Other Sisters who worked in Japan are Sisters Monica Mary, Joan Michael, Alice Lorraine, Lioba Catherine and Grace Elizabeth. In 1971, another Japanese Community, the Sisters of Nazareth, was able to assume charge of this work, and the Sisters of the Transfiguration withdrew.

MCKINNEY AND DALLAS, TEXAS

During Mother Louise's second term a new work was undertaken in Texas. In 1967 the Sisters accepted the invitation of The Rt. Rev. Charles E. Mason of the Diocese of Dallas to undertake work at the Holy Family School in McKinney, Texas. His ministry worked for the care and health of Mexican-American children who had been taken to the fields as their mothers picked cotton. The children learned English, and the routine of school life would enable them to fit more easily into the public schools in which no Spanish was permitted. The school was integrated; it included both Black and "Anglo" students. Two of the children of different ethnic backgrounds became good friends, and they went on to finish their education to become pediatricians.

There were many Sisters who worked there at various times: Sister Mary Evelyne and Sister Joan Michael were both there for over ten years. Sister Mary Evelyne was away from the house for a time to study at the Christ for the Nations school in Dallas. Sister Jeanette Clare was in charge of the children's meals. Sister Althea lived in McKinney. She had earlier conducted a pre-school at St. Phillip's in Dallas, as reported in the Chapter on Outreach for Ministry. Other Sisters who served there for varying periods of time were Sisters Margaret Alice, Leinaala Josephine and Elizabeth Anne. Novices or Sisters in first vows were often sent there as part of their training. Consequently, there were frequent changes of Sisters. Sister Jacqueline Marie and Sister Johanna Laura were there as Novices. Sister Mary Elizabeth and Sister Grace Marie were there under first Vows.

In June, 1977 the Sisters left McKinney to work at St. Philip's School in south Dallas. They lived in the rectory of Epiphany Episcopal Church and commuted to the Center on weekdays. Sister Laura Mary was in charge from 1977 through 1978.

In 1983 the situation changed as the Diocese of Fort Worth was separated from the Diocese of Dallas. The Bishop of the formerly combined Diocese of Dallas became the Bishop of the new Diocese of Fort Worth, and there was a new Bishop in Dallas. The Community withdrew from the ministry there in 1983, and returned to the Mother House in Glendale, Ohio.

ST. LUKE'S HOUSE
1979-1988
LINCOLNTON, N.C.

In September, 1979, the Community of the Transfiguration accepted the invitation of Bishop Weinhauer, the Episcopal Visitor of the Community of the Transfiguration and the vestry of St. Luke's Episcopal Church, Lincolnton, North Carolina, to undertake the work at St. Luke's House, a small retreat and conference center on the grounds of St. Luke's Church.

The retreat center had been the dream of the Rev. James Radebaugh, a former Rector of St. Luke's Church. It was paid for by an anonymous donor, and much of the work was done by volunteers. The building was completed sometime in 1977. By the time the House was completed, Fr. Radebaugh had moved to a parish in Florida.

The first administrators of the House were the Rev. and Mrs. James Stone, who lived in the House, and a charismatic group called "The Open Door Community". Fr. Radebaugh's successor as rector, the Rev. Peter Shea, became a member of this group. After about a year, the group felt called to move to another location and St. Luke's House was vacant.

It was then that Bishop Weinhauer issued his invitation to the Sisters to come to administer the House as a more traditional retreat center. Two Sisters visited the House in Easter Week, 1979, and two others came on a weekend in July to further inspect the building and to meet with members of the congregation. In September the Community voted to accept the invitation. The first two Sisters took up residence in November, 1979.

St. Luke's Church provided the alterations necessary for a house staffed by three Sisters instead of a group of people. Except for the plumbing, the work was done by the men of the parish. The upper floor consisted of two bedrooms and a bathroom, to be used by either individual guests or groups. One room, too small for a bedroom, was used as an Oratory where the Sisters usually recited their Offices.

The large space downstairs was divided by a pair of closets into a meeting room which also served as a Chapel for the Eucharist, and a dining area. It was planned for a group of about 20 people. The Sisters had their own apartment at the back of the House.

The first two Sisters, Sister Monica Mary and Sister Mary Grace, took up residence on November 6, 1979. Sister Priscilla Jean joined them in January. In the beginning, the arrangement with the Bishop and the vestry of St. Luke's Church was made for a two year trial period. A new agreement, slightly amended, was signed on October 4, 1981 when the Sisters agreed to continue as a regular ministry of the Community.

The Sisters were responsible to the Bishop, not to the Vestry, although obviously they had to work in cooperation with the parish, and were involved a good deal with its ongoing life. In the beginning there was no Rector, Fr. Shea having gone with the group. Daily Eucharist was celebrated by the Rev. Dennis Fotinos, Rector of St. Peter's Church, Denver, North Carolina, and by two retired priests who lived in Lincolnton: the Rev. H.M. Kennikell and the Rev. Jack Wooley. Later when the Church had a Rector the Sisters attended weekday services at the Church and were also served by clergy from neighboring areas. The first three Sisters worked as a team with no designated Superior. Each undertook particular on-going responsibilities, and they took turns with cooking and housekeeping duties. A neighbor was engaged for cleaning in the guest area. The Sisters took care of their own apartment, which included the kitchen. They considered employing someone to cook for groups, but this proved impractical because of the irregularity of the schedule. and the Sisters soon learned that they were quite able to do it themselves.

Located at the southeastern edge of the Diocese, the Sisters were conveniently located for ministry in the Diocese of North Carolina, the Diocese of Western North Carolina and the Diocese of Upper South Carolina. The Bishops of both North Carolina, Western North Carolina and especially Bishop Beckham of Upper South Carolina, welcomed them.

The pattern of ministry that developed at the House included a variety of activities. The Sisters usually initiated three events every year: a School of Prayer, a Retreat intended primarily for Associates, and one other Retreat or Quiet Day. These retreats were the so-called "classic" retreats, with silence. The Associates' Retreat was always led by a Sister from the Mother House. The other two events might be led by one of the Sisters here or by a conductor from outside. They provided Quiet Days for parish groups such as Altar Guilds and Daughters of the King. A number of vestries and other parish groups came for working retreats. For several groups, a visit to St. Luke's House became an almost annual event. Others came just once or twice. The majority of these groups were from the Diocese of North Carolina. We were very conveniently located near the city of Charlotte. Parishes in this Diocese seemed likely to invite a Sister to come to the parish, sometimes for a Quiet Day, more often for a program for the ECW, or adult Christian Education.

Usually the Sisters did one or more Vacation Bible School programs during the summer. These might have been almost anywhere in the country, for sometimes requests were passed on from the Mother House. Because we were small, and a family type of place, we could provide for individuals more easily than most larger retreat or conference centers, so we had a number of individual guests. They often called their visit a retreat. It was, for them, a retreat from the routine of daily life in a prayerful environment. The amount of silence and the way of keeping it were up to the individual. Sometimes a person will come at fairly frequent intervals over a period of time. Some come sporadically, and some never came again. Perhaps the personal contact with individuals, whether encountered in group situations or as individual guests, was the most valuable part of the work, although it is impossible to measure.

Cursillo began in the Diocese during that first year The Sisters were active in that, thus getting to know people from all over the Diocese. To give them "visibility" Bishop Weinhauer appointed each Sister to a Diocesan committee: Christian Education, Liturgy and Music, Commission on Ministry. The Bishop was interested in promoting the vocational diaconate, so he was particularly pleased to have Sister Priscilla, a Deacon, there.

We tried to treat St. Luke's Church as any other parish by making appointments rather than committing ourselves to any ongoing responsibility. This kept us more available for appointments away from Lincolnton, and we did not want them becoming dependent on us for things they would normally do. However, while Sister Mary Elizabeth was there she acted as parish administrator. We attended ECW meetings, occasionally helped with the Sunday School, and occasionally preached. Both the ECW and the vestry came to prefer St. Luke's House as a meeting place.

It was the intention of the Community to have three Sisters on the staff. This was possible during the first four years. In the fall of 1983, Sister Mary Grace requested a leave of absence to go to school. (She eventually left the Community.) Sister Priscilla Jean was transferred to our new work in the Dominican Republic. Sister Hilary replaced her for a short time, but she was also waiting to be sent to the Dominican Republic. Sister Mary Elizabeth was the only replacement available for the remainder of the year. Sister Jacqueline Marie came in the fall of 1984. At that time Sister Monica was officially named Superior of the Branch House.

Bishop Weinhauer retired at the beginning of 1990. The Rt. Rev. Robert H. Johnson was consecrated as coadjutor in March, 1989. Since the Rule calls for a "periodic review" of our Branch Works, it seemed appropriate to do this at this time of transition in the Diocese. The work was going on as usual and to the extent of the physical capabilities of two Sisters. In reality, the greatest problem was that of having sufficient Sisters to staff the House. In 1990 Sister Monica returned to the Mother House to stay. Sister Jacqueline continued at St. Luke's House. Sister Lydia Magdalene and, later, Sister Eleanor Grace were sent to Lincolnton.

In 1990, Chapter voted to withdraw from this ministry, and the House was closed as of April 1, 1991. The building continued to be used by St. Luke's Church.

THE DOMINICAN REPUBLIC 1980-PRESENT

CENTRO BUEN PASTOR

The island of Hispaniola, was discovered by Columbus in 1492. Four centuries later the island is the site of two independent countries: the Dominican Republic which occupies two-thirds of the island, and Haiti. The Episcopal Church in the Dominican Republic was founded in 1897 in San Pedro de Macorís by English-speaking migrants from the British West Indies who brought their Anglican faith with them when they arrived in San Pedro to work in the sugar cane industry. They were people profoundly committed to Christ, and many arrived with bibles and prayer books under their arms.

It became part of the Episcopal Church in 1913. However, it remained under the supervision of Diocese of Puerto Rico. During its early years, the church actively established itself in this country primarily with the help of missionary priests. The church was sincerely dedicated to serving and meeting the pastoral needs of Anglicans there. During its first 60 years, most Anglican services were conducted in English. In the early 1950's American missionaries "nationalized" the Church by instituting services in Spanish. Today Episcopal services are in Spanish with the exception of one service every Sunday at Epiphany Church.

In 1961 the Dominican Republic was recognized as a mission diocese of the Episcopal Church, Province IX. The Rt. Rev. Paul Kellogg became the first resident Bishop, and sought to solidify the Church's expansion.

Sr. Ann visiting neighbors.

In 1972, the Rt. Rev. Telésforo Isaac was elected as the first Dominican-born Bishop. Under his leadership the Church truly became a Church of and for the Dominican people. He retired as Diocesan Bishop in 1991. Since then he has served as interim Bishop of other dioceses. He remains active in the Dominican diocese and was director of the diocese's first vocational Deaconate.

The Sisters of the Transfiguration had visited the Dominican Republic several times from Puerto Rico. Sister Esther came over at least once. Sister Priscilla came over in 1976 to give a Lenten retreat and a conference on the religious life. After hurricane "David", a category 5 storm, devastated the island in 1979. Sisters Ann, Mary Luke and Hilary came down for 6 weeks to stay in Santana-Bani to help with relief work and be a calming presence among the people. Their stay was temporary and their purpose was to help hurricane victims.

In May 1984 the Sisters returned to study the social needs of D.R. Based on this investigation, they made a commitment to help the children and families in the Barrio Los Flores. Bishop Telesforo asked the Sisters to come to establish a more permanent mission there. In 1984 Sister Hilary and Sister Priscilla received visas that allowed them to begin a long-term mission in that country. Bishop Isaac first asked them to serve in San Pedro de Macorís. At first they taught at San Esteban School. Sister Priscilla tells of their experience, "At that time we taught at San Esteban School, lived in the vicarage and helped with the Church. We were the Altar guild along with the young people. Everyone time the church door opened we were there. Every time that there was a funeral or a wedding within the parish or among the clergy we were there. We went to conventions and Diocesan do's. We were a Presence, I guess. Bishop Isaac took us under his wing. When we came to town, Doña Juanita, his wife, drove us around shopping as we had no vehicle at the time. We ate at his place every time we came into town. It was great."

The Sisters quickly branched out from San Esteban, building a street ministry in the poorest barrios. They got to know the children and their needs and became advocates for those who could not speak for themselves. The more they looked the more desperate needs they saw, and the more creative they had to become.

Among the problems encountered were race and class prejudice, lack of basic services such as clean water, joblessness, overcrowded schools, families who could not afford school uniforms and shoes and books for their children, lack of health care and scarce medical supplies, malnourished children, lack of pre-natal and postnatal care and overcrowded and primitive housing. Sister Priscilla and Sister Hilary walked through Las Flores with a first aid kit. Medical students gave first aid and referred people to the Public Health doctors for pre-natal care and teaching. The Sisters did what they could. Sometimes they parked the "Blue Nun" van and worked out of the back. It had their name in large letters plastered all over the side. And so began a permanent, challenging, and time-stealing feature of the work–fund-raising.

In 1989 the Sisters began a new mission in the neighborhoods (barrios) of San Pedro. El Centro Buen Pastor (Good Shepherd Center) was established initially to provide nutrition services to malnourished children in the very poor barrios of Las Flores and Filipina. Barrios have sprung up in adjacent areas, which the Center also serves. All of these poverty stricken shanty neighborhoods are characterized by poor or non-existent sanitation, lack of potable water and electricity, environmental contamination, illiteracy, unemployment, and lack of health care. The results of these extremely poor economic and living conditions are malnutrition and high rate of illness and mortality, especially among women and children.

On Sundays and some weekday mornings there is a worship service with a small but growing congregation. The congregation at the service is made up of young people and older ones. It is sad but also hopeful to see so many children being cared for by the grandmothers. The young people, including pre-teens, help prepare for the services, read the Lessons, and help put things away afterwards.

Gathering in front of Centro Buen Pastor.

In 2005, the Rector of San Esteban celebrated the Eucharist. Later, another Priest became his assistant and also served Buen Pastor.

Monday though Friday there is a primary school, an elementary school, nutrition program, and a clinic dispensary. There are not enough public schools to accommodate all the school-aged children of school age and many families can not afford to go to the public schools. They do not have enough money for shoes and books. Gifts from friends make it possible for the Sisters to help with these needs. The Sisters frequently prepare food baskets to take to needy families.

The clinic serves mostly women and children, but men and women of all ages receive help for minor injuries. The government pays for some part time doctors and nurses and gives some help with medicine. The nutrition program had to be closed periodically, because of lack of funds, but it has reopened. Many malnourished children have been fed.

The Sisters' support and influence has helped the people in the barrio to obtain more education and more medical assistance A nurse in the clinic, a woman from the barrio, is the first person there to obtain a college degree and is now an RN. Her sister will graduate in 2009. The Sisters report that many of the people now attending the mission were attracted by the medical assistance they received. Health care continues to be provided through the clinic and dispensary. In 2004 there were four government doctors and a new primary health care program. There are agencies in Santo Domingo, the capital, who arrange care for children with special needs, even sending them for medical care in the United States. Parish groups in the United States have helped to care for children sent to their cities. The Sisters spend a great deal of time transporting children with their guardians to and from San Pedro de Macorís and Santo Domingo.

Every year the Sisters are visited by teams of volunteers with money and labor from parishes in the United States. Several parish groups have come over at least once, especially from the Tampa Deanery in Florida, and others have come several times. They have contributed funds, time and energy to put up new buildings and to repair old ones. They have helped to build and a new larger Chapel. They have also brought doctors and nurses for much needed medical care.

Over the years the work has steadily expanded particularly in the field of education. The school grew substantially. A grade was added each fall. Sister Jean Gabriel reported in 2004 that there were 121 children in classes from preschool, (maternal) three year olds, kindergarten and pre-first grade through fourth grade. Positions for three teaches and a principal were now funded by the government. They planned to add anther grade each year, as space became available, until they had pre-school through eighth grade.

Four years later she reported that they had begun construction on a new primary school building. They were looking forward to April, 2009 when El Centro Buen Pastor will celebrate 20 years of the Centro's being open. The new school will have been expanded to eight grades in time to be dedicated at this time. There is now an average yearly enrollment of 200-270 students from nursery through eighth grade.

In 2001 they began a vocational education program. From 2001 to 2003 they graduated nearly 300 students, most of them young and many of them family bread winners who formerly had no job skills.

Another part of their work those first few years was to have conferences on the religious life for all of the Episcopal schools. When Sister Hilary went home for health reasons the first time, Sister Jean Gabriel came down to help. Sister Hilary's health did not allow her to serve permanently in the Dominican Republic, although she was there as often as her doctors would permit. She spent a total of ten years serving at the Center. Between her times there, she has worked at fund raising in the States, as well as developing and maintaining a vast correspondence with friends, Associates and other supporters. With time it became clear, however, that another Sister was needed. From 1985 through 1989 Sister Jean Gabriel served for several short stints in the Dominican Republic, and in 1991 returned to work with Sister Priscilla on a more permanent basis. Together they continued to share God's love with those who

Sr. Priscilla and young children.

are too easy to overlook. In 2000 Sister Priscilla returned to Ohio, so Sister Johanna became part of the team. She returned to Glendale in 2005, and Sister Priscilla once again went to serve there.

Fourteen other Sisters have served there for short periods of time. These include Sister Marjorie Hope, Sister Althea Augustine, Sister Rachel Margaret, Sister Nadine Elizabeth, Sister Diana Dorothea and Sister Monica Mary.

Sister Monica who was there for a short time in 2005—6, remembers U.S. Customs, an unfamiliar language, and pesos instead of dollars. She soon observed the contrast between the living conditions of the people in the barrio at Las Flores, with unpaved roads, lack of electricity and potable water and the wealthier areas with paved roads and nice houses. She was surprised to see that there were American style grocery stores and the availability of many things we at home take for granted, for those who have money to pay.

Children at an activity table.

At Christmas the children had a Nativity pageant, and the Sisters happily prepared Christmas presents for the children at the Center. These gifts, like the scholarships for the school, and many other ways in which they help are the gifts of friends in the United States. The Rt. Rev. Julio C. Holguin Khoury was elected in 1991. He was born in San Francisco de Macorís. He is also serving as interim Bishop of the Diocese of Cuba. The Diocese has entered into a significant period of growth, thanks to committed clergy and lay leaders.

Storytime.

INDEX

A

Abplanalp, Fritz, 62, 112, 120, 139
Acolytes, 265
Ada Francis, Sister, 63-65, 90, 219
Ada Julian Walpole, Sister, 192
A Follower's Story, xi-xii, 11-12, 17, 20, 22, 41-42, 44, 82, 138, 154, 161-162, 216, 221, 229, 232
Agnes Margaret Newchem, Sister, 189
Albertina, Sister, 243
Alice Lorraine Reid, Sister, 85, 146, 157-160, 166, 194, 256-258, 276, 287
All Angels' Day, 26
Allin, John, 77, 164
All Saints' Day, 42, 136, 226
All Saints' Sisters of the Poor, 10, 156
Altar Guild, 46
Althea Augustine King, Sister, 85, 95-97, 143, 146, 193, 220, 272, 281, 289, 303
American Book of Common Prayer, 52
American Expeditionary Force, 107
Amy Martha Arch, Sister, 186, 244
Anderson, Janet, 236
Angela Hannah Eliot, Sister, 127, 191
The Angelus, 71-72
Anglican Cathedral, 235
Anglican Church, 5, 7, 10
Anglican Communion, 5, 199
Anglican Sisterhoods, 10
Anna Grace, Sister, 161, 186, 245
Anna Mary, Sister, 139-140
Ann Margaret Davis, Sister, 157-158, 166-167, 171 195, 282
Anti-Poverty Program, 275
Aoba Jo Gakuin, 286
Ascension Day, 247
Ascot Priory, 43

Ash Wednesday, 13
Associate Mission, 11-12, 14
Associates of the Community, 86-88
Associates' Rule, 86
Atlantic Transport, 36
Austin, Julia, 61

B

Barbara Margaret, Sister, 189
Bat Cave, 18, 27, 29, 89, 117, 138, 161, 176, 181, 215-216
Beatrice Martha Henderson, Sister
  as first Novice Director and, 81-82
  Bat Cave and, 216
  Bethany Home for Children, 30-34, 46-51
  Diocese of Southern Ohio and, 132
  early years of, 10-11, 15
  family of, 4
  Feast of Transfiguration and, 3
  F. E. Lund and, 228
  first Chapter meeting of the Community and, 68
  first diocesan convention and, 7
  first meeting of Eva Lee Matthews and, 11
  "Fresh Air Camp" and, 23-24
  growth of community and, 60-65
  House of Women and, 11-12, 15-16, 60, 70, 181
  letters from Sister Helen and, 232
  Mother Eva's birthday feast and, 122
  parish and social services work, 19-23
  retirement of, 137-138
  rule modification and, 72-73
  St. James School for Boys and, 224-225

story of the Chapel and, 58-59
trip to England and, 35-45
visits to Convents and, 39-44
Bechtel, Nellie, 22
Beekley, Mary Jane, 133
Beresford, Margaret, 50
Bethany Home Aid Society, 31
Bethany Home Chronicle
  China and, 234-235
  first issue of, 50
  General Convention (1937) and, 137
  Mary Jane Beekley letter and, 133
  mountain girls and, 215
Bethany Home for Boys, 30-34, 138-139
Bethany Home for Children, 30, 46-51, 64, 70, 87, 106-107, 121, 126-127, 131-134, 148-150, 159-161, 219
Bethany Home for Girls, 33-34
Bethany Home Village, 47
Bethany Mission House, 18-20, 28, 70, 181, 209
Bethany School, 148-149, 155-156, 158, 166
Binsted, Norman, 285
Black History Week, 271
Black, William G., 59
Blanchard, Robert W., 59
Blessed Sacrament, 52, 54, 57, 63, 120, 131, 182, 200, 221, 224, 227, 229
Block, Karl M., 140, 251
Board of Missions, 92, 222, 266
Book of Common Prayer, 57, 122-124, 135
Borg, Marcus, 172
Boynton, Charles F., 144, 281
Boys' and Girls' Club, 276
Boy Scouts, 34, 261, 265
Branch Houses, xiii, 51, 87, 89, 94, 102, 119, 132, 153, 164
Breidenthal, Thomas, 59
Brookins, Charles, 107
Browning, Edmond L., 250
Burgess, John Melville, 155, 264-265, 272
Burton Tower, 117

C

Cane, Patricia, 173

Cannon, Harriet Starr, 114, 145
Canon Law, 4, 76, 166
Canterbury Cathedral, 38
Capacitar Program, 173
Carina Elsa, Sister, 177
Carolina Mountain Land Conservancy, 176
Caroline Mary Cochran, Sister, 34, 60, 185, 244
Carroll, James, 77, 165
Catholic Movement, 4, 9
Chang, Joan, 235
Chapel of the Transfiguration
  beginning of, 105-106
  carvings and, 112-113
  chapel bells and, 116-120
  dedication of, 108-111
  windows and, 113-115
Chapter of Faults, 84
Chen Ngai, Sister, 241
Cherry, Margaret, 63
Chester Cathedral, 39
Children's Hospital Cooperative Society, 23
China, 33, 48, 51, 54, 56, 61, 64, 73, 80, 91-93, 102, 114, 132, 145-146, 182-183, 185-188, 190-191, 197, 221-242, 244-245, 264, 285
China Inland Mission, 233-234
Ching, Frank, 227
Christ Church, 10, 55
Christ for the Nations school, 289
Christ Hospital, 231, 263
Christina Margaret Ludt, Sister, 190
Chronology of community history, 180-184
Church Divinity School of the Pacific, 175
Church League, 23
Church Missions House, 240
Church of England, ix, 9, 53, 67, 97, 122-123, 243
Church of the Advent, 95, 144
Church of the Incarnation, 253
Cincinnati Public Library, 267
Cincinnati Symphony, 269
Clara Elizabeth, Sister, 34, 62-63, 65, 74, 109, 111-113, 115, 138-141, 248,

251-253
Clare Marie, Sister, 197
Clayton, David, 156
Cleveland, Grace Matthews, 4, 131
Cleveland, Harlan, 4, 28, 274
Cleveland, James, 109
Cleveland, John, 110
Cochran, Caroline, 34
Cole, Mark, 97
Colmore, Charles, 77, 144, 281
Community Chest, 31, 33
Community of St. Francis, 165
Community of St. John the Baptist, 10, 156
Community of St. Mary, xv, 5, 16, 114, 145, 154, 156, 165-166, 193
Community of St. Monica, 11
Community of the Holy Spirit, 165
Community of the Resurrection, 9
Community of the Transfiguration, ix, xi, 3, 10, 12, 15, 47, 62, 74, 136, 138, 161, 169, 225, 247, 254, 265-266, 274, 291
Companions of the Community of St. Mary, 5
Conference of Anglican Religious in the Americas (CAROA), 144, 170
Confucius, 235
Connick, Charles J., 113
Constance Anna Hayes, Sister, 4-5, 48, 116, 186, 225, 238, 239, 240, 242
Constance Johanna, Sister, 166
Convent of St. Boniface, 237
Coolie Shelter, 232
Cooper, Hilda, 95
Coral Cross, 244-245
Crafts Wright Place, 24, 30
Craighill, Lloyd, 237
Cram, Ralph Adams, 107-108
Crypt Church, 262
Cultural Revolution, 236
Curry, Michael, 272
Cursillo program, 99

D

Damron, Anthony, 77, 156, 247
Dawson, Paul, 149
Deaconess Sisters of St. Andrew, 154

Dean, Myrtle, 140
Deaver, John, 127-128, 164-165
Deborah Ruth Powell, Sister, 34, 185, 225, 242, 245
Decker, Martha, 176
Declaration by novice community practices, 199-200
Diana Dorothea Doncaster, Sister, 127, 175, 198, 258, 303
Dickerson, Robert, 264
Diocesan Board of Missions, 266
Diocesan Convention, 20
Diocese of California, 251
Diocese of Cuba, 303
Diocese of Dallas, 289-290
Diocese of Fort Worth, 290
Diocese of Hawaii, 248
Diocese of Indianapolis, 166
Diocese of Massachusetts, 264
Diocese of Nebraska, 14
Diocese of North Carolina, 293
Diocese of Northern California, 175, 251, 254, 257
Diocese of Puerto Rico, 297
Diocese of Southern Ohio, 59, 132, 260, 269, 275
Diocese of Tohoku, 146, 285
Diocese of Upper South Carolina, 293
Diocese of Western North Carolina, 157, 293
Divine Office, ix, 71, 83, 88, 112, 123, 154, 160
Dominican Republic, 94, 97-98, 159, 165, 169, 184, 195-197, 283, 295, 297-303
Dorf, Martha Schickel, 172
Dorothy Mary Lanvermier, Sister, 188, 264
Dotson, John, 28
Draper, William, 287

E

Edith Constance, Sister, 61, 64, 73, 85, 90, 109, 140, 222, 225-227, 231, 233-234, 242
El Centro Buen Pastor, 299-300, 302
Elda Magdalene Smith, Sister, 197, 233, 242, 285

Eleanor Grace Narkis, Sister, 99, 177, 198, 295
Eleanor Mary Meyers, Sister, 106, 185, 219, 229-230, 242
Elizabeth Angela Cleveland, Sister, 189
Elizabeth Anne Coles, Sister, 127, 196, 289
Elizabeth I, 37
Ellis Victoria, Sister, 11, 15, 60, 106
Ely Cathedral, 37
Emily Faith, Sister, 188, 242
Emily Francis, Sister, 193, 268
England, Charles, 263
Epiphany Episcopal Church, 290
Episcopal Children's Hospital, 263
Episcopal Church
  Book of Common Prayer and, 121
  Canon Law of, 4, 76, 166
  canons of, 52
  Catholic Movement and, 4, 9
  Church of England and, 243
  Dominican Republic and, 297
  feasts and, 122
  General Convention (1937), 136-137
  General Theological Seminary of, 9
  House of Bishops and, 170
  Iolani school and, 244
  Richard Frye and, 119
Episcopal Church Women (ECW), 257, 281
Episcopal Seminary, 175
Epting, Christopher, x, 77, 164, 166
Espy, Walter, 262
Esther Fifield, Sister, 90
Esther Mary, Sister, 90, 127, 142, 152-154, 157, 162, 189, 247, 256, 264-265, 269, 272-273, 281-283
Ethel Bertha, Sister, 26, 28, 60-61, 90, 219
Eucharist, ix, 9, 49, 71, 83, 88, 109, 112, 120-121, 123-124, 126, 131, 145, 148, 155, 160, 164, 166, 199, 247, 257, 261, 292, 300
Eva Dorothea Ely, Sister, 93, 151, 193, 220, 249
Eva Mary Matthews, Mother
  Bethany Home for Children, 30-34, 46-51
  Bishop Vincent's sermon and, 5-7
  burial of, 111-112
  China visit and, 226
  death of, 13, 57, 103, 138
  early years of, 8-9, 15
  family of, 4, 7
  Feast of Transfiguration and, 3
  F. E. Lund and, 228
  first Chapter meeting of the Community and, 68
  first diocesan convention and, 7
  "Fresh Air Camp" and, 23-24
  growth of community and, 60-65
  House of Women and, 11-12, 15-16, 60, 70, 181
  illness and, 24-26
  Jerusalem Cross and, 75
  last years of, 101-104
  parish and social services work, 19-23
  pilgrimage to the Holy Land, 17
  policies for missions and, 89-98
  purpose of the Rule and, 66-76
  reconciliation and, 57-58
  Sisterhood of St. Mary and, 16-17
  social ostracism and, 8
  St. James School for Boys and, 224-225
  trip to England and, 35-45
  University of Oxford, England and, 9-10
  vision for the Community and, 79
  visits to Convents and, 39-44
  writings on Religious Life and, 170
Evans, John Marvin, 271
Evelyn Ancilla Hetherington, Sister, 93, 98, 137, 190, 248, 266, 272, 275
Eve of the Transfiguration, 88

F

Faith Marguertite Ocley, Sister, 191, 216, 281
Falls of Lahore, 38
Farlander, Arthur, 253-254, 256
Fasts, 5, 67
Feast Day, 59, 72, 121-122, 126, 155, 243, 247
Feast of St. Michael, 30
Feast of the Confession of St. Peter, 154

Feast of the Transfiguration, 3, 86, 124, 157, 166, 229
Feasts of St. Joseph, 122
Feng Ai, Sister, 235
Feng Ngai, Sister, 241
Fifield, Esther, 260
Fingal's Cave, 37
First Evensong of Advent IV, 115
Fleming, James, 268
Flower Guild, 23
Ford Museum, 271
Foreign and Christian Missionary Society, 223
Fotinos, Dennis, 292
Founders' Day, 247
Frances Helen, Sister, 146, 194
Frances Mabels, Sister, 189
Franciscan Health Center (FHC), 96
Francis, James, 269-270
Fresh Air Camp, 23-24
Frye, Richard, 119

Gabriel Katherine Cooper, Sister, 195
Galera de Menores, 281
Gardner, Wallace J., 137
General Convention (1910), 91
General Convention (1937), 136-137
General Convention (1976), 124
General Convention (1979), 122
General Convention (2007), 123
Georgiana Faith Ellis, Sister, 193
Gertrude Christine, Sister, 185
Giovanni, Nicki, 271
Girl Reserves, 265
Glendale College, 33
Glendale High School, 50
Golden Jubilee, 114
Good Shepherd Center, 299
Good Shepherd Convent, 41
Gore, Charles, 9
Gowen, Vincent, 228
Grace Elizabeth Ludt, Sister, 137, 190, 237, 242, 287
Grace Marie Galluccio, Sister, 195, 289
Great Depression, 259, 263
Great Wall of China, 235
Greenwood, Westwell, 263-264

Grey, Jane, 75, 102, 108, 111
Griswold, Frank, 164
Guild of Carillonneurs, 118

Habits, 7, 74-75, 141, 187, 192, 207, 251
Halladay, Richard, 166
Hall, Katherine Kittle Kennedy, 93
Hamer, Frank, 110
Hanchett, Lani, 248
Harriet Monsell, Mother, 114
Harrison, C. Edward, 265-266, 268
Harrison, Ruth Chapman, 268
Havner, Alice, 256
Hawaii, 43, 93, 98, 115, 132, 142, 154, 162, 182, 185-188, 191-192, 243-250, 260, 266
Hayes, Anna, 102
Head Start Program, 275-276
Head Start School, 270
Healing ministry, 125
Heather, Roger, 127
Helena Miriam Lambert, Sister, 137, 190
Helen Veronica Farrell, Sister, 85, 98, 185, 222, 225-226, 228, 230, 242, 245
Hilary Mary Moores, Sister, 85, 127, 146, 159, 162, 197, 216, 283, 295, 298, 299, 302
Hilda Cynthia Baskin, Sister, 49, 187
Hindle, James, 149
Hobson, Henry, 262
Hollaway, Willis, 271
Holy Baptism, 2, 49, 67, 203, 205, 226, 247
Holy Communion, 4-5, 52, 98, 104, 115, 120, 148, 199, 223
Holy Cross Home for Crippled Children, 90, 102, 219
Holy Cross House, 102, 132
Holy Family Church, 153
Holy Family House, 153
Holy Family School, 289
Holy Name Church, 282
Holy Trinity Church, 281
Holy Trinity School, 143, 281-282
Hoover, Herbert, 231
Hope Mary Kunkle, Sister, 198
Hospital San Lucas, 282

House of Women, 11-12, 15-16, 60, 70, 181
Howard University, 265
Hughes, Marion Rebecca, 115
Hunter, James, 262
Huntington, Daniel T., 61, 91-93, 221, 223-224, 227, 229, 233, 227
Huston Hall, 24, 30

I

Ignation Spirituality Project, 173
Irene Augustine, Sister, 62, 65
Isaac, Doña Juanita, 299
Isaac, Telésforo, 159, 298-299
I. T. Verdin Company, 117

J

Jacqueline Marie Curtis, Sister, 87, 195, 289, 295
Japan, 143, 146, 154, 156, 160, 183, 187, 190, 192-194, 222, 232, 236, 238-240, 249, 255, 285-287
Jean Benedict Lynch, Sister, 193, 220
Jeanette Clare Abbey, Sister, 146, 192, 285, 289
Jean Gabriel Crothers, Sister, 196, 301-302
Jenkins, Thomas, 137
Jerusalem Cross, 17, 74, 75, 87-88, 105
Joan Michael, Sister, 166, 193, 287, 289
Joanna Mary Waterman, Sister, 187, 242
Johanna Laura Moseley, Sister, 97-98, 196, 283, 289, 302
Johnson, Irving, 11, 14-15, 17, 55-56, 76, 79, 110-111, 114, 137
Johnson, Mary, 106
Johnson, Robert H., 295
Jordan, Boyd, 116
Josephine Martha Hanes, Sister, 188
Julia Margaret Hayes, Sister, 162-163, 190, 281
Juliana Justin Sweikert, Sister, 196

K

K-8 Day School, 175
Kairos Prison Ministry, 198
Kairos program, 99
Kang, Martha, 240

Katherine Helen Barry, Sister, 187
Keese, Grace, 15
Keiser, Marilyn, 164
Kellogg, Paul, 297
Kennedy, Harry Sherbourne, 93, 247-248, 250
Kennedy, Katherine Kittle, 250
Kennikell, H.M., 292
Khoury, Julio C. Holguin, 303
King David, 113
King Ethelbert, 38, 115
King Harold, 39
King Kamehameha IV, 243
Krumm, John M., 59, 155

L

Lake Erie College, 97
La Mothe, John Dominique, 248
Lauds, 83, 123-125, 156
Laura Mary Wood, Sister, 194, 272, 275-276, 290
Leinaala Josephine Folk, Sister, 127, 192, 220, 289
Lent, 13, 46, 143
Leonard, William A., 90, 102, 111, 219, 229
Lesser Feasts, 5, 67
Lewis, Gerald, 137, 260
Lillian Martha Steineman, Sister, 186
Lincoln Heights Elementary School, 268-269
Lincoln Heights Recreation Department, 275-276
Lincoln, James Otis, 251
Lincoln, Nellie, 140-141
Lioba Katherine Shipps, Sister, 143, 146, 192, 256, 285, 287
Littell, S. Harrington, 248
Littledale, R. F., 67
Lois Mary Sook, Sister, 193
Louise Magdalene Hoehn, Sister, 87, 142, 145, 147, 150-151, 156-157, 189, 232, 235-240, 257, 263-264, 283, 285, 289
Lucy Caritas Burgin, Sister, 191, 220, 236, 242, 245, 248
Lund, F. E., 223, 228
Lydia House, 252

Lydia Magdalene Mathews, Sister, 36, 160, 196, 257, 295
Lydia Margaret Jensen, Sister, 187
Lynn, Connor, 156
Lynn Julian Browning, Sister, 198

M

Mabel Lioba Snow, Sister, 90, 186
Madeleine Mary Stansburg, Sister, 141, 186, 251-252
Marcelle Louise Meisel, Sister, 195
Marcia Francis McCauley, Sister, 127, 198
Margaret Alice Allen, Sister, 162, 197, 281-282, 289
Margaret Dolores, Sister, 63, 65, 163, 215
Marian Therese Miller, Sister, 198
Marie Helen Bender, Sister, 189
Marilyn Elizabeth Kennedy, Sister, 197
Marion Beatrice Jones, Sister, 188, 248
Mariya Margaret Hester, Sister, 192, 285-286
Mariya Margaret, Sister, 143, 146
Marjorie Hope Harkness, Sister, 141, 191, 251, 255, 281-283, 303
Martha Mary Armstrong, Sister, 109, 187
Martin Luther King Day, 271
Mary Agnes, Sister, 136, 190
Mary Catherine Matthews, Sister, 114, 150, 162, 187, 260, 261
Mary Elizabeth Ammon, Sister, 190
Mary Elizabeth Roll, Sister, 195
Mary Elizabeth, Sister, 85, 98, 127, 158
Mary Evelyne Tookey, Sister, 173, 194, 281, 289
Mary Grace Parkin, Sister, 148, 195, 292, 295
Mary Joseph, Sister, 136, 188
Mary Luke Evans, Sister, 159, 173-174, 195, 216, 276-278, 298
Mary Raphael McCoy, Sister, 192
Mary Veronica Hooten, Sister, 162, 197, 281
Mason, Charles E., 289
Maternity Society, 23
Matthews, Elizabeth, 150

Matthews, Grace, 8, 103
Matthews, Jane, 8, 16, 103
Matthews, Marianna, 114
Matthews, Mary Ann, 8
Matthews, Mortimer, 4, 7-8, 24, 109, 225-226, 262
Matthews, Paul, 4, 7-9, 14-19, 22-23, 25-26, 28-29, 33, 56, 58-59, 67, 76-77, 90, 102, 104, 108, 110-111, 113, 131, 135, 137, 140, 228-229
Matthews, Stanley, 8, 262
Mays, Samuel, 271
Melinda Boyd, Sister, 177
Merton, Thomas, 169
Metropolitan College of Music, 33
Meyer, Albert, 118-119
Meyers, Albert, 156, 165
Miami River, 108
Minuth, Fred, 249
Miriam Jeanne Campbell, Sister, 196
Mitchell, LaVerne, 271
Moeller Organ Company, 127
Monica Mary Heyes, Sister, 85, 93, 119, 125, 127, 151, 156, 162, 166, 171, 194, 249-250, 287, 292, 295, 303
Moore, Mabel, 127
Morag Michael, Sister, 44, 154
Morse, Walter, 236
Mother Foundress Day, 112, 115, 122, 142, 164, 233, 259, 262
Mother's Meetings, 19, 22, 215
Myrtle Catherine Dean, Sister, 191

N

Nadine Elizabeth Schilling, Sister, 174, 196, 303
Nakamura, Timothy, 146
Naomi Mercedes, Sister, 146, 197
National Association of Christian Communities (NAACC), 170
National Association of Episcopal Schools, 175
National Church Ecumenical Office, 77
National Women's Auxiliary, 264
Neale, Alan, 103
Neale, John Mason, 67, 114
Neal, Emily Gardiner, 125
Nelson, Frank, 55-56, 58

New England Teachers' Travel Bureau, 36
Nieb, Arthur, 107
Novices, training of, 83-84
Novitiate
    organization of, 84-85
    purpose of, 78-85

O

Oakes Home Corporation, 55
Oblates, xiii, 88, 166, 198
Office Book, 45, 67, 124-126, 196
Ohio Reformatory for Women, 99
Olive Rachel Bechtel, Sister, 185, 219
Olivia Mary Matthews, Sister, 73, 82, 85, 114, 139-140, 142-145, 150, 160, 186, 239, 244, 247, 253, 260-261, 263-266, 272, 276
Open Door Ministry, 95-96, 144
Oratory, 31-32, 198, 221, 224, 252, 283, 292
Oratory of the Convent, 18
Orchard Corners, 132
Order of Deaconesses, 205
Order of Emmaus Pilgrims, 165
Order of St. Anne, 35, 156, 165
Order of St. Benedict, 156
Order of St. Gregory, 165
Order of St. Helena, 156, 165
Order of St. Monica, 60
Order of the Holy Cross, 61, 97, 156
Order of the Most Holy Trinity, 243
Organ, design of, 127
Oriole Mary Oatman, Sister, 191
Osborn, Winn, 256
Oxford Movement, 9

P

Parker, Sandra, 165
Paula Harriet Bray, Sister, 109, 111, 187, 248
Paula Irene Brown, Sister, 127, 146, 163, 194
Payne, Edward, 164
Pei Ai, Sister, 241
Peking Language School, 235
Peterson, Vivan, 77, 145
Petit and Fritsen Company, 116

Pez, Cheryl, 149
Piersawl, Fannie, 264, 269-270
Pitts, Susie, 273
Plainsong, 125-126
Pontifical Eucharist, 164
Porter, Noel, 254
Powell, Deborah, 34
Powell, F. C., 35-36
Presbyterian Church, 8
Price, Kenneth L., 59, 164
Price, Percival, 117, 165
Priem, Cynthia, 165
Princeton High School, 265
Princeton Junior High School, 269-270
Princeton Theological Seminary, 9
Priory Expansion Program, 246
Priscilla Jean Wright, Sister, 97-98, 119, 159, 162, 175, 195, 216, 281-283, 292, 294-295, 298-299
Priscilla Lydia Sellon, Mother, 115
Prisoners, ministry and, 98-99
Proctor and Gamble Company, 7
Proctor, William A., 7
Proctor, William Cooper, 33, 106
Protestant Evangelicalism, 9
Puerto Rico, 77, 87, 94, 98, 119, 143-146, 152-153, 158-159, 162-163, 182, 190-197, 235, 255, 265, 281-284, 297-298, 281-284, 297-298
Pusey House, 9

Q

Queen Emma, 243, 247
Queen Emma Square, 244-245
Queen Liliokalani, 246
Queen Victoria, 43
Quiet Days, 136, 293

R

Rachel Margaret Phillips, Sister, 125, 174, 196, 303
Radebaugh, James, 291
Ramsharan, Carlisle, 268
Ranfurly Children's Home, 144
Ranfurly Home for Children, 96-97
Rebecca Louise, Sister, 146, 194
Red Cross, 56
Reed, Mary, 273

Religious Life, xvi, 4-5, 10, 35-36, 61, 67, 69, 79, 119, 153-154, 157, 160, 170, 202, 241, 282, 298, 302
Religious Orders, 7, 9, 16, 35, 67, 91
Religious Rule, 3, 16, 241
Restarick, Henry B., 93, 243, 248
Rhoda Pearl Pignel, Sister, 190
Rickshaw Coolie Shelter, 226, 229, 232
Roberts, Florence, 115
Roberts, Laura, 115
Roberts, Lois, 256
Robinson, Pearl, 50
Robinson's Opera House, 263
Roman Catholic Franciscan Health Center, 96
Roman Catholicism, 9-10
Rosebud Reservation, 98
Rose Marie, Sister, 85
Rose Marie Thorn, Sister, 188
Rule of Life, 16, 62, 101, 207, 255
Rule of Prayer, 71-74
Ruth Magdalene Kent, Sister, 85, 111, 116, 118, 165, 187, 225, 230, 235, 242
Ryan, Pat, 171-172

S

Sahs, Barbara, 88
Saint Mary's Hall, 90
S.A. Minnehaha, 36
Sanibel Island, 103
Sarah Elizabeth Niles, Sister, 196
Schantz Organ Company, 127
Sears, Lillian, 105
Sellon, Priscilla Lydia, 243-244
Sen, Sun Yat, 222
Sewing School, 19, 22-23, 27, 260
Shea, Peter, 291-292
Shek, Chiang Kai, 222, 234
Shou Ngai, Sister, 241
Shrove Tuesday Pancake Supper, 265
Silbereis, Richard, 126
Singing Tower, 116-117
Sisterhood at the Church Charity Foundation, 62
Sisterhood Life, 6, 205, 207, 210
Sisterhood of St. John the Divine, 156
Sisterhood of St. Mary, 16-17
Sisterhood of the Holy Nativity, 156
Sister of the Most Holy Trinity, 247
Sisters of Divine Love, 286
Sisters of Holy Love, 241
Sisters of Nazareth, 287
Sisters of St. John the Baptist, 10, 41, 43, 114, 165
Sisters of St. John the Divine, 166
Sisters of St. Margaret, 67
Sisters of St. Mary the Virgin, 44-45
Sisters of the Holy and Undivided Trinity, 10
Sisters of the Holy Nativity, 165
Sisters of the Holy Rood, 44
Sisters of the Tabernacle, 136
Sisters of the Transfiguration, 12, 33, 43, 55, 115, 120, 141, 221-222, 243-244, 251-258, 287, 298
Skystone-Ryan Inc., 171
Society of St. Anne, 232
Society of St. Francis, 154
Society of St. John the Evangelist, 10, 35, 156, 236, 286
Society of St. Margaret, 10, 36, 114, 165
Society of the Most Holy Trinity, 43
Society of the Transfiguration, 3-4, 59, 73, 75-76, 110, 223
Spanish American War, 243
A Spark of Love, 282
Spinner, Ralph, 118-119
Standing Committee of the Episcopal Church, 122
Standing Liturgical Committee, 153
St. Andrew's Cathedral, 244, 246-248
St. Andrew's Church, 22
St. Andrew's Priory, 43, 98, 132, 139, 162, 232, 260, 266
St. Andrew's Priory School for Girls, 93, 142, 243-250
St. Ann's Home, 146
St. Augustine's Chapel, 11
St. Barbara's Mission, 271
St. Barnabas Day, 108
St. Barnabas parish, 15
St. Boniface, 221
St. Boniface Convent, 240
St. Bride of Ireland, 115
St. Cuthbert, 37

St. Dorothy's Camp, 160
St. Dorothy's House, 255
St. Dorothy's Rest, 94, 140, 141, 251, 256
St. Edmund's Camp, 34
St. Edmund's Home, 34
St. Elizabeth's Home, 147
St. Ethelburga, 115
St. Faith's Chapel, 39, 133-134
St. Francis Chapel, 115, 119
St. Francis of Assisi, 122
St. Frideswide, 115
St. George's Chapel, 42
St. Gregory's Priory, 247
St. Hilda of Whitby, 115
St. James Church, 77, 97-98
St. James Compound, 223
St. James School for Boys, 224, 238
St. John Baptist Community, 36
St. John Baptist Day, 11
St. John Baptist School, 61
St. John's Home, 95, 97, 144, 154, 219-220
St. John's Orphanage, 64, 90, 132, 219
St. John's Social Service Center, 96
St. Lioba's Boarding School, 221, 234, 238, 240
St. Lioba's Chapel, 226
St. Lioba's Compound, 223, 230
St. Lioba's Day, 224, 232
St. Luke's Church, 7, 18, 22-23, 157, 201, 291-292, 294-295
St. Luke's Day, 14, 113, 137, 140
St. Luke's Episcopal Church, 291
St. Luke's Episcopal Hospital, 143, 281, 285
St. Luke's House, 291-296
St. Martin's in the Fields, 38
St. Mary's Memorial Home, 87, 147-148, 156, 158, 161, 167, 171
St. Mary's School, 61
St. Mary's Society, 46
St. Mary the Virgin, 125, 281
St. Matthew's Parish Day School, 256
St. Matthias Church, 14
St. Michael's House, 115, 162, 282
St. Monica's Band, 265
St. Monica's Center, 259, 264-268, 270, 272

St. Monica's Hobby Clubs, 265
St. Monica's House, 153, 273, 275-276
St. Monica's Recreation Center, 173, 272-279
St. Nicholas Day, 47, 59
St. Paul's Cathedral, 22, 37, 39
St. Philip's Church, 95, 268
St. Philip's School, 153, 290
St. Phillip's Recreation Center, 95
St. Simon of Cyrene's Church, 135, 156, 164
St. Simon's Church, 114, 164, 267, 275
St. Simon's Council, 265
St. Simon's Day School, 266-267, 271, 273
St. Simon's High School, 272
St. Simon's Mission, 142, 153, 259, 262-272
St. Simon's Primary Day School, 263
St. Simon's School, 143, 268, 270
St. Simon's Sunday School, 271-272
St. Stephen's Day, 127
Stanley Memorial Hospital, 225, 230
Stanley Rowe Towers, 147
Starr, Eddie, 271
Stasney, Jon, 95
Stenson, Marvin, 271
Stephanie Helen McNichols, Sister, 98, 192, 246
Sterling, W. S., 33
Stone, James, 291
Symons, Canon Gilbert, 260
Symons, John Prower, 109, 116-117, 127

T

Tabor Ministry, 173-175
Teh Ai, Sister, 241
Teh Ngai, Sister, 241
Teresa Marie Martin, Sister, 148, 157, 160, 163, 167, 177, 197
Teresa Ruth Clark, Sister, 193, 282
Theodora Eleanor, Sister, 189, 268, 269, 272
Thomas, Doris, 276
Thomas-Feren, Toni, 88, 173
Thompson, Herbert, 59, 164
Thurlow, Edward, 221
Thurlow, Frank, 227

Tintern Abbey, 38
Tower of London, 38
Transfiguration Day, 7, 225, 235, 237, 239
Transfiguration Quarterly
  Associates and, 87
  Bat Cave and, 216
  beginning of, 144
  chapel bells and, 116
  debut of, 51
  letters from Sister Constance and, 232
  Sister Diana Dorothea and, 258
  writing by Sisters and, 163
Transfiguration Spirituality Center, 171-174
Transfiguration Sunday, 155
Trenholme, E. C., 124
Trinity Church, 165
Trinity School for Ministry, 276
Turner, Theodore, 268

U
United Church of Christ, 165
United States Supreme Court, 8
University of Cincinnati, 215
University of Hawaii, 162, 250
University of Michigan, 117
University of Pittsburgh, 162
Ursula Elizabeth Rogers, Sister, 143, 146, 166, 192, 248, 250, 281, 285, 286
U.S. Customs, 303

V
Vacation Bible School, 260, 294
van den Blink, Johannes, 77, 166
Veronica Sacha Meyers, Sister, 186
Vespers, 40, 123, 126
Victoria Elizabeth Hughes, Sister, 194
Vincent, Boyd, 4-7, 10, 17-19, 30, 52-54, 56-58, 201-211
Virginia Cecilia Wiley, Sister, 127, 191, 242, 245, 267, 272, 276

W
Walter-Perry, LaVone, 88
Wang, Arthur, 237
Watts, James, 263
Weinhauer, William G., 77, 157, 164-166, 291, 294-295
Welles, Edward, 77
Wellesley College, 8
Welles, Pauline, 12, 15
Welles, Samuel, 12, 33
West, George, 261
Westminster Abbey, 39
Williams, John Albert, 14
Wilson, Arthur G., 136, 260-261, 263-265
Windsor Castle, 42-43
Winifred Agnes Willcox, Sister, 191, 266, 268, 272
Wood, Richard, 149
Wooley, Jack, 292
World War II, 142-143
  attack on Pearl Harbor and, 245
  Kunming as Allied military center and, 240
  Norman Binsted and, 285
Worthington, George, 14
Wylie, Samuel, 77, 155

Y
Yellow Fever epidemic, 5
Young Churchmen, 265
Young Peoples' Fellowship, 265
Young People's Recreation Center, 264